WINGS AND SPACE

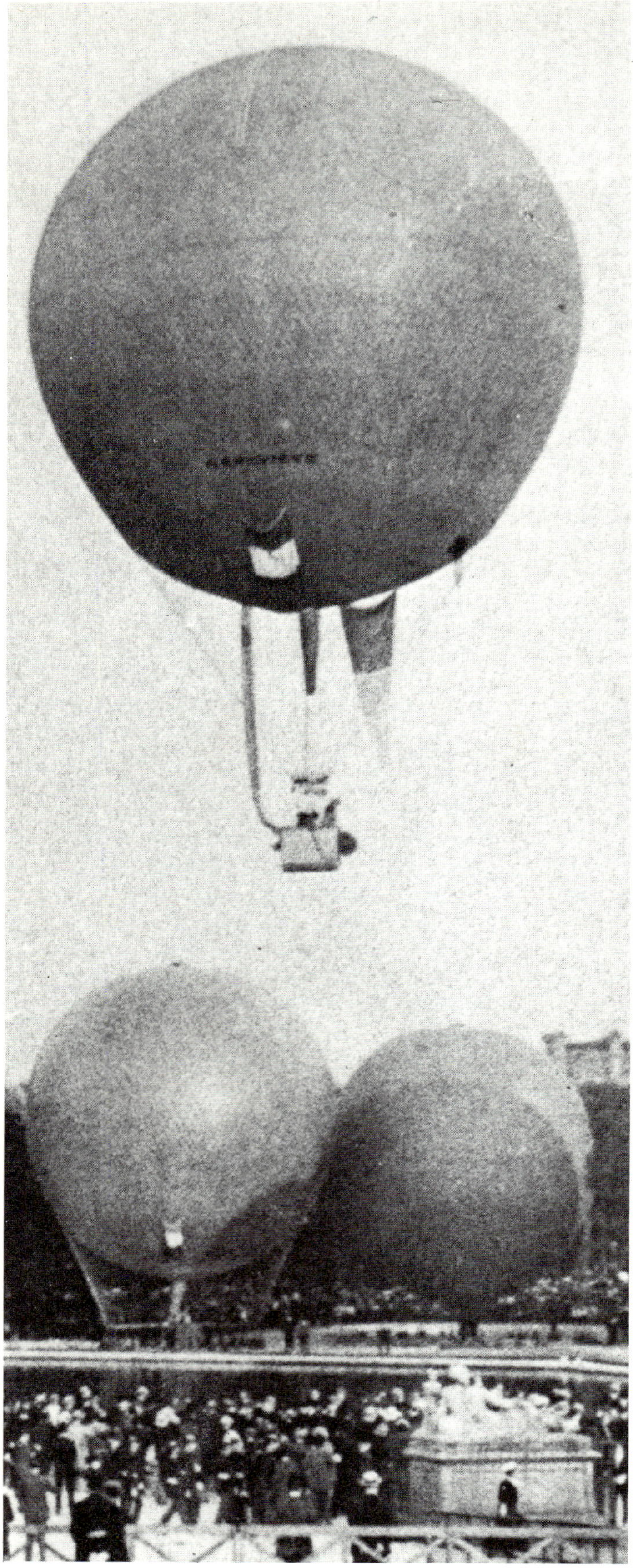

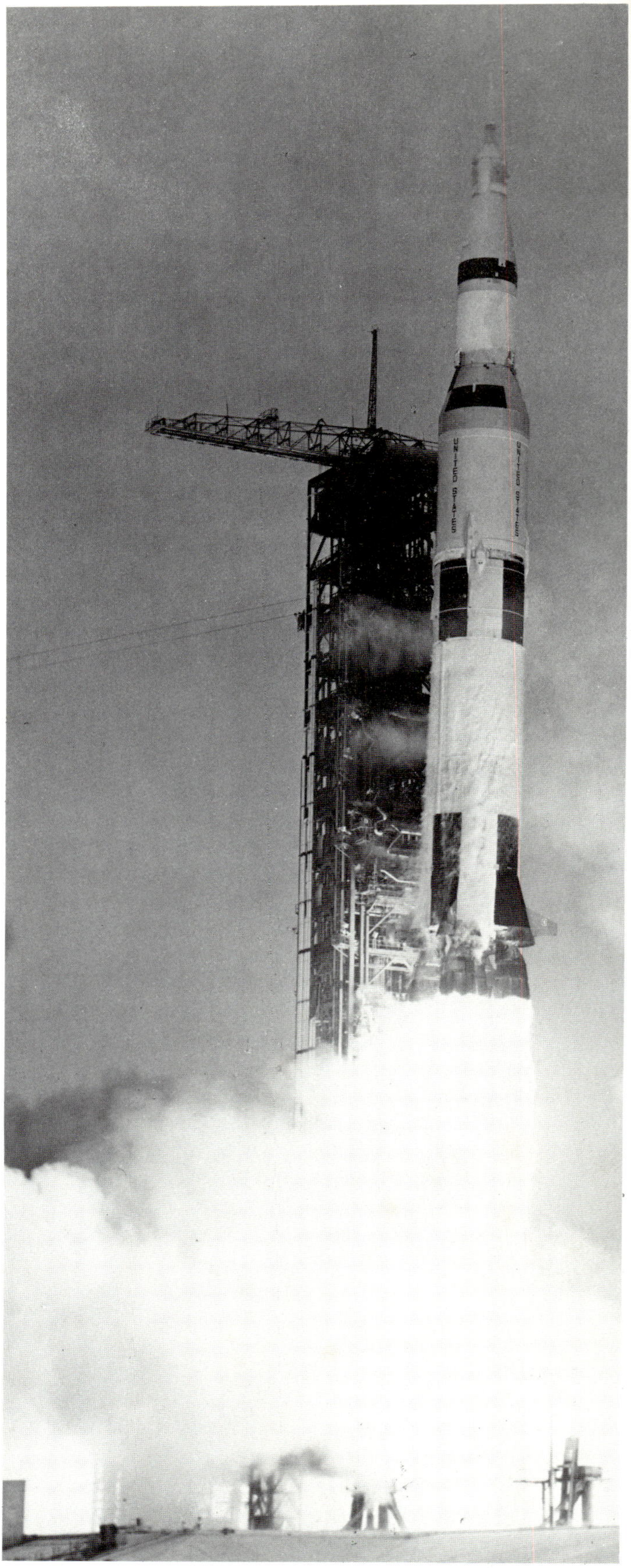
UNITED STATES
UNITED STATES

WINGS
AND SPACE

JOHN CHAPLIN

LONDON

IAN ALLAN

First published 1970

*For my Father and his grandchildren,
Christopher, Paul and Jeremy . . .*

SBN 7110 0150 2

*Published by Ian Allan Ltd, Shepperton,
Surrey and printed in the United
Kingdom by Jarrold & Sons Ltd, Norwich*

Contents

Introduction

1941: *The Second World War was at its height and Orville Wright, the man who – watched by his brother Wilbur – had made the first proper flight, was celebrating his 70th birthday. This was the message he sent to the world: "Neither my brother nor myself ever thought when we took off in our plane all those years ago, that our invention would or could ever deal out so much destruction. That wasn't our idea at all. We always believed the aeroplane would be an instrument of peace . . ."*

Man and Superman

Above: *The ancient symbol of freedom, the flying man. The figure is the Greek god Hermes. He has a winged helmet, winged sandals and his staff is entwined with two serpents representing release.*

The aeroplane is a symbol of freedom.

It represents, in the mind of man, a way he can liberate himself from his restricted and imperfect daily life on Earth.

This is why flight, and the things that fly, have held a magic attraction for human beings down the ages. For man – especially the thinking and so-called modern civilised man – is in constant conflict with himself.

There is always a battle going on between his conscious mind and his inner, unconscious mind. It is a battle of good against evil, of adventure against discipline, of freedom against security. It is a battle between what man would really like to do and what his duty tells him he ought to do.

And what man really would like to do is escape to a freer, better world where he can achieve his wildest dreams. In his heart he doesn't want to be a man at all. He wants to be a superman.

When an aircraft lifts itself free from the Earth, the people in it – whether they realise it or not – are making a token gesture to themselves that they are on their way to that better world.

This longing for freedom is why every year nearly a million people visit the world's busiest international airport at Heathrow, London, just to watch the aeroplanes. They see the great airliners soaring into the sky and imagine that they are making that same gesture of release.

Journalists often have to go to airports to cover stories for their newspapers and, after returning from an assignment of this kind, one reporter remarked: "When I am at an airport and see aircraft taking off, it always makes me angry that I am not going too."

That reporter felt angry because he had been watching his own dreams of freedom coming true for someone else . . . the passengers he had seen fly away.

Flying was invented by four different kinds of creatures before man finally learned the secret himself.

The insects, the birds, the great saurian reptiles and the bats all conquered the air and, for thousands of years, man looked on with envy.

Evidence of the idea of human flight and the urge of men to copy the flying machines of nature has been found in the works of art of the earliest civilisations.

And men seem to have decided that, because they could

Below: *The Superman that man created: the comic strip hero hurtling through the air on another mission against evil.*

NATIONAL PERIODICAL PUBLICATIONS, NEW YORK

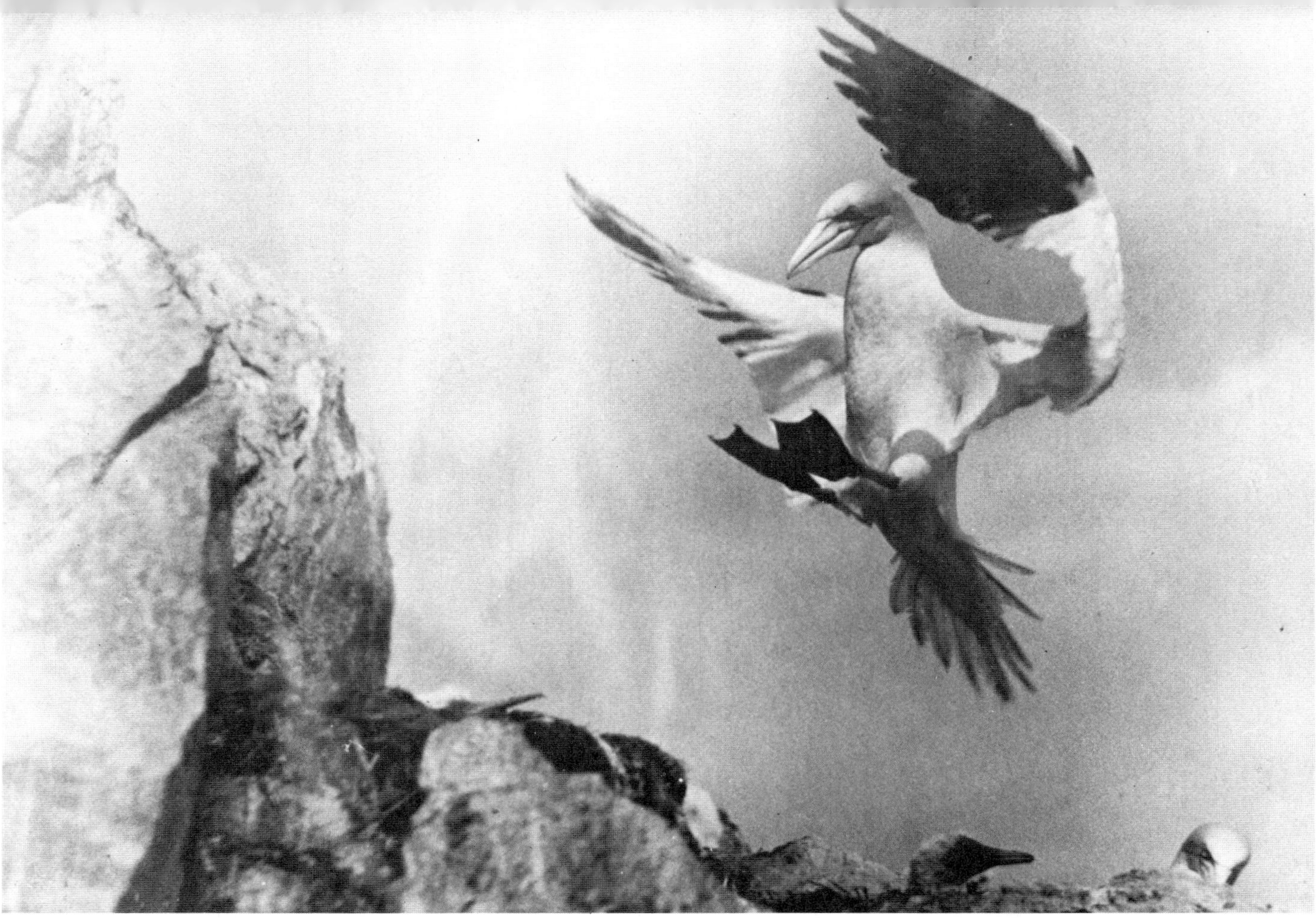

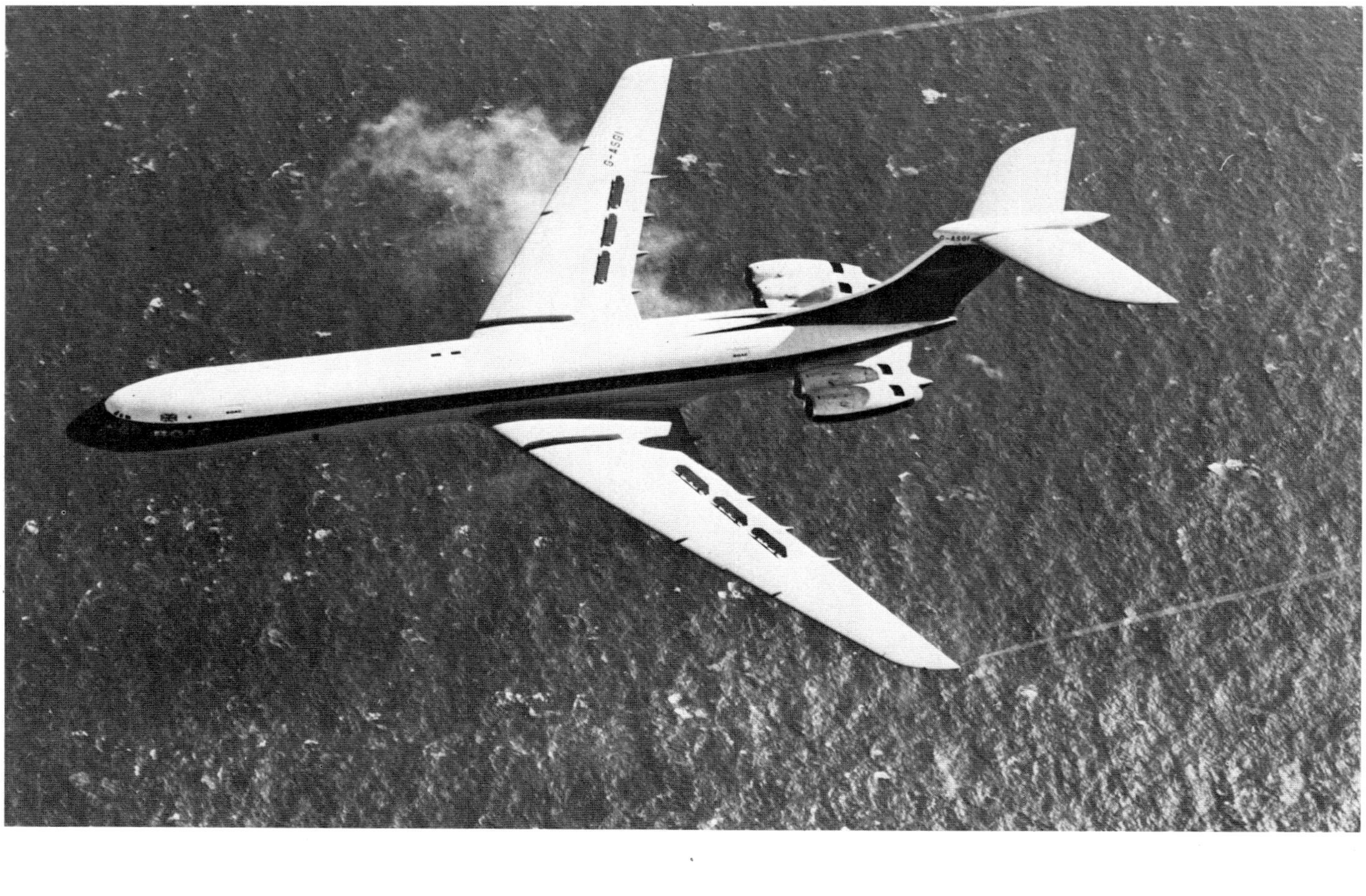
G-ASGI

the Moon and dominate the world.

But it soon became obvious that Earth-launched missiles would be faster and more accurate. Moon-launched missiles would be detected and destroyed long before they had time to reach their targets.

And so the space race became one for international glory, and some people believe that the competition has prevented a third world war breaking out.

On October 4, 1957, Russia put up the first man-made satellite, Sputnik 1. The world marvelled and Western scientists were surprised at its weight, 184 lb. They thought a decimal point had been left out somewhere and the proper weight should have been 18·4 lb.

Space progress was rapid after that. Within 12 years America's giant 3,000-ton Saturn V rocket was able to blast 120 tons of astronauts and their equipment to the Moon.

In the years between Russia notched up an impressive list of firsts in the space spectacular:

April 1961: First man in space, Yuri Gagarin.

June 1963: First woman in space, Valentina Tereshkova.

October 1964: First multi-manned spacecraft.

March 1965: First space walk, Alexei Lenov.

By then America's manned and unmanned space programme was overhauling Russian achievements. But both countries were considering the best way of making a Moon flight.

Should a space platform be built close to the Earth which could be used as a launching base, or should the journey be made in a single flight?

Russia chose the jumping-off platform. America decided on the direct route and the National Aeronautics and Space Administration's rocket development team, headed by Von Braun, designed the multi-stage Saturns.

Then came disaster, for both Russia and America.

In January 1967 three American astronauts died when fire engulfed their space capsule during launch-pad tests. In April Cosmonaut Vladimir Komarov was killed when his spacecraft Soyuz 1 crashed as it returned to Earth.

Apollo underwent major design changes. The sort of atmosphere that the astronauts breathed was altered and new, fast-opening hatches were fitted. The work set America's manned space programme back two years.

Then, in December 1968, the three-man Apollo 8 crew made a flight to within 70 miles of the Moon's surface. They proved it was possible to get there.

Two more Apollo missions followed.

Apollo 9 tested the spidery Moon landing vehicle in Earth orbit. Apollo 10, in May 1969, tested it in Moon orbit. It was detached from the parent spacecraft and went through all the motions of an actual landing ten miles above the Moon. Everything worked.

All that Apollo 11 had to do was make the landing.

The chosen crew, Armstrong, Aldrin and Collins, were all airmen, all fighter pilots.

This is how they carried out the most audacious and heroic achievement in the history of human endeavour:

Above: *The Saturn V rocket, with its Apollo spacecraft, begins its journey to the launching pad. The entire assembly is called the "Stack" and consists of: three rocket stages with the Lunar landing craft encased in the third stage; a service module containing instruments and supplies; the Apollo command module which is the astronauts' cabin. The tall spike-like section at the top is the launch escape system which can be used to lift the command module to safety if there is an emergency during the launch.*

The Stack is taken from the rocket assembly building by the "crawler" – the world's largest tracked vehicle – to the launching pad. The 3½-mile journey, which takes place six weeks before blast-off, lasts seven hours.

Above: ***Blast-off:*** *Apollo 11 lifts away from Pad 39 at Cape Kennedy bound for the Moon. Two hours and forty minutes before lift-off astronauts Armstrong, Aldrin and Collins had strapped themselves in their couches for the final stages of the count-down. They lie on top of a rocket that is 363 ft high – as tall as St. Paul's Cathedral in London. It weighs 3,200 tons of which 2,780 tons is fuel – liquid oxygen, hydrogen and kerosene. When the engines are ignited and the slow first stage of the ascent begins fuel is being burned at the rate of 15 tons every second.*

Left: *At a height of 40 miles and a speed of 6,000 mph the first stage of the rocket separates and falls away. The five engines of the second stage ignite and burn for 6½ minutes.*

Above: *The second stage burns out and falls away. The third stage of the rocket then pushes the spacecraft into orbit round the Earth at a height of 115 miles and a speed of 17,400 mph. After careful checks, to see that everything on board is working properly, the third stage is relit to increase Apollo's speed to almost 25,000 mph. At this speed the spacecraft is pushed out of Earth orbit towards the Moon. But it cannot escape from the pull of Earth's gravity entirely and, if anything goes wrong at a later stage of the flight, Apollo will merely swing round the Moon and return to Earth.*

Right: *The command and service modules separate from Saturn's third stage. By the delicate firing of small steering rockets the spacecraft makes a "U" turn in space to connect with the Lunar landing craft and draw it free. The third stage of the rocket is then abandoned to orbit the sun and Apollo begins its three-day journey to the Moon.*

Above: *As Apollo gets further away from the Earth it starts to slow down, like a ball does when it is thrown into the air. At 20,000 miles speed is down to only 2,700 mph but at this point the pull of the Moon takes over and speeds the spacecraft up again until it is travelling at 5,600 mph. As it passes behind the Moon Apollo's main engine is fired to brake it into lunar orbit.*

Right: *Astronauts Aldrin and Armstrong, who are to make the Moon landing, crawl from the command module into the Lunar landing craft along the connecting tunnel. The two craft separate and the Lunar landing craft's engine is fired to bring it out of orbit and line it up for a touchdown. The command module, with Collins on board, continues to circle above.*

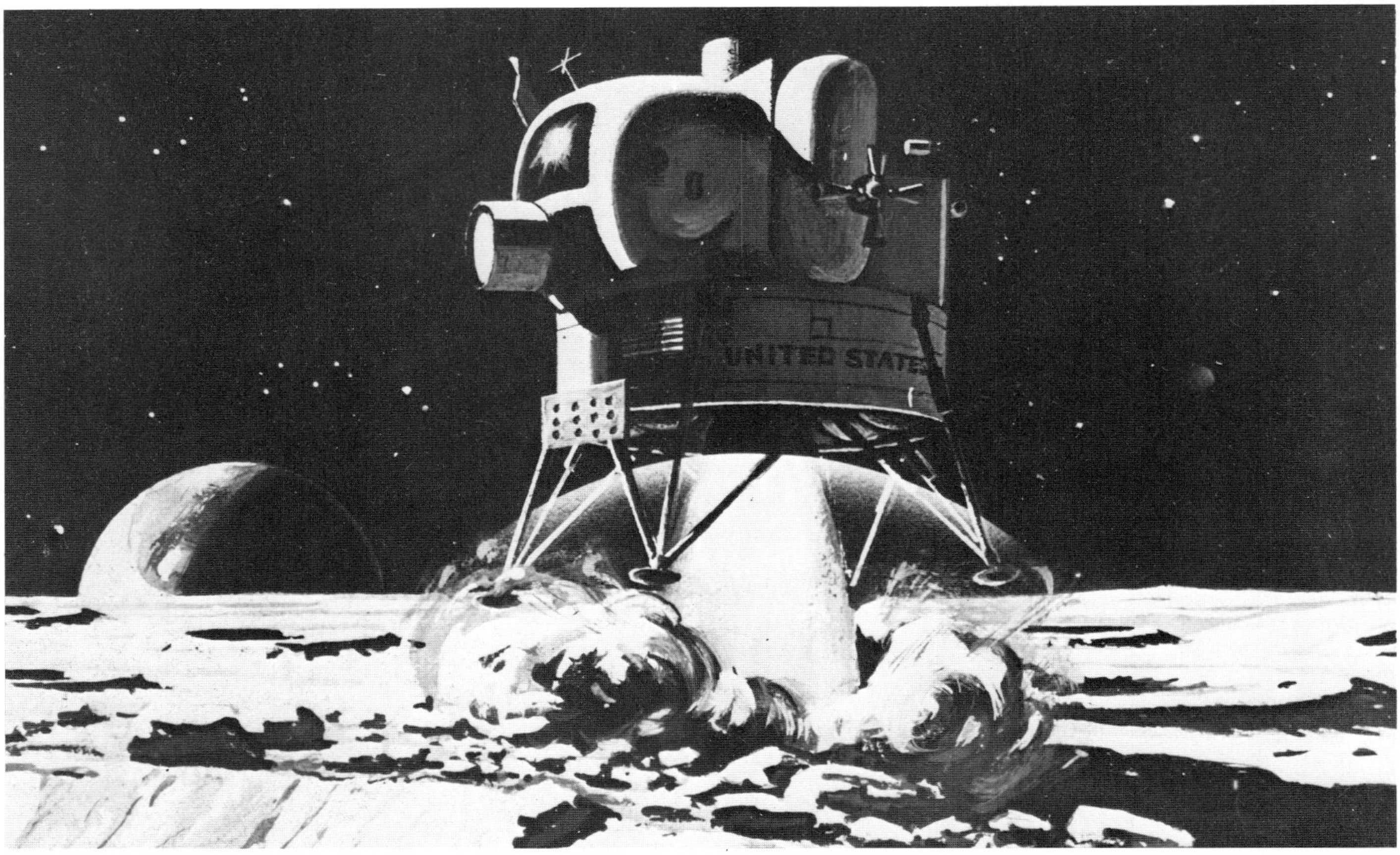

Above: *The final descent is automatically controlled by computer until the last few seconds. Then Armstrong, the lunar landing craft pilot, takes over and uses small control jets to pick his landing site. The actual touchdown is cushioned by the craft's four shock-absorbing spidery legs.*

Right: ***Man on the Moon:*** *This is how it actually happened. Neil Armstrong is already on the surface. He took this photograph of Edwin Aldrin inching his way down the last few rungs of the Lunar landing craft's ladder. On his back the pack containing oxygen and cooling water to keep him alive on the airless Moon.*

Above: *After carrying out experiments, collecting samples of Moon rock and beaming television pictures back to Earth the two astronauts are safely back inside the Lunar craft. Now comes the most vital moment of the whole operation – blast-off from the Moon. If their engine fails there can be no hope of rescue. But for Armstrong and Aldrin everything went according to plan. The lower half of the Lunar landing craft is used as a launch pad and the ascent engine thrusts the two spacemen away from the surface and back into orbit ready to link up with the command module again.*

Above: *With the use of the small control jets the two craft come together in a nose-to-nose position. After locking together the two men in the Lunar landing craft crawl back into the command module and the Lunar craft is set free to circle the Moon alone.*

Left: *The main engine boosts Apollo to 5,600 mph, pulling it out of Moon orbit and setting it on course for the Earth. As the craft begins to get near its home planet its speed increases to nearly 25,000 mph.*

Left: *Just before re-entering the Earth's atmosphere the command module separates from the service module. It weighs only six tons and is the only part of the 3,200-ton rocket that set out which returns to Earth.*

Above: *The effect of the command module hitting the Earth's atmosphere is the same as when a match is struck. As it "rubs" against the air it gets hotter and hotter. To protect the astronauts from the blistering heat of 5,000 deg. F. the spacecraft has a two-inch thick shield which is turned forward. And it has to enter the atmosphere at the right angle. Too steep and the heat would burn it up. Too shallow and it would "bounce" off into space.*

Below: *Six miles above the Earth parachutes open to steady the spacecraft during the last stage of the descent, and finally the main parachutes drop it gently into the ocean. The astronauts are then picked up by hovering helicopters.*

"Them crazy boys... name of Wright"

Right: *Huffman Prairie, 1904: The second Flyer takes to the air. In the background the line of trees indicates the Springfield turnpike road where the trams ran. It would have been from there that Ed and Jim saw the crazy Wright boys going through their paces.*

Zooom! A strange machine sailed over the treetops, skimming the roof of an electric tramcar on the road below. The machine looked something like a flying chicken coop and made a noise like a combine harvester going full blast.

"Heavens, Ed. Whazzat? Ed, whazzat?" The question came from one of the startled passengers in the tram, which was on the hourly run taking it past a piece of rough, open pasture-land known as Huffman Prairie, just outside the American town of Dayton in the State of Ohio.

Ed and his companion craned their necks to watch the machine sweep away low over the fields. It had two rigid, wing-like planes braced with wires, two smaller planes sticking out in front and a sort of tail at the back. They could also see a figure lying flat on the lower wing who seemed to be actually driving the contraption through the air.

It was 1904. Only birds could fly, and that thing up there was no bird. No wonder the passenger in the tram nearly jumped out of his skin.

But it was nothing new to Ed. After the machine had passed out of sight he replied: "Tain't nothin', Jim. Just one o' them crazy boys we got here. Name of Wright. Dern fools, tryin' to make a machine that can fly. Both crazy – always was. Y' can't go agin' nature."

The man flying the machine . . . name of Wright . . . was Orville, one of two local brothers who had a bicycle shop in Dayton. The other brother, Wilbur, was also riding in the tram that day and could not help overhearing the conversation that had taken place.

It is just one of the legends surrounding the Wright brothers and if this particular incident really did happen it probably caused Wilbur a great deal of amusement.

The year before he and Orville had not only "gone agin'" nature, they had made nature work for them, too, and built a machine that *could* fly.

The other two passengers in the tram had seen something that was going to change the world. They were already living in the air age . . . and didn't know it.

But they were not alone.

So many well-publicised attempts to fly had failed dismally and disastrously that most people had stopped taking the idea seriously.

Flying was something to be made fun of, and the general public – even those living near Huffman Prairie – believed that it was impossible.

Three years later, in 1907, when the United States Government at last issued details of the sort of aeroplane it would be prepared to buy, the War Department was even then thought to have taken leave of its senses.

*

The Wright family were Americans of English and Dutch descent. They could trace their ancestry back to John Wright who owned Kelvedon Hall in Essex in 1538. One of his descendants, Samuel Wright, emigrated to the United States.

The Dutch ancestor was a Van Cleve who went to live in America in the 17th century and whose name Wilbur and Orville gave to one of their bicycles.

The brothers were the sons of a clergyman, Bishop Milton Wright of the United Brethren Church. There were also two elder brothers and a younger sister, Katherine, in the family.

One of the first contacts Wilbur and Orville had with flying came in the autumn of 1878. Their father came into the house one night with something partly hidden in his hands. Before his sons could see what it was he tossed it into the air. Instead of it falling to the floor, as they expected, it flew across the room and fluttered for a while against the ceiling.

When it finally sank to the floor Wilbur and Orville saw that it was a toy helicopter. But, with what they described as "sublime disregard for science", they at once nicknamed it a "bat".

It was made of cork, bamboo and paper with twin airscrews that were driven in opposite directions by rubber bands. The "bat" was delicate and, in the hands of two enthusiastic young boys – Orville was seven and Wilbur was eleven – it survived for only a short time. But it made a lasting impression on them.

The little helicopter interested them so much that they built and flew copies of it – an indication of their desire to experiment on their own which was to be so important to them later on. Their models got bigger and bigger, but the boys were puzzled by the fact that the bigger they made

Above: **Before:** *Maxim's monster was depicted like this in the British Petroleum Company's film* The Power to Fly, *surrounded by the elegant ladies and gentlemen of the 1890s.*

Above: **After:** *The reality. Maxim's monster at the end of its test run, slewed across the smashed check rails. A sad end for a magnificent machine.*

Left: *Otto Lilienthal making a flight in one of his biplane gliders. It was Lilienthal's death that ignited "an unquenchable enthusiasm" in the Wright brothers which led them to solve the problem of flight.*

Below: *The final disaster: Professor Langley's aerodrome crumples up and falls into the Potomac River after hitting its launching gear in 1903.*

Below: *Octave Chanute's own drawing of his 1896 glider showing his system of wing bracing.*

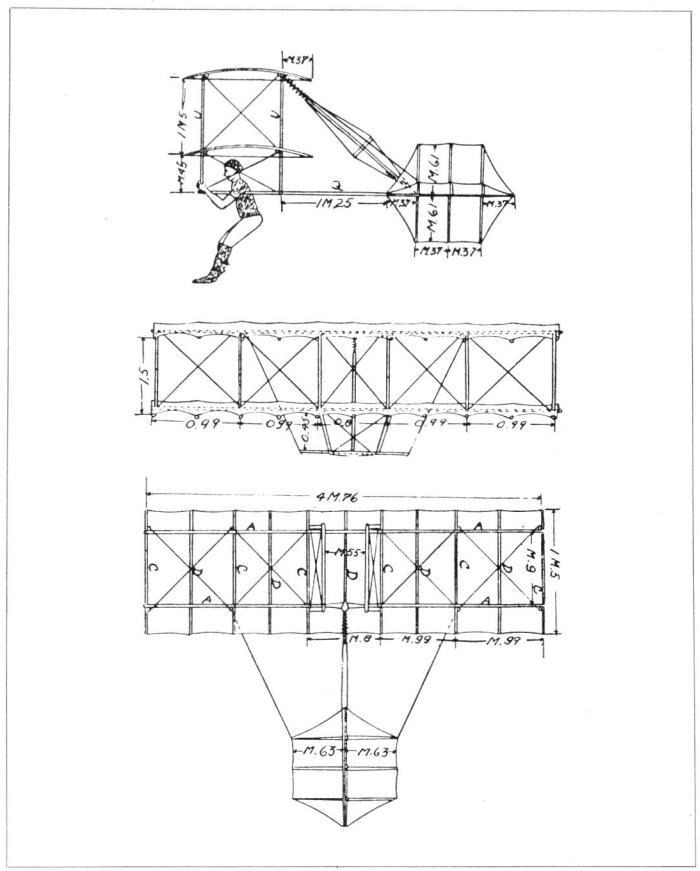

them the less they flew. They didn't know at the time that a machine twice as big as the original needed eight times the power to fly it.

It was a problem they were to meet again . . . and conquer.

They went on to become expert kite flyers. But Wilbur did not attach too much importance to this as an indication of what was to come because, as he later pointed out, most boys are good at flying kites. And soon they had to give up the pastime. Though the sport fascinated them they decided, as they got older, that it was "unbecoming to boys of our ages".

Neither of them went on to college when they left school.

Instead they were soon earning their own livings. They became journalists, writing, printing and distributing a small magazine and several weekly papers.

Then, in 1892, they opened their bicycle shop and, from selling and repairing other people's machines, they began to make their own. As well as the Van Cleve, another of their models was prophetically called the Wright Flyer.

The business provided Wilbur and Orville with enough money to support them and pay for their hobby – the study of flight, by men and birds.

They neither smoked nor drank, and there seems to be no record of them going out with girls. Early years were spent in contact with the Church which was an ideal influence

Above: *The Wrights' first full-sized glider being flown at Kitty Hawk in 1900.*

Left: *The second glider, with the front horizontal elevator, crunches into the sand after one of the Wrights' 1901 flights at Kill Devil Hills.*

Below: *Ready for the off: Side view of the first practical aeroplane, Wilbur and Orville's 1903 Flyer at Kill Devil Hills.*

Top right: *Nearly there: the third glider piloted by Wilbur soaring above the dunes.*

Right: *Moment of history: With Orville lying flat on the lower wing the Flyer lifts itself shakily from its starting rail leaving Wilbur to stare in wonder at the miracle of man's first flight.*

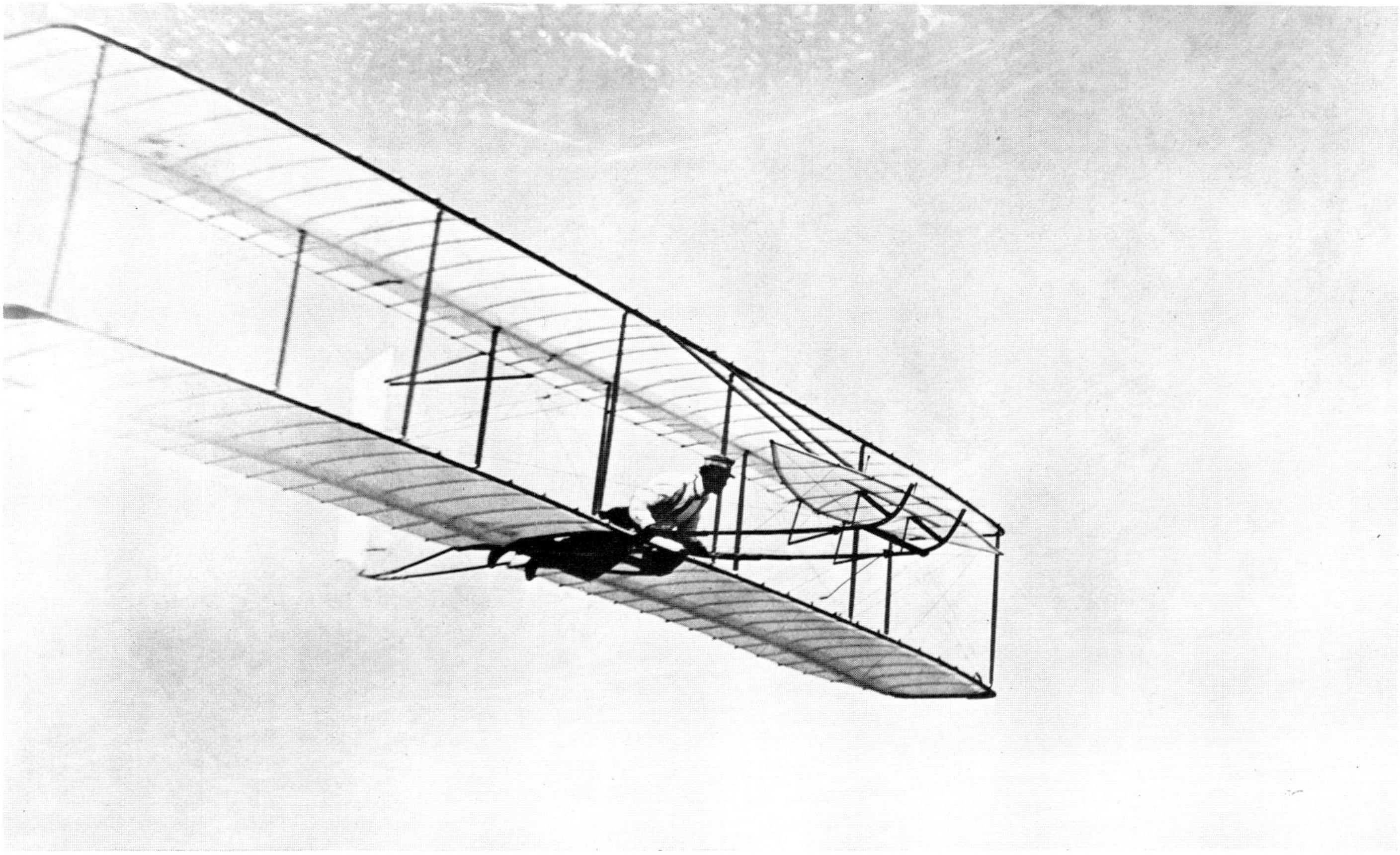

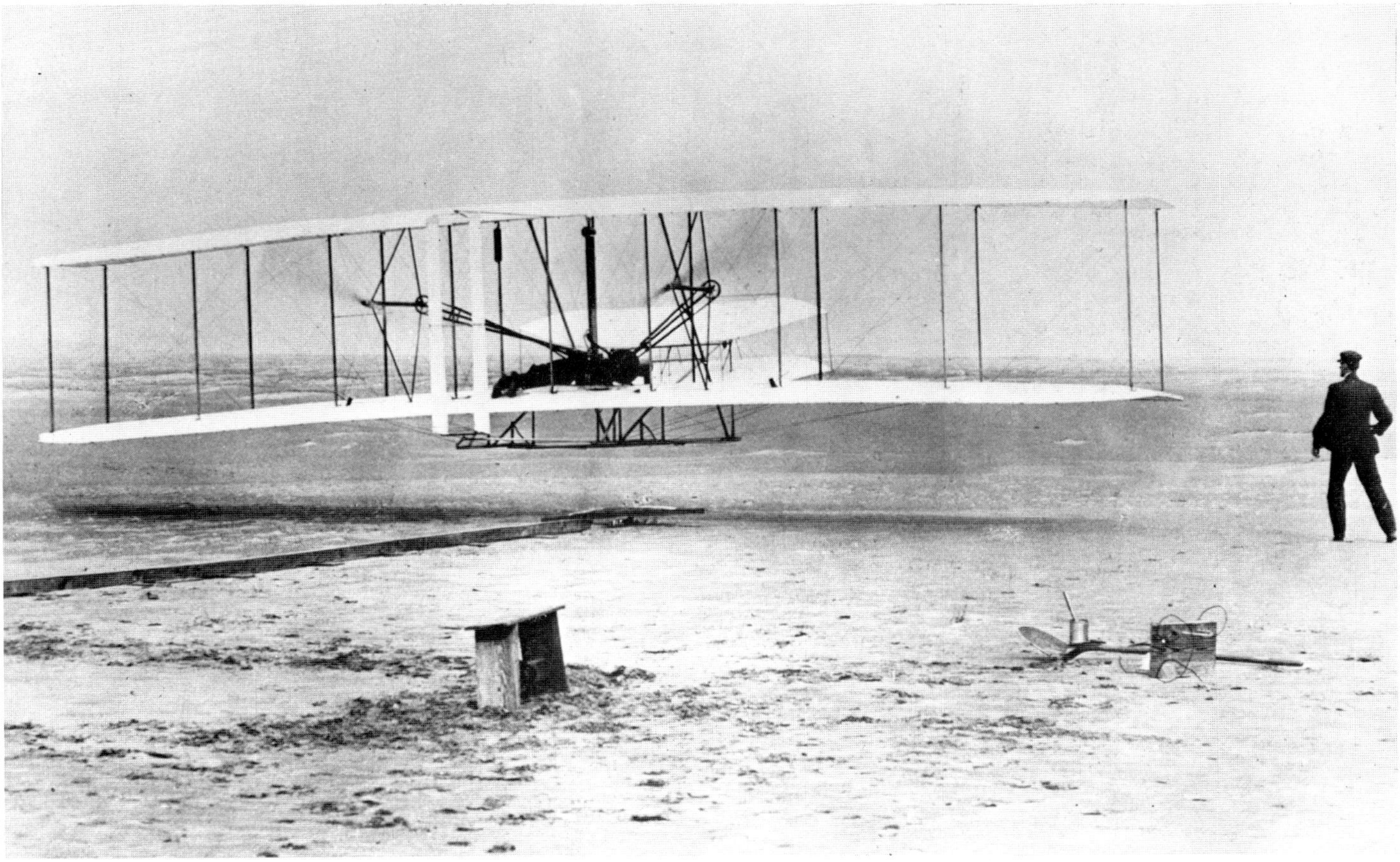

to fit them for the task they were to set themselves.

It produced two men of honesty, integrity, singleness of purpose and modesty. They had a supreme indifference to worldly pleasures, but though they preferred work they were not dull boys by any means. They did not lack a sense of humour, nor were they remote from the need that all of us have to escape from the worries of the world and work.

Orville, for instance, played a little private joke on some newspapermen one day in 1911.

By then everything the brothers did was news, and reporters flocked to see their soaring experiments at the now famous Kill Devil Hills in Dare County, North Carolina. The newsmen spotted a rod with a bag-like object on the end sticking out from the leading edge of the wings on one of the gliders. They asked Orville what it was, and back came the deadpan reply: "It's a special stabilising device."

The next editions of the papers carried the news that the Wright brothers were trying out a new "secret" stability device.

What Orville hadn't told the newsmen was that the "secret" device was just a bag of ordinary sand hung on the end of the rod to bring forward the glider's centre of gravity.

And Wilbur could escape into the world of fantasy. Children soon discovered that he was an authority on fairies. Griffith Brewer of the Royal Aeronautical Society of Britain, who was a long-time friend of the Wrights and the first Englishman to fly with Wilbur in France, revealed Wilbur's fairy-hunting expeditions. He wrote: "Who could know

more about such charms than the man who acquired their principal accomplishment?

"Several children will remember to the end of their lives how he hunted for fairies in the box borders in the gardens, and how, although never really successful, he nearly caught them several times."

But the characters of Wilbur and Orville, which produced the original thought and determination that enabled them to solve the problem that had baffled men for centuries, also proved to be something of a drawback to them.

One quality they both did not have was showmanship. Francis McClean, another of the early British flying enthusiasts, remarked: "If they had been showmen they would have been world famous in 1903."

When President Franklin D. Roosevelt invited Orville to a dinner on December 17, 1943, to celebrate the fortieth anniversary of the Wrights' first flight, Orville replied: "I am sorry that inabilities as a speaker compel me to decline any speaking part in the programme." And at the dinner he became very annoyed when he was manœuvred to a microphone and urged to say a few words.

Had the Wrights been showmen, events which could have denied them the credit for the achievement which is now recognised as a turning-point in the history of the world might never have happened.

But they did. And it was the old iron will and determination of Orville, working on alone after Wilbur had died of typhoid in 1912, that in the end overcame them.

Four years after the Wright Cycle Company opened in Dayton news reached Wilbur and Orville of the death of Otto Lilienthal, the German gliding pioneer.

Lilienthal is credited with being one of the four men – along with the Wrights and Sir George Cayley – whose genius contributed most to the achievement of true powered flight.

He was the first to build and actually fly heavier-than-air craft with consistency. He was an engineer who studied the problem of flight in detail and published his findings in a book called *Bird Flight as the Basis of Aviation*. The book inspired many other would-be aviators including the Wrights, though the brothers later had to revise Lilienthal's conclusions.

From 1891 he made and flew monoplane and biplane gliders, launching himself first from a springboard and later from an artificial hill he built near Berlin. He made about 2,000 flights, some further than 270 yds.

Lilienthal controlled his gliders with the movements of his body. His head and shoulders protruded above the mainplanes and the rest of his body and legs swung free beneath the glider. He demonstrated that, in a properly designed aircraft, it was possible for men to fly.

His experiments continued until 1896 when he was about to fit a carbonic acid engine to a glider with flapping wing-tips. On August 9 he was making a routine flight in one of his monoplanes in gusty conditions. He was in a shallow glide when the wind forced up the nose of the craft, bringing it to a dead stop in mid-air.

Lilienthal was caught in a stall, a deadly trap for airmen which, even today, can be fatal. It happens when an aircraft's wings are "attacking" the air at too steep an angle. They lose the ability to keep it up in the air and the pilot loses control.

Realising what had happened, Lilienthal tried to force his body forward to bring the nose down to regain flying speed and control. But it was too late. The glider crashed from a height of about 50 ft and Lilienthal died of his injuries the following day.

The tragedy was the spark that ignited an "unquenchable enthusiasm" in the Wright brothers that was to lead them to immortality.

From then on the brothers' interest in flying became less and less of a hobby and more and more a serious undertaking. They wrote to the Smithsonian Institution in Washington for information on the subject of flight. From the books that were sent to them they learned about the work on aviation done in the past by others, like Cayley and Leonardo da Vinci.

They also learned about the work that had been done in their own time, by men like:

Sir Hiram Maxim: He was an American living in England who invented the modern machine-gun. In the early 1890s he built a giant aeroplane of steel and canvas that weighed nearly four tons. It was powered by two 180 hp steam engines.

Left: *Alone after two attempts to demonstrate the Flyer to the Press at Huffman Prairie in 1904, the Wright brothers discuss their temporary troubles.*

Right: *The assisted take-off device being used in France. Willing helpers pull the Flyer back along the starting-rail to link it up with the catapult.*

It was completed in 1894 and tested at Baldwyns Park, Kent. It was a magnificent machine, with enormous lifting surfaces criss-crossed with bracing wires and struts.

A railway track was laid down for it to run along, and there was an outer rail to STOP it rising into the air. The idea was not to make a free flight. Even if the machine had flown there was no means of proper control.

The test was purely to find out the lifting power of the engines and wings.

But Maxim's monster seemed to have a mind of its own. On the day of the trials it lumbered off down the track and, after about 1,000 ft, developed so much lift that it not only raised itself from the rails but burst through the check rails as well. Out of control it crashed back to earth, embedding itself in the turf of Baldwyns Park.

Surprisingly Maxim ceased work on developing his machine, considering his experiments complete. They had cost £20,000.

He later wrote: "The experiments have led me to believe that the flight of man is possible with a steam engine." But he went on to advise young engineers who wanted to become airmen to "turn their thoughts in the direction of the petroleum motor . . . I believe it is the petroleum engine that will drive our flying machines." There was also:

Samuel Pierpoint Langley: Professor Langley became the Wright brothers' chief rival. He nearly pipped them at the post in 1903 with one of his machines, which he called "aerodromes". And years after his death people were still trying to prove that he did beat them into the air.

Unlike the brothers, with their lack of advanced formal education, Langley was a man of many brilliant parts: architect, astronomer, physicist and mathematician. He had many years' start on the Wrights, having studied flight and experimented with models from the late 1880s.

He was secretary of the Smithsonian Institution, and it was to him that Wilbur and Orville wrote for the books that started them off on their own study of flight.

With the help of a £20,000 grant from the American Government Langley had a full-sized man-carrying aerodrome ready for testing in the fateful year of 1903.

The petrol engine was now really coming into its own and Langley's assistant and pilot, Charles Manly, built a five-cylinder, 52 hp power unit that was fitted to the tandem-wing monoplane to drive its twin propellers. The plane had a wing span of 48 ft and a tubular-steel-framed fuselage.

Two attempts were made to get the aerodrome into the air, both from a houseboat on the Potomac River, Washington. The first was made on October 7 and the second on December 8. Each time the plane fouled the launching mechanism – a catapult to help the aerodrome take off – and it dived straight into the water.

With a roaring, grinding noise, the aerodrome – with Manly at the controls – just toppled over the side of the boat. On both occasions Manly was rescued, wet but unhurt.

And the newspapers were scornful of yet another failure. "Perhaps," said one, "if Professor Langley had only thought to launch his airship bottom up, it would have gone into the air instead of down into the water." Langley, who was then 69, had neither the spirit nor the money to carry on.

But his was the final failure. Nine days after the aerodrome's second test the Wrights' first Flyer was as brilliantly successful as Langley's machine had been such a damp and dismal flop.

The other man the Wrights learned about was:

Octave Chanute: Another American, and a civil engineer, Chanute was probably the world's greatest authority on aeronautics living at that time. The Wrights began writing to him about their ideas and the "disease" that had afflicted them . . . that flight was possible to man.

Chanute was in his sixties. He carried on where Lilienthal had left off, though he was too old to actually pilot gliders himself. He introduced a way of bracing biplane wings based on a method of building bridges. It was called the Pratt truss and used struts and diagonal wires to strengthen wings. It was still being used on aeroplanes in the 1930s.

But Chanute also gave himself the task of keeping aviation enthusiasts throughout the world informed of latest developments. The Wright brothers sought his advice and he became their friend, encouraged them and publicised their work.

By reading about the failures of other men, Wilbur and Orville learned what not to do. They reached the conclusion that the secret of flight was control in the air.

They had little time for the efforts of Maxim, Langley or the Frenchman Clement Ader who, in the late 1890s, made some attempts at flight with curious bat-winged machines which he called "avions".

Lilienthal had been the most successful of all, but both he and an Englishman, Percy Pilcher – who had also made some progress with gliders – had been killed because they had not learned how to overcome the vital problem of control.

Wilbur and Orville were equally sure that it was wrong to try and imitate the birds and build flapping-wing aeroplanes. But they did not think that they could learn nothing at all from the birds.

They felt, too, that if men were to fly they had to get up there . . . and fly. Though Lilienthal had spent five years gliding, they worked out that he had spent a total of only five hours actually in the air. It seemed incredible to them that he had accomplished so much in such a short time.

Control. How to solve the mystery. That was the big question. The method used by Lilienthal and Pilcher – shifting the weight of the body – was "incapable of expansion". They would have to find another way.

They knew how big their task was. Wilbur was under no illusions about it: "When we studied the story of loss of life, financial disaster and final failure which had accompanied all attempts to solve the problem of human flight, we understood more clearly than before the immensity and difficulty of the problem we had taken up", he wrote.

But they did solve it, and the big secret finally came from . . . the birds.

Wilbur had noticed the way that pigeons and buzzards adjusted the tips of their wings as they glided, first one way and then the other, so that they achieved lateral – side-to-side – balance in flight. It was done by using the action of the air instead of moving their weight.

Adjusting the tips of the wings. That was it. And so man at last learned to fly, not by imitating the birds, but borrowing from them.

How the Wrights finally hit on a way to use the wing-twisting action of the birds was described by Alec Ogilvie of the Royal Aeronautical Society in his Wilbur Wright Memorial lecture in 1922. He said:

"Wilbur was explaining to Orville, their sister Katherine and a Miss Harriet Silliman what he wanted.

"He was using an old open-ended cardboard box which had probably contained puffed wheat, or some other strange American breakfast food, to illustrate his remarks.

"As Wilbur was holding the box by the two ends and twisting it about, he suddenly realised that in his hands he had a biplane structure firmly braced in two planes but able to be twisted at the two open ends, and that this was just what was wanted for the lateral control of a flying machine."

The brothers set to work and built a model to test their ideas. It was a biplane kite with the wing-twisting – or warping as it became known – built into the five-foot span.

World fame for Wilbur: One of the kings who came to see him fly in France, King Edward VII talks to Wilbur at Le Mans.

Success at last: The army is interested and, in 1908, Orville takes a new Flyer to demonstrate it to the authorities.

The wing-tips were made flexible and the warping was done by pulling on cords held in the hands. The kite also had an "extra adjustable surface", a tailplane.

It worked. So the following year, 1900, they decided to build a full-sized glider.

The craft was a biplane with a 17 ft span. It was the machine that was eventually to lead to true powered flight. And so the aeroplane can claim to be solely a product of the 20th century.

That first full-sized glider built by the Wrights was the "great-grandfather" of their 1903 plane in which man finally took to the air.

Wilbur and Orville consulted the United States Weather Bureau and were told that a barren North Carolina sand bar was one of the windiest places in the country. It was a stretch of beach between Albemarle Sound and the Atlantic Ocean.

The Wrights chose as their testing ground a five-mile area near the village of Kitty Hawk which, even today, has a population of only about 250 people. There was another reason, besides the wind, that made it just what Wilbur and Orville were looking for.

There were hills to launch their gliders from. These were the Kill Devil Hills, and a 60 ft granite memorial now stands on the spot where the first powered flight began.

Wilbur and Orville first went there in September 1900 to assemble their new glider. Its construction was based on the calculations they had read about, but with the addition of

Triumph into tragedy: Orville's crash at Fort Myer in 1908 in which he was seriously injured and his passenger killed.

wing-warping and a front horizontal elevator. The wings were set at a dihedral angle – a shallow "V"-shape – which gives automatic lateral stability.

The glider was tested with and without a pilot. It was designed to fly with a man on board in winds of 15 to 20 mph, but the brothers found that winds of about 25 mph had to be blowing before it could get enough lift, even with the pilot lying prone to lessen resistance.

The flights they did make were kept down to a height of five or six feet. They were determined not to take unnecessary risks. In one of his first letters to Chanute, Wilbur had told the old man that he feared flying could possibly cost him his life – let alone money.

The next year, 1901, with a new and bigger glider, they went to Kitty Hawk again, this time flying from the dunes at Kill Devil Hills.

They had discovered that wings set at a dihedral angle were of practical use only in calm air, and that they tended to produce a continuous rocking motion. So Wilbur and Orville decided to build a machine that would not tend to right itself.

They would rely on the pilot's skill with the controls to keep the machine level, and make it as immune as possible to wind gusts. To achieve this they "arched" the wings from tip to tip – the exact reverse of what their predecessors had always done – which gave a drooped look.

The 1901 glider's wings also were more deeply curved, and the warping cables were operated by a hip cradle which the pilot could swing to the right or left. But though they made flights of several hundred feet the machine proved to be less controllable than the first one, in some cases flying better backwards than forwards

Its poor performance convinced the Wrights that there was something basically wrong with the calculations they had been following. They went back home to Dayton, threw everyone else's ideas on one side, and decided to rely entirely on their own investigations.

They built a crude wind tunnel to study air pressures and the action of air flowing over different wing shapes in an effort to find out what was going wrong.

In the autumn of 1902 the results of their research were used as a basis for a third glider, again slightly bigger than the others, and with a fixed vertical double fin at the rear.

The fin was to give them their last bit of trouble. It made the glider spin. Their early flights that year usually ended in disaster until they decided to hinge the fin and link it to the wing-warping controls so that they operated together.

With this arrangement they found they were able to make smooth, banked turns. Nearly 1,000 flights were made, the longest over 600 ft. Wilbur and Orville now felt that they knew enough to build a machine and know exactly how it would behave in the air.

They were on the verge of practical flight. All they had to do was add the power.

The 1903 machine, which they called the Flyer after their bicycle, was what today would be called a "real do-it-yourself" job.

It was made of spruce and ash, wood carefully selected to combine strength and lightness, and nailed and glued together. The wings were covered in muslin and braced with ordinary piano wire.

The brothers tried all the well-known motor manufacturers to find a suitable engine. But they soon discovered that the manufacturers were "too busy" to build them an engine. The real reason for their refusal was almost certainly that none of them wanted to be associated with the Wrights' crazy ideas about man-carrying flying machines.

The setback did not bother Wilbur and Orville for long. They built their own engine. They designed a four-cylinder, 12 hp unit and, with the help of their machinist, had it on test within six weeks.

Propellers were also a problem. There were no suitable ones being manufactured at the time, so they built those themselves as well. They decided that the Flyer should have two so that the engine could act on a larger volume of air than if there was only one propeller.

They took the completed machine to their Kitty Hawk camp in September. There they found that the wind, the shifting sand and the weather had moved their old hut. So they set to work on a new building and getting the previous year's glider ready for some flying practice before the attempt to get the Flyer off the ground.

The first morning back at camp did not start too well. The coffee-pot kept boiling over.

But Orville observed that the hills were in the best shape for gliding. He was confident that things would go well. And by November both the brothers were more sure than ever that the Flyer would be a success.

There had been problems. The propeller sprockets kept coming loose. But that had been fixed by the application of a little of Arnstein's patent hard cement.

Then the propeller shafts twisted while the engine was being test run, and Orville had to go all the way back to Dayton to get new ones made. He did not arrive back until December 11.

Three days before, Langley's aerodrome had made its second dive into the Potomac River.

And the world, or that part of it that still had any glimmer of interest left in manned flight, was more sure than ever that it was impossible.

On December 14 the Wright brothers were ready to prove everyone wrong.

They brought out the Flyer and signalled to their friends at the Kill Devil Hills Life Saving Station to come and watch. Orville described how it was decided which of the brothers should make the first flight: "We tossed up a coin . . . and Will won."

Wilbur climbed into position on the lower wing and the engine was started. But they had trouble freeing the rope that held the Flyer back on its starting-rail. When they did release it the plane ran down the rail, rising into the air about 15 ft. But the climb was too steep and, after travelling a few yards, it crashed back into the sand. It was all over in three and a half seconds, and the rudder was damaged and one of the front landing skids broken.

Wilbur put it down to "a trifling error due to lack of experience". But even though the test failed, neither he nor Orville now had any doubt at all that they were going to fly.

The first thing to do was repair the damage. This was completed, and conditions were again favourable, by December 17 even though it was bitterly cold, and the beach puddles were covered in ice.

Before they went home for the winter Wilbur and Orville were determined to know whether the Flyer was as good as they thought it was. Nothing would stop them now.

Once again they put out a signal for the men at the life-saving station. Four men and a boy turned out on that historic day: W. S. Dough, A. D. Ethridge from the station, W. C. Brinkley from Manteo, John T. Daniels, and the boy, Johnny Moore from Nags Head. Orville set up a camera to record the event and Daniels was to operate the shutter.

This time it was Orville's turn to take the controls. The engine was run to get it warm, the twin propellers made flashing circles behind the wings and the silent beach awoke to a sound like a reaper working in a distant field.

It was 10.35 am. The wind speed was 22 mph. The 60 ft starting-rail, laid down on level ground, faced into the wind.

The Flyer, its skid landing gear resting on a small truck fitted with rollers made from bicycle wheel hubs, was ready to go.

There was no difficulty in releasing the holding rope this time. With Wilbur at one wing-tip to steady the plane, the Flyer began its take-off run.

It was up after trundling along for 40 ft. Shakily it rose free from the earth and flew waveringly on for 12 seconds to land safely 120 ft away. The air speed had been about 30 mph.

There were no wild scenes of delight. In fact the Wrights thought that their effort – sensational as it was after their years of hard work, and centuries of striving by others – "very modest compared with the birds".

But it was the first flight in the history of the world in which a machine carrying a man had raised itself by its own power . . . had sailed forward on a level course without reduction of speed, and had finally landed without being wrecked.

Three more flights were made that day.

Wilbur made one of 11 seconds an hour later. Orville then took over the Flyer again at 11.40 am and flew for 200 ft in 15 seconds. Then Wilbur took off once more at midday and made a flight of 59 seconds covering 852 ft.

All the flights were made as close to the ground as possible, and there was little room for errors of judgment. On this last flight Wilbur found the elevator highly sensitive and, in trying to bring the Flyer's nose down, he over-corrected and the plane struck the ground damaging the elevator.

The little group stood around talking over the events of the morning. As they did so a gust of wind overturned the Flyer, breaking part of a wing and bending the propeller chain guides.

The Flyer never flew again. But the age of the flying machine had arrived at last.

Orville sent a telegram to his father telling him of the success, and asking him to inform the Press. Some newspapers did print the news. Bishop Wright reported "flaming headlines" in the *Cincinnati Enquirer*, and that he was besieged by reporters wanting pictures of Wilbur and Orville and their plane.

But by all accounts the Press reports were highly exaggerated. It was not until the New Year, January 1904, that a factual account of the first flight appeared in the *Chicago Daily News* after the Wrights had given a statement to the Associated Press. But they banned pictures of the Flyer and their methods.

The flight was not the end of their work. It was the beginning. They had a machine that could fly. What they now wanted was a really practical aeroplane – a safe, reliable machine that could fly long distances – "to present to the world for some serviceable purpose".

Until they were satisfied – and to protect their invention from spies who wanted to copy it and take the credit – they would keep themselves to themselves as much as possible.

It was to take another two years of hard work before Wilbur and Orville had the aeroplane they wanted, and another three years before they were able to convince anyone in authority that the flying machine had come to stay.

In 1904, with a new Flyer to test, they stayed nearer home. A Dayton banker, Torrence Huffman, lent them the 90-acre prairie eight miles outside the town.

When the plane was ready for its first trial the Wrights notified all the local newspapers. About 50 people turned up to see the flight but, with a wind of only three miles an hour blowing and an engine that refused to work properly, the plane twice failed to get off the ground.

The first time the brothers tried to take off, the Flyer just slid off the end of the starting-rail without rising at all. The second time it managed a glide of 60 ft. The Press went away and didn't bother to return.

But the engine trouble was only temporary. The brothers went on to make about 100 flights during the season, concentrating on mastering the control of the Flyer in the air. Eventually they were able to fly in a complete circle and land back at the starting-point.

The Huffman prairie was a marshy field and covered in molehills. These hazards, and the fact that the wind speed in the area was much lower than at Kill Devil Hills, led them to develop an assisted take-off device. This was a weighted derrick at the rear of the starting-rail which, through a system of pulleys and ropes, catapulted the Flyer into the air.

At the end of the year's trials they were making progress. Wilbur had made their longest flight so far. It had lasted five minutes and enabled him to make almost four circuits of the prairie. But they found that the Flyer tended to stall in tight turns.

The following year, with a new and "stretched" version of the Flyer, this problem was finally overcome. The wing-warping and rudder controls were disconnected so that the pilot could operate them independently. It gave them the absolute control they had been after.

Now they set out to prove the plane's reliability and endurance. On October 5 a flight of over 24 miles was made, the Flyer staying in the air for 38 minutes.

It was less than Wilbur and Orville had hoped for. Originally they had planned to make a flight lasting one hour, but one of them forgot to fill the reserve fuel tank and the Flyer ran out of petrol.

They had, to all intents and purposes, conquered the air. They now had a plane that, according to Orville, was capable of travelling "hundreds of miles in a single flight".

It was in this year, 1905, that the Wrights first offered the Flyer to the American Government, and were turned down flat.

They tried to interest the British and the French, too, but they had no success there either. Disappointed, and becoming increasingly bitter, Wilbur and Orville stopped flying. For two and a half years neither of them left the ground.

They spent the time building more planes. And when, in 1907, the Government offered £5,000 for a heavier-than-air machine, they were not caught unprepared.

The contract said the plane must carry two people 125 miles at not less than 36 mph, conditions which the newspapers at the time described as "drastic".

Wilbur and Orville took one of their Flyers to Kill Devil Hills and tested it to make sure it could meet the requirements, altering it so that the pilot sat upright, fitting a passenger seat, bigger petrol tanks and a larger engine.

Orville was to demonstrate a new Flyer for the Army in the autumn of 1908, while Wilbur went to France to make public exhibition flights in Europe. Orville began his tests in September, at Fort Myer, near Washington.

His first flight, before an audience of a few soldiers, threw the whole town into disorder. Later the same day he flew again, and every man, woman and child who could turned up to watch.

But his triumph turned to tragedy. On the 17th Orville took up a Lieutenant T. E. Selfridge as a passenger. One of the propellers split in mid-air and the Flyer crashed out of control from about 75 ft. Orville was seriously injured. But Selfridge was killed, the first man to die while making a powered flight.

Wilbur had been flying in France since August. His first flight, at the Hunaudières racecourse, near Le Mans, on the 8th was made before a highly critical audience of doubting French aviators and Pressmen. He took off, and in exactly 1 minute 45 seconds – the time it took to make two short circuits – he revolutionised European aviation.

He was able to write and tell Orville that his flights had caused "excitement beyond comprehension. The French", he wrote, "have simply become wild." Soon enthusiasts from England were making trips to France to see him.

Griffith Brewer recalled the time that Charles Rolls, founder of the Rolls-Royce car firm, heard that he was catching the night train to Paris and invited him to dinner. The two men were old friends and had competed in many balloon races together.

At dinner Rolls inquired in a whisper: "Brewer, why are you going to Paris?" Brewer replied: "Don't tell anyone, but I am going to see Wilbur Wright fly."

Rolls laughed and said: "Well, don't tell anyone, but I have just returned from seeing him fly."

"From that moment," Brewer said later, "we kept our balloons for pleasure races and accepted the arrival of mechanical flight."

It was not only Wilbur's flying that staggered them all, but the "astonishing simplicity" of the Flyer. One English enthusiast, Dr. F. W. Lanchester, was not at all impressed with the way the plane had been built. He commented on its "crudity of detail" and said that it was "almost a matter of surprise that it holds together".

Lord Northcliffe, proprietor of the London *Daily Mail*, whose prizes were to do so much to spur the advance of aviation, thought the machine looked "very rough".

Mr. C. G. Grunhold, a prominent member of the Aero Clubs of France and Britain, remarked: "I had always taken it that the surfaces of the plane should be absolutely air-proof to ensure resistance, but that this idea is a fallacy was proved by a rent in the under-plane large enough to put your hand through; and here and there the loops employed

to attach the canvas of the planes to the framework were missing.

"In fact, in one place, a portion of the canvas was attached by what looked suspiciously like a bootlace."

In spite of all this, it was noticed that "the Wright machine appears not to come to pieces, but continues to fly day after day without showing any signs of weakness or disintegration".

Wilbur was winning world fame, and "kings and lesser men" flocked to see his flights. He gave the Europeans the "push" they needed to lift their attempts to fly out of the groping stage to a point where they were producing really practical aeroplanes.

In 1909 the American Government finally bought a Wright machine for the Army, and with Flyers being built in France and Britain the fight to prove that man could fly was over.

The following year the Wrights designed a plane with a wheeled undercarriage for the first time. They also built a racing plane, the Baby Wright, which had no forward elevator. This was moved to the rear with the rudder, and the shape of the aeroplane as we know it today was complete.

But the Wrights were no longer the undisputed masters of the air. They had been teaching others to fly, and those to whom they had shown the way were taking over from them.

Wilbur and Orville – who had recovered from his Fort Myer crash – had other battles to fight, in the courts, to protect their invention. Then, after Wilbur's death in 1912, Orville was faced with one of the biggest challenges of all.

He had a row with the Smithsonian Institution over who had actually been the first to fly.

Langley's aerodrome, which had crashed into the Potomac River in 1903, was lent to Glenn Curtiss, one of the Wrights' chief American rivals, in 1914. The machine was tested again on a lake, and afterwards it was exhibited at the Smithsonian with the claim that it was the first man-carrying machine in history capable of sustained free flight.

Orville was furious. He refused to let the Institution have the 1903 Flyer and sent it instead to the Science Museum in London, where it was seen for the first time by the general public on the museum's opening day, March 20, 1928.

It was not until 1942 that all claims for the Langley machine were dropped. An American expert on the Wrights, Fred C. Kelly of Pennsylvania, sent to the Institution a list of alterations that had been made to the aerodrome for the 1914 trials.

There had been about 15 major changes. Included among them were modifications to the wings and their trussing, the controls, propellers and engine. But even after these "improvements", the aerodrome had only managed to rise into the air for a maximum of five seconds.

The Smithsonian climbed down and officially recognised that the Wrights had been the first men to fly. Orville gave permission for the Flyer to be returned to America but, as the Second World War was at its height, he decided it should stay in Britain until "transportation is less hazardous".

He also gave permission for a replica of the Flyer to be built for the Science Museum, which hangs there to this day. But, to be sure it was absolutely accurate, he insisted on correcting the drawings because he had found that the Flyer's "right side actually is four inches longer than the left".

And so, on December 17, 1948 – 45 years after the Flyer's finest hour – the frail little plane was taken back home and presented to the Smithsonian Institution. But Orville was not there to see it. He had died in the January at the age of 76.

The label that the Institution placed on the Flyer is a fitting epitaph for Orville and his brother. It said: ". . . By original scientific research the Wright Brothers discovered the principles of human flight. As inventors, builders and flyers, they further developed the airplane, taught men to fly, and opened the era of aviation."

Left: *The Flyer goes home: the plane is handed over to the American Air Attache at the Science Museum in London before being shipped back to the Smithsonian Institution.*

On their way home from Europe in 1909 the Wright brothers visited Shellbeach, England's Kill Devil Hills, where much of Britain's early aviation history was made. Here they pose with many of the important British flying pioneers of the day, including the Short Brothers – who built Wright machines under licence and later went on to produce the famous Empire flying boats – and the future Lord Brabazon. This unique picture shows, standing from the left: J. D. F. Andrews, Oswald Short, Horace Short, Eustace Short, Frank McClean, Griffith Brewer, Frank Butler, Dr. W. S. J. Lockyer and Warwick Wright. Seated from the left: J. T. C. Moore-Brabazon, Wilbur Wright, Orville Wright and C. S. Rolls who was killed in a Wright biplane a year after the photograph was taken.

Birds fly, why can't I? The idea that obsessed men for thousands of years and inspired the "tower jumpers" to imitate the birds.

Beware of imitations

It was a very long time before anyone began to realise that man would only achieve effective flight through scientific methods, and not by trying to imitate the birds.

The doubter was an Italian scientist, Giovanni Borelli, whose writings were published in Rome in 1680 after he had carefully studied the problem. He concluded that men's muscles were too weak for them "to be able to fly craftily by their own strength".

As far as we know no human-powered flight, sustained and controlled, has ever been made, though in theory it is now thought to be possible by using the latest light-weight materials. It would be expensive to build a suitable craft, and require a "pilot" capable of great physical effort. Scientists believe that such a man could fly under his own power, but extremely slowly and not very high. It is also doubtful that his flight could last long.

But for thousands of years dedicated men, visionaries and plain cranks were obsessed with the idea: "Birds can fly, why can't I?"

And from their attempts to find the answer, many of which were doomed to end in injury and sometimes death, grew fanciful myths, machines and legends.

They appear in the stories of ancient China, **Persia**, Rome and Greece. And it is from Greece that the most famous of all flying legends has been handed down. The story of **Daedalus and his son Icarus.**

Daedalus was a mythical Greek sculptor, architect and inventor exiled on the island of Crete. But he angered King Minos and decided to make wings out of feathers and wax so that he and Icarus could escape to Italy.

With the adventurous spirit of youth Icarus tried to be clever and flew too high. His impetuousness took him too near the sun, which melted the wax holding the feathers of his wings together, and he fell to his death in the sea. We now know, of course, that long before Icarus got anywhere near the sun the air would have become too thin for him to breathe and he would have been driven to a lower altitude by the cold.

Another legend tells of the exploits of **King Bladud,** founder of the city of Bath and father of Shakespeare's King Lear. He is supposed to have ruled Britain in the 9th century BC and is credited with making an attempt to fly

The most famous flying legend of all, the story of Daedalus and his son Icarus. The adventurous Icarus about to plunge to his death in the sea after flying too near the sun.

This is the type of aeroplane that really put Europeans into the air – the Box Kite – developed by Henri Farman and the Voisin brothers in France. Many of the early pioneers earned their "wings" on Box Kites. The type was used by White and Paulhan for the first epic long distance contest, their London to Manchester Race in 1910.

Successful killer: A First World War SE 5a, sometimes claimed to be the outstanding British fighter plane of the 1914–18 war. It had a range of 250 miles, a top speed of nearly 140 mph and twin machine-guns. This one belongs to the Shuttleworth Collection of historic aircraft in England.

Hawker Hart: In some ways a "blend" of old fashioned biplane and the coming monoplane fighter. Note the extensive streamlining of the sharp nose. The Hart was a between-the-wars, high performance military aircraft. High performance for its day. In fact its top speed was under 200 mph.

Vacuum: *In 1670 an Italian Jesuit priest, Francesco de Lana, thought of fixing four giant copper globes to a boat. By removing all the air from them he hoped to give the "air ship" the necessary lift. The central sail was to propel the ship along. The flaw in de Lana's idea was that globes thin enough to provide lift would have been collapsed by the pressure of the air outside them. With all the air removed from them, globes thick enough to stand up to the outside pressure would have been too heavy for the ship to get off the ground. The device was never built, and de Lana seems to have been discouraged from further experiments because he was convinced that God would not allow anyone to succeed in building a machine that would actually fly. De Lana reasoned that such things could be used to bring destruction to people below: "Fireballs and bombs could be hurled down . . . and cities could thus be destroyed, with the certainty that the airship would come to no harm, as the missiles could be thrown from a great height." Bombs, missiles. Curiously nuclear-age expressions for someone living nearly 300 years ago.*

Left: **Muscle Power:** *A French locksmith called Besnier attempted man-powered flights in 1678 with a simple flapper device. It consisted of two poles balanced on Besnier's shoulders. On the ends of each pole were hinged flaps that opened out as they came down and folded together as they were moved upwards. They were operated at one end by hand and at the other by the feet through a rope attachment.*

Below: **Magnetism:** *Another Jesuit, Laurenco de Gusmao, designed his "Passarola" in 1709. It was an ornithopter complete with bird's head, wings, tail and an overhead sail. It was to have been held up in the air by two magnetic globes. It is thought that early engravings are the work of a misinformed artist, and a model, by no means as fanciful as the one depicted, may have been flown by Gusmao as a glider.*

over ancient London with artificial wings. Like Icarus, he also fell to his death after crashing into his "launching pad", the temple of Apollo.

Now, nearly 3,000 years later, American astronauts have flown to the Moon in their spacecraft Apollo, which is named after the Greek sun-god.

About midway between these two events an English monk called Oliver of Malmesbury had a shot at "tower jumping". He made his bid to conquer the air in the 11th century AD and lived to tell the tale, even if he wasn't exactly able to walk away entirely unscathed. He broke his legs after flying more than a furlong with wings tied to his hands and feet. After the crash he complained that the reason for his failure was that he had forgotten to equip himself with a "tail".

It was in the 15th century that the human mind – and one mind in particular – began to come to grips with the problem it had set itself.

Leonardo da Vinci, the man who painted the *Mona Lisa*, and was sculptor, poet, composer, scientist and philosopher, turned his vast talent to the study of the new art of human flight.

But even Leonardo – recognised as "one of the outstanding creative geniuses of human history" – was firmly convinced that muscles of men would be sufficient to lift a flying machine. His notebooks contain numerous **flapping-wing devices** (ornithopters) based on his studies of the birds. About 1500 he drew a detailed design for a helicopter.

It had a screw-shaped (helix) rotor which is said to have inspired Igor Sikorsky who eventually became the world's leading pioneer of helicopters.

The helicopter was one of Leonardo's two important inventions. The other was his drawing of the parachute, which he described as "a tent made of linen of which the apertures have all been stopped up", to enable a man to "throw himself down from any great height without sustaining injury".

Leonardo died in 1519. But no one had the chance to examine his ideas and follow them up. His manuscripts lay hidden for over 300 years, and it was not until the late 19th century that his work in the field of aeronautics was given any serious consideration. By the time this happened he had been overtaken.

In the meantime men went on trying to perfect an aeroplane. And with no suitable source of power they thought of using all sorts of things to get one into the air: vacuum, magnetism, steam, clockwork, gunpowder, twisted rubber bands, gas, compressed air and, yes, good old human muscle power.

They were to meet with consistent failure for more than 200 years. Then, one November day in 1783, two men borne by a device of linen and paper rose triumphantly into the sky above Paris. Their "engine" was a fire of wool and straw. Men's "loftiest aspiration" had been achieved at last, but not in an aeroplane. The device of linen and paper was . . . a balloon.

Muscle Power: One of the last attempts by the old style "tower jumpers" was made by the 62-year-old Marquis of Bacqueville in Paris about 1742. A large crowd gathered to watch him after he announced that he was going to try and fly the Seine with the aid of artificial wings. He climbed to the top of his mansion overlooking the river, leaped into space . . . and crashed ungracefully onto a washerwoman's barge, breaking a leg.

Steam: One hundred years later in 1842 William Henson, of Chard in Somerset, patented his Aerial Steam Carriage. His work was inspired by Cayley whom he called "the father of aerial navigation". Henson's design is acknowledged to be the first for a modern powered aeroplane. It was a high-wing monoplane with a 150 ft span and a cabin slung underneath. There was a tricycle undercarriage, a fan-shaped tail unit with a vertical rudder, and twin pusher propellers. The machine gave rise to a grand scheme for an "Aerial Transit Company, with the object of flying letters Goods and passengers from place to place." Many ambitious illustrations appeared showing Henson's "Ariel" – as it was called – over London and even China, India and the Pyramids of Egypt. The project earned considerable ridicule from the cartoonists of the day. With his friend John Stringfellow, Henson tested a model in 1847, but its steam engine was too heavy and not powerful enough to sustain flight. Henson gave up and emigrated to America. But Stringfellow carried on alone, experimenting with several more models. One of them was launched from a wire the following year, and though it seems to have achieved some sort of flight – either a glide or powered "hop" – opinions are divided on whether it was capable of a sustained performance. Discouraged, Stringfellow abandoned his experiments for 20 years.

Facing page upper: *The "trusty" that failed: A JU87 Stuka dive bomber relied on by Hitler's Luftwaffe to batter the way ahead for the Führer's army. But it failed him when it came to fight its own kind in the air. It proved to be just as slow as the old fashioned biplanes and easy prey for the fast British fighters in the early days of the Second World War.*

Above: *The defender that became the attacker, America's B17 Flying Fortress. Originally intended to keep raiders well away from the American coasts, it became one of the Allies' heavy bomber force which was to be the key to victory in the Second World War.*

Facing page lower: *And this is one of the planes that ruined the Stuka's reputation, the Hawker Hurricane. The plane was a high-speed peace-time experiment, but it turned out to be one of the most formidable fighting machines in the history of aviation, taking over from the RAF's older generation of biplane fighters.*

Below: *One of "The Few", the famous Spitfire. A descendant of the British Schneider Trophy seaplane race winners it fought, with the Hurricane, the might of the Luftwaffe in the Battle of Britain. The Spitfire was so respected – even by its enemies – that one German pilot asked Luftwaffe chief Hermann Goering to equip his squadron with Spitfires if he wanted the British cleared from the skies.*

Above: *Clockwork:* *A French naval officer, Felix Du Temple, used clockwork to power a model in 1857. It took off, maintained flight and landed safely – the first fixed wing aircraft to leave the ground unaided. It had swept-forward wings with a dihedral, a 12-bladed tractor propeller which "pulled" from the front instead of "pushing" from behind, a tricycle undercarriage, a tailplane and rudder. The machine was built and tested in 1874 with a hot-air engine. Launched down a sloping ramp it managed a short "leap" with a young sailor aboard as pilot. The event is claimed to be the first time a man-carrying powered plane left the ground, but still it was not a powered "flight".*

Below: *Another "tower jumper" comes to a sticky end. Oliver of Malmesbury crashes to earth and blames his lack of a tail for his failure.*

Over the Channel in England a ten-year-old boy heard about the astonishing event. The boy was the young Sir George Cayley. He was to provide the key to the secrets of the age-old dream.

Cayley decided to concentrate on powered flight, and he wrote: "My object was to leave out the unwieldy bulk of the balloon altogether and to make use of the inclined plane propelled by a light first mover . . . I am fully convinced that this mode of aerial navigation is practicable, and will, ere long, be accomplished."

He was the first to really understand, and set down, the principles of mechanical flight. Cayley did not ignore the birds. He also studied them, but applied what he learned to man's particular needs.

The problem, he wrote, was this: "To make a surface support a given weight by the application of power to the resistance of air." Unfortunately, even for Cayley the right sort of power was still not available as his "light first mover". The steam-engines of the day were far from light.

Cayley experimented with "lift" and, from his observations of the wings of birds, concluded that it was best obtained with an inclined and curved plane. His researches led him to build a simple **kite-like glider** in 1804 which is claimed as the first real aeroplane, and earned him the title of the "true inventor of the aeroplane".

The glider's mainplane was set at a six-degree angle on a five-foot pole. It had a movable tail consisting of "two planes crossing each other at right angles", the basic design

Rubber Bands: *Alphonse Penaud was another Frenchman, and a pioneer of significance. He built what he called his "Planophore" which had a motor of twisted rubber bands. It was no more than a toy of 20 inches in length, but it was the first flying machine to have built-in stability. It had mainplanes with dihedral tips, a fixed tailplane and a pusher propeller, a layout that became standard. Penaud flew it in public in 1871. Then, in 1876, he produced an idea for a very forward-looking amphibious plane which contained practically all the needs of a modern aircraft. It was to have been a passenger-carrying machine with broad wings, rear elevators, a vertical rudder, retractable undercarriage, an enclosed engine and a glass cockpit cover. There were twin tractor propellers and the steering surfaces were to be operated by a single "control column". Even instruments were included: an aneroid pressure indicator (altimeter), anemometer (presumably a form of air speed indicator), compass, and a type of artificial horizon to help the pilot keep the craft straight and level in flight. But Penaud could find no one with enough faith in his project to provide financial backing and the machine was never built. At the age of 30 in 1880, dispirited, in poor health and discouraged, Penaud committed suicide.*

for all modern aeroplanes. Cayley was able to vary the glider's centre of gravity with a sharp weight which could be stuck into the pole at any point.

He recorded that "it was very pretty to see it sail down a steep hill". And it gave him the idea for a "larger instrument".

There was little doubt in Cayley's mind that he had formulated the principles of what he called "this noble art". In asking an editor to publish one of his essays on flight in 1809 he wrote: ". . . In the course of much attention to this subject, I may be expediting the attainment of an object that will in time be found of great importance to mankind." He was right.

Cayley discovered the need to streamline and to stabilise a craft in the air as well as control it, and pointed out that the chief basis for stability was for the wings to be set at a dihedral angle – a shallow V shape.

He built his "larger instrument", a full-sized **man-carrying glider**. A young boy is said to have been lifted off the ground in it and carried several yards during a downhill flight. Cayley's granddaughter was a witness at another demonstration about 1853 when the family coachman flew across a small valley near Brompton Hall, Cayley's Yorkshire home.

According to her account of the happening, the coachman got himself clear of the machine and told Sir George: "I wish to give notice. I was hired to drive, not to fly."

Cayley died four years later. The value of his work in the field of aviation is regarded today as incalculable. But his interests were wide, and during his life he contributed much to the development of artificial limbs, theatre acoustics, hot-air engines, railway equipment, education, land reclamation, artillery and philosophy. He also found time to invent the self-righting lifeboat, caterpillar tracks for tractors, the tension wheel – forerunner of the spoked bicycle wheel – and become an MP.

"Aerial navigation" was the name Cayley gave to flying. He thought it gave dignity to something that, at the time, was the subject of a great deal of public ridicule.

But no matter how ridiculous the pursuit of flight appeared to most people, there were men who were prepared to weather the scorn, as there must be for any new idea to succeed.

The pace of progress began to quicken. Just ten years after the death of Cayley a son was born to the Wright family in the New World of America. His parents called him Wilbur. The dream of many men throughout thousands of years was merely a generation away from fulfilment.

The Balloon
goes up

It was raining at five o'clock on the afternoon of August 27, 1783. But no one in the crowd of 50,000 French citizens gathered in the Champ-de-Mars in Paris rushed for shelter.

They had been waiting all day while a young physicist called J. A. C. Charles struggled to fill a 13 ft diameter fabric and rubber globe with hydrogen gas, commonly known as "inflammable air" because it burned so fiercely. But it was also very much lighter than ordinary air and had great lifting power.

At last the globe was ready and Charles released it. The balloon rose above the heads of the crowd and, after two minutes, it vanished into the low-lying clouds.

The performance had been watched by Benjamin Franklin, the American envoy in Paris. When it was all over someone in the crowd near him remarked: "Interesting. But what use is it?"

Franklin looked at the speaker and answered with another question: "What use," he said, "is a new-born baby?"

Fifteen miles away, in the village of Gonesse, the puzzled locals saw a strange monster descending on them from the sky. They thought it was something from another world and they were afraid.

The large sphere had appeared suddenly and silently from out of the clouds and bounced gently to earth in a field. For an hour the people of Gonesse watched it lying there. Then, gaining courage from their numbers, they attacked.

Setting about the balloon with pitchforks, they were even more frightened when the escaping hydrogen "hissed" back at them. So they tied the thing to the tail of a horse which ripped it to shreds in a cross-country gallop.

The Government issued a proclamation to tell the people that the new flying globes, far from being "an alarming phenomenon", were merely machines which could not possibly cause any harm. And, some day, they might even "prove useful to the wants of society".

Fortunately there had been no one in Charles's balloon, or he might have been attacked, too.

But a short time later, at six minutes to two o'clock on November 21, two men made the first aerial voyage in history.

Their names were Jean-François Pilatre de Rozier, a young doctor, and the Marquis d'Arlandes, an infantry officer. It was their flight that the boy who was to become Sir George Cayley heard about over in England.

The two men made a five-mile trip across the rooftops of Paris in a hot-air balloon made by two brothers, Joseph and Etienne Montgolfier, who were papermakers in the town of Annonay.

They had discovered that hot air could be made to lift a balloon by watching the smoke and sparks leap into the air from the kitchen fire. And they experimented with small silken bags before building a balloon, with an "engine" of blazing wool and straw, big enough to carry two people.

De Rozier had made several tethered ascents in October, but his trip with d'Arlandes was the first free flight made by men.

The effect on the civilised world was similar to that of the first manned Moon landing in July 1969. It was hailed as a feat of supreme courage and the birth of a new age of discovery for men on Earth.

But it was not long before the flying men – the aeronauts – became more adventurous.

The first cross-Channel balloon flight was made only 14 months after de Rozier and d'Arlandes's journey across Paris.

Another Frenchman, Jean-Pierre François Blanchard, and an American-born doctor, John Jeffries, took off from Dover on January 7, 1785. They landed safely at Calais only after throwing everything movable overboard – anchors, brandy, food, ballast – even Blanchard's trousers were sacrificed.

Ballooning quickly became a craze, as a sport for racing, and as a spectacle at fairs and carnivals. Thrill-hungry fairground visitors paid for rides or watched daredevil parachute descents.

There was even a wedding in a balloon high above New York in 1865.

And, of course, balloons were used in war.

The French Republican Army used a captive balloon for observing during the Battle of Fleurus in 1794, the Federal Army used a balloon during the crossing of the Rappahannock River during the American Civil War in 1862, and during the siege of Paris during the Franco-Prussian War in 1870–71 66 balloons left the city. They carried over 100 passengers, mail and carrier pigeons which later flew back to Paris with messages on microfilm.

Many long-distance flights were attempted, like the 804-mile epic by John Wise – who dreamed of crossing the Atlantic by balloon – between St. Louis and New York in 1859.

But the big "gas-bags" had a severe handicap. They could not be steered. They were completely at the mercy of the winds.

Numerous ingenious ideas were put forward to overcome the problem. Blanchard and Jeffries carried oars on their cross-Channel flight. Great paddles, hand-operated fans, sails and rudders, even harnessed birds were all considered as possible power and steering devices.

It was not until the last few years of the 19th century, when the petrol engine appeared, that steerable balloons – dirigibles – were successful.

The dirigibles were elongated, sausage-shaped balloons with power units and passengers slung in gondola-like cars underneath. In their most refined and famous form they were known as Zeppelins after the German airship pioneer Count Ferdinand von Zeppelin.

The Count launched his first Zeppelin in 1900 and within ten years his airships had introduced the first aerial passenger services in Germany. Up until the outbreak of the First World War five Zeppelins carried over 35,000 passengers 170,000 miles without a single mishap. It was a proud record, but one that was to be sadly shattered.

A balloon with sails, one of the ways they tried to solve the problem of control.

The Zeppelins were enormous structures. The first was nearly 420 ft long, 38 ft round. The famous *Graf Zeppelin*, which made a round-the-world flight in 1929, was 772 ft long and 100 ft round at its widest part. It had five engines giving a combined power of 2,650 hp and a maximum speed of 80 mph.

And the Zeppelins were stately, elegant, smooth and luxurious. In sharp contrast to the uncomfortable, noisy, dirty and unreliable new heavier-than-air craft called aeroplanes.

The gigantic airships were like aerial hotels, with spacious lounges, splendid dining-rooms, promenade decks. The *Hindenburg*, described by its commander, Captain Max Pruss, as the "best and finest ship for travellers", had a cabin for every one of its 72 passengers, hot and cold water, air conditioning, even a grand piano on board.

But their great bulk and slowness made them vulnerable to the weather and, when they were used as bombers to raid England between 1914 and 1918, they fell easy victims to the nippier fighter planes.

A year after the war ended, and only a month after the first non-stop Atlantic crossing by an aeroplane, the British airship R-34 flew the Atlantic both ways.

But it was the German *Graf Zeppelin* and the *Hindenburg* that pioneered transatlantic passenger travel in the 1930s when heavier-than-air planes had not been developed enough to make the long trip.

Then a series of disasters overtook the airships.

Britain's R-101, on a flight to India in 1930, burst into flames and crashed in France. Fifty-four people died.

The American airships *Akron* and *Macon* were also wrecked with the loss of 76 lives.

On May 3, 1937, the *Hindenburg* left Germany with 97 passengers for its first flight of the year across the Atlantic.

Just after seven o'clock in the evening three days later the giant 804 ft airship approached its mooring tower at Lakehurst, New Jersey. The mooring cables were lowered and the *Hindenburg* sank slowly until it was less than 200 ft above the ground.

Captain Pruss had brought his ship in under a thunderstorm and he was in the control car supervising the landing when he heard an explosion.

Flames licked at the 2,500,000 cu. ft of highly inflammable hydrogen in the great fabric gas-bag of the *Hindenburg*. The fire engulfed the tail section and swiftly swept the whole length of the ship.

Twisted, flaming girders crumpled to the ground before the eyes of the horrified spectators who were watching the landing. Screaming passengers leapt for their lives. Thirty-six didn't make it. Many of those who did were badly burned.

The cause of the tragic end of the *Hindenburg* is still a mystery, though it is believed that leaking hydrogen may have been ignited by lightning.

But the end of the *Hindenburg* was also the end of the balloon age. The aeroplane was taking over.

The years
of adventure

Three years after the Wrights' epic achievement at Kitty Hawk, a millionaire Brazilian airship pioneer, Alberto Santos-Dumont, astounded Europe by flying 200 ft in a strange, swan-like machine at Bagatelle, near Paris.

It was the start of the most adventurous and romantic period in man's struggle to master the air.

Dumont's plane, the **14 bis**, was built by the Voisin brothers, Charles and Gabriel, two French gliding enthusiasts. It was of bamboo, covered with fabric, and had box-kite wings with a pronounced dihedral. Control was by another box-kite arrangement set forward on the end of a long "neck". The 50 hp Antoinette engine was placed at the rear, and when in flight the plane appeared to be travelling backwards.

The pilot stood upright, and Dumont flew those 200 ft at 25 mph.

The Wrights were still virtually ignored in America, and so little information about them had filtered through to Europe that Dumont believed, when he took to the air that day, October 23, 1906, he was the first man to succeed in flying a heavier-than-air machine.

Mr. C. G. Grunhold, an eyewitness of that first flight, recalls how, in the cold, damp air of the autumn evening, the little crowd stood about waiting for Dumont. The general flimsiness of the great box-kite suggested to Grunhold that it would be "at the mercy of the slightest ground current".

But Dumont "mounted" the machine and started the engine. The aeroplane, which was fitted with cycle wheels, ran for a few yards along the ground then suddenly rose into the air. It flew steadily for a while, and then began to rock visibly. "Santos cut off his ignition at once," says Grunhold, "and his descent was distinctly abrupt."

The landing caused some damage to the 14 bis. "But what did a broken elevating plane and a couple of wheels matter in such an hour of victory? A power-driven machine had flown."

The official observers, like Grunhold, were so overcome by Dumont's effort that they forgot to check the whole distance of the flight. But a month later, at Bagatelle again, they must have been more alert. Dumont flew 722 ft and was awarded the French Aero Club's prize for the first flight of 100 m, a "world record".

Dumont's success led him to make two bold prophecies in a newspaper interview reported on November 16, 1906. He said:

"I am quite certain that within five years people will be aeroplaning to the same extent as they are now using motor-cars, and as the cost of an aeroplane will be much less than that of a motor-car, the aeroplane will be in more universal use.

"I assert unhesitatingly also that aeroplanes will be far safer than motoring, and the percentage of fatal accidents will be less."

Only the second of these prophecies was to prove accurate.

The aeroplane does not cost less than the motor-car because it is a much more complicated piece of machinery, especially today. In Dumont's time there were no vast banks of instruments to tell a pilot what was happening to his aeroplane at any time. There were no fitted radios, radar, hydraulic systems, navigational aids.

A modern intercontinental jetliner now costs about £3,000,000, and you would have to be quite well off to afford to own and fly even a small club plane. And piloting an aircraft, of course, takes a lot more skill and knowledge than driving a car.

Which is one reason why Dumont was right about fatalities in the air. It is unfair to try and compare the number of deaths from road accidents with deaths from aeroplane accidents. The two types of transport are so different, but it is estimated that within ten years flying will be the safest form of travel there is.

During the year following Dumont's flights at Bagatelle, a French manufacturer of motor-car headlights, Louis **Blériot**, produced the **monoplane** – an aeroplane with a single wing, instead of the two-winged biplane – the forerunner of the monoplanes we know today.

Blériot's had a fuselage with an airscrew in front, a rudder tail unit with combined elevators and ailerons.

Aviation was beginning to progress. The Wrights had competition in America from a young motor cyclist called Glenn Curtiss. Helped by the inventor of the telephone, Alexander Graham Bell and others, who formed the Aerial Experiment Association, Curtiss built the **June Bug**. This was a biplane with movable wing-tips which he flew for a

The strange, swan-like machine in which Santos Dumont took to the air at Bagatelle, Paris, in 1906. So little news about the Wrights had travelled to Europe that Dumont thought he was the first man to fly.

mile before several hundred people at New York in July 1908.

The flight brought him far more public recognition than the Wrights had received. But the wing-tip control surfaces brought him into conflict with the brothers, who took him to court accusing him of infringing their wing-warping patent. The Wrights won the case, and Curtiss later moved his wing-control surfaces in between the mainplanes.

People were now beginning to recognise the value of the Wrights' work. Orville was commissioned to prepare a machine for military trials for the American Government. While he stayed at home Wilbur went to France to perform a series of demonstration flights.

He amazed the struggling French pioneers. At first they had been sceptical, but after watching the ease with which he turned, banked and flew figures of eight, their doubts vanished. One of them, Leon Delagrange, remarked: "We don't even exist."

What was it like to fly in those fragile little machines?

Frank Hedges Butler, founder of the United Kingdom Aero Club and a "veteran of nearly every conceivable form of locomotion, including 120 free balloon ascents and a voyage in a dirigible ballon", was taken for a **flight by Wilbur Wright**.

Wilbur's headquarters had been set up at the Hunaudières racecourse near Le Mans. Butler described the experience in the February issue of *London Magazine* in 1909. Everything he had experienced before "was as

Competition for the Wrights: Glenn Curtiss flying his June Bug in which he covered a mile at New York in 1908.

nought," he wrote, "compared with the prospect of actually flying.

"It was the happiest moment of my life. Mr. Wright escorted me to a seat situated exactly in the middle of the front of the aeroplane, and he occupied the seat on my left.

"This struck me as the embodiment of mechanical cleverness. The effect of the arrangement is . . . astonishingly simple. The aeroplane was weighted on my right in such a manner as to be balanced to a nicety by Mr. Wright and his levers on my left.

"Directly I took my seat I pulled my cap well down on my head, for fear it might blow off and become entangled in the machinery . . . the engines were running smoothly [Butler was referring to the twin propellers operated from the single engine]. The next instant Mr. Wright was in his place, the starting weights began to descend and the aeroplane made a dart down the declined rail some 20 yds long. The first movement reminded me somewhat of a switchback in its early stages.

"The thrust of the propeller blades speedily increased the pace at which we were travelling, and before the end of the runner was reached we were off the earth and gracefully soaring upwards.

"Mere words can only convey an imperfect impression of what it feels like to fly . . . at one moment you seem to be in the most perfect transport of unalloyed joy, and the next you are overwhelmed by the supreme satisfaction of having at last established a conquest over the air.

"Although we were rushing along at something like 40 miles an hour, the prevailing sensation was one of absolute security. The perfect composure of Mr. Wright was contagious. There he sat with a lever in each hand. The one on the right steered and deflected the wings; that on the left regulated the planes in front, and so controlled the altitude of the machine. The idea of flying from Paris to London was growing into a commonplace reality.

"We rose at will to the height of the treetops, and gracefully dipped down to within a few feet of the earth . . . the left lever moved slightly, and away we soared again. . . ."

Then Wilbur Wright piloted his passenger gently back to earth. After that no wonder Butler was moved to comment: "I am convinced that he [Wright] has a great deal up his sleeve, that he has made infinitely vaster discoveries concerning the art of flight than he has yet proclaimed to the world, and moreover I believe that the stupendous import of his knowledge is not fully comprehended by Mr. Wright himself."

Butler followed this graphic description of flying in those early days with an interview with the colourful S. F. Cody, Aviator Expert to the British War Office. Cody was an American-born adventurer who dressed like a cowboy and built the War Office a biplane that they called **British Army Aeroplane No. 1**.

In the interview Cody hinted that he was considering his prospects of winning the £10,000 prize being offered for the first London to Manchester flight.

Above: *Cody's British Army Aeroplane No. 1, the machine he built for the War Office.*

Below: *A flight with Wilbur Wright: Wilbur takes up a passenger during his demonstrations in France. Here he flies over the smart carriages of some of the people who came to watch.*

Above left: *The Avro Triplane, one of A. V. Roe's experimental aircraft. It was covered with brown paper and powered by a 9 hp engine.*

Above: *The first enclosed cabin aeroplane of 1912.*

Below: *A. V. Roe about to swing the propeller of one of his biplanes in which he made a few brief "hops" at Brooklands in 1908.*

Butler concluded by observing: "It would be futile to speculate on the amazing possibilities which have been opened up by this latest addition to the world's wonders. Once across the Channel by aeroplane, and England no longer remains an island enjoying splendid isolation. New phases of life will spring into being, and a new order of things will perforce obtain."

The aeroplane, and that French car headlight manufacturer, were to end England's "splendid isolation" within six months.

In the meantime Lieutenant-Colonel J. T. C. Moore-Brabazon (later Lord Brabazon) made history in England.

The aviation writer Harry Harper described the details in a letter to Mr. O. Pulvermacher at the *Daily Mail* on March 5, 1929. He wrote:

"Though Mr. A. V. Roe did make a brief 'hop' of about 75 feet at Brooklands as long ago as June 8th, 1908, the Royal Aero Club holds that this machine did not travel far enough through the air to come under the heading of 'free flight'.

"The Club has now decided officially that the British subject who made the first flight in a heavier-than-air machine in the British Isles was Lt. Col. J. T. C. Moore-Brabazon.

"Col. Moore-Brabazon's flight was made at Shellbeach, Isle of Sheppey, on May 2nd, 1909, in a **French Voisin biplane**.

"He rose from 50 to 80 feet high, and flew for a distance of from a quarter to half a mile."

Brabazon, like many other English pilots, had gone to the French to learn how to fly.

But mostly it was a case of getting into a flying machine and finding out for yourself. Brabazon gave this description of one of his early flying experiences:

"You were sitting out on the front wing, nothing underneath you and nothing to hold you in. Very alarming I always found, when you got up to any height at all. . . .

"The side planes were operated by my feet, the rudder by my left hand and the elevator by my right. It was very difficult really. I don't know how we did it."

And it was Brabazon who became the holder of the Royal Aero Club's pilot's licence No. 1 for being the first Briton to fly a circular mile in an all-British-built machine in October.

A. V. Roe was destined to become equally as prominent as Brabazon. The former Merchant Navy officer later founded the Avro Company which produced the Second World War Lancaster bombers, one of the most successful aircraft ever built, and other famous types.

But in those early days Roe was experimenting with biplanes and triplanes. He crashed so often at one period that he was prosecuted as a menace to public safety. He called his aircraft "avroplanes" and it was he who built the first enclosed cabin aeroplane in 1912. His 1911 biplane led to the First World War Avro 504, three of which were to carry out the first long-range strategic bombing raid in flying history.

But it was Louis Blériot who woke up the world to the

Above: *The arrival at Dover: Blériot and his wife surrounded by welcoming crowds after his 37-minute historic flight.*

Left: *Louis Blériot leaves Calais and sets out to conquer the English Channel.*

possibilities of the aeroplane by conquering the Channel early on the morning of July 25, 1909. It was an event that had, as well as the drama of the achievement itself, a great behind-the-scenes drama, too.

Hubert Latham, a colourful half-English, half-French character who smoked cigarettes in a long holder, set out to make the crossing on July 19 in an **Antoinette monoplane**, designed and built by Leon Levavasseur. But on the way over his engine failed and he landed in the sea, to be rescued by a French ship.

Latham ordered another plane so that he could try again when the weather improved.

But Blériot had set up headquarters on the coast and, kept awake by a burn on his foot, he decided early on July 25 that the wind had dropped enough for him to have a chance of success. In his **XI monoplane** fitted with a 25 hp Anzani engine – half the power of the Antoinette – he took off from a field near Calais and headed out to sea. He had no compass to tell him his direction, or any other instruments.

By the time Latham's helpers realised Blériot was heading for England, and not just testing his plane, the wind had risen again and Latham never took off at all that morning.

Out over the sea Blériot was peering into the gloom. . . . "I was alone, isolated, lost in the middle of the foamy sea, seeing nothing on the horizon, not even a boat. Those ten minutes seemed long to me and truly, I was happy to catch sight of a gray line which detached itself from the sea. It was the English coast."

He landed near Dover Castle. It had taken just 37 minutes to cover the 20 miles from France. Blériot hit the headlines round the world, receiving a hero's welcome in London and Paris.

Thinking men in England saw that the flight had a sinister prospect, too. Sir Alan Cobham, later to set up records for flights within the British Empire, observed: "The day that Blériot flew the Channel marked the end of our insular safety, and the beginning of the time when Britain must seek another form of defence besides ships."

The sporting Latham, determined not to be beaten, tried again to fly the Channel two days after Blériot. But once more his engine let him down.

He was back in the air again the following month at the now famous Rheims Air Meet. It was the world's first flying meeting and nearly all the pioneer pilots competed except the Wrights. At last the general public could see for themselves just what these new miracle machines could do.

Nearly 40 aircraft took part. Glenn Curtiss won the speed award, the Gordon Bennett Trophy, with an average of 43 mph. Henry Farman, the son of an English newspaperman living in France, set up an endurance record in an improved plane of his own design. It was powered by a revolutionary rotary engine – the main centre shaft stayed still while the cylinders spun round it – called a Gnome. He flew for 3 hours 4 minutes and 50 seconds while covering 112 miles.

Latham won the altitude award with a height of 500 ft in his Antoinette.

Another pilot at the Rheims meeting was Louis Paulhan. He is reported to have flown "extremely well" at the time. Within a year his name was to be on everyone's lips, like Blériot's. He was to capture the *Daily Mail*'s £10,000 prize for the first London to Manchester flight from his English rival Claude Grahame-White.

The offer had originally been made in 1906. A sceptical competitor mockingly came out with a counter offer of another £10,000 for the first person to fly to Mars and back within a week.

Now, only 50 years later, we are about to take the first steps to making flights to the planets a practical possibility, though a trip to Mars will take much longer than a week.

To win the London to Manchester prize pilots had to fly the 186 miles in 24 hours and not make more than two stops for fuel.

On Saturday, April 23, 1910, White – an early pupil of Blériot's – made an attempt in a **Farman biplane** powered by a 50 hp Gnome with a pusher propeller. Monday's edition of the *Mail* carried the following report:

"Mr. Grahame-White achieved glorious failure. . . . He flew 115 miles across England creating new records for cross-country flight. A crowning misfortune overtook him last evening, his aeroplane being overturned while at rest by a squall, and seriously damaged."

No longer, said the *Mail*, was it possible for the "doubters to cherish scepticism". To White belonged the credit of

having administered the "final blow to national indifference in regard to aviation".

He had set out at dawn from Park Royal, near Acton, "outpacing the swiftest motor-cars that pursued him by road. He flew the 83 miles to Rugby without mishap."

After taking off again high winds forced him down at Hademore crossing, Whittington, two and a half miles from Lichfield. The plane was damaged enough for him to give up. But White said he would try again as soon as the machine was repaired.

At this point Paulhan came on the scene. After finding White's effort "admirable" he announced that he was going to enter for the prize himself, promptly registering at the Royal Aero Club.

Two days later, April 27, the two men were racing each other across the sky in their **Farmans. Paulhan took off from Hampstead** at 5.31 pm. **White left Wormwood Scrubs** 58 minutes later, having worked night and day to get his plane ready to fly again.

He and his mechanics decided to get some sleep before attempting the flight the following day. But White was woken by friends telling him that Paulhan had started. White remarked: "I must go at once. If Paulhan is ready to break his neck, I am going to break mine too." And – in spite of more high winds – went.

The contest held the world enraptured. In New York special editions of the evening papers reported the latest progress of the two airmen. In Paris special bulletins were posted at leading hotels.

And from Berlin a dispatch revealed: "Aeroplanes are to be used for the first time as weapons of war in the forthcoming Kaiser manœuvres of the army and navy . . . and the flight will be studied in all its detail by the German staff for any possible tactical lessons."

Enormous crowds watched White and Paulhan head north into the dusk. And Paulhan won in 12 hours, half the time allowed. His actual flying time was four hours and two minutes.

Darkness forced White to land at Roade, 60 miles from London. Paulhan reached Lichfield by 8.10 pm, 57 miles ahead of White.

In an attempt to catch up White flew off again while it was still dark, becoming the first man to fly at night in Britain. He steered with the help of the lights from railway signal-boxes below, and a friend drove up to Crick where he shone his car headlights on the wall of an inn to show White he was heading in the right direction.

Nearer and nearer White flew to his rival. But with ten miles still to go he came down again at Polesworth because of high winds. And he spent the next hour alone hanging on to his plane to stop it being blown over once more.

Paulhan started the second leg of his flight at nine minutes past four, flying straight to Manchester where he was greeted with almost hysterical enthusiasm.

It was Brabazon who took a pig up with him around this time to prove that the time had come when pigs *could* fly.

Left: *The Rheims Air Meet: Glenn Curtiss putting his aeroplane together before winning the speed award at 43 mph.*

Below: *Ready for the race to Manchester: Grahame-White's Farman being rolled from the hangar at Wormwood Scrubs.*

The "impossible" had been achieved by these "magnificent men" in their frail flying machines, and their numbers were beginning to increase.

In France there were 353 certified pilots, Britain had 57, Germany 46, Italy 32, Belgium 27 and America, where it all began, 26.

Aviators were becoming more and more adventurous. In 1911, piloting a specially built Wright biplane, a young motor cyclist called Calbraith (Cal) P. Rodgers flew across the United States. His journey from New York on the Atlantic to Pasadena on the Pacific was packed with incidents.

He was out to capture a prize of nearly £18,000 offered by another newspaper chief, William Randolph Hearst, for the first coast-to-coast flight in under 30 days.

The trip took him 49 days. He left New York on September 17 in his plane, which he called the *Vin Fiz* after the soft drink made by his sponsors. He was followed – and sometimes led – by a special train containing his wife, mother, mechanics and spares.

Twenty thousand people saw him land at Pasadena on November 5 with one leg in plaster. He had crashed 19 times, made 69 stops – many unplanned and 23 in the State of Texas alone – and the *Vin Fiz* had been repaired so many times that it finished the journey with only the rudder and one strut remaining of the original machine that set out. Rodgers covered the 3,220 miles in an actual flying time of 82 hours and 4 minutes.

In spite of Rodgers's troubles, machines, engines and airframes were becoming more reliable.

Geoffrey de Havilland, another famous name in British aviation, who had become the British Government's first test pilot and designer, produced his BE 2 biplane. One of these aircraft set up a British height record of 13,000 ft.

Then, in 1913, the Schneider Trophy race for seaplanes was introduced. It was a competition that was to have farreaching effects on the development of aeroplanes, even on history itself. The Mediterranean was conquered by the Frenchman Roland Garros. He made the 460-mile crossing in 7 hours 53 minutes in a Morane-Saulnier flying from St. Raphael in the south of France to Bizerta in Tunisia.

And in Russia Igor Sikorsky – later to perfect the helicopter – was building four-engined cabin biplanes capable of carrying 15 passengers. They were to lay down the pattern for all future large, multi-engined aircraft. It also seems to have started a trend in Russia, which has specialised in big aircraft right up to the present day.

The men who flew were beginning to turn their eyes towards farther horizons. Prizes were offered in 1914 in Britain and America for flights across the Atlantic and round the world.

Both had to wait. The aeroplane was going to war.

Above: *Victory for Paulhan: at the end of the race the Frenchman is greeted by enormous crowds.*

Right: *The Royal Aero Club's pilot licence No. 1 which went to Moore-Brabazon for being the first Briton to fly a circular mile.*

Below right: *Even pigs fly: Brabazon prepares to prove it by taking a well-strapped-in piglet for a flip.*

Below: *An artist's impression of Sikorsky's "Grand" of 1912, the first multi-engined aircraft. It had a wing-span of 92 ft and was powered by four 100 hp motors. Sikorsky later built an improved plane, the Ilia Mouriametz, which could carry up to 15 passengers.*

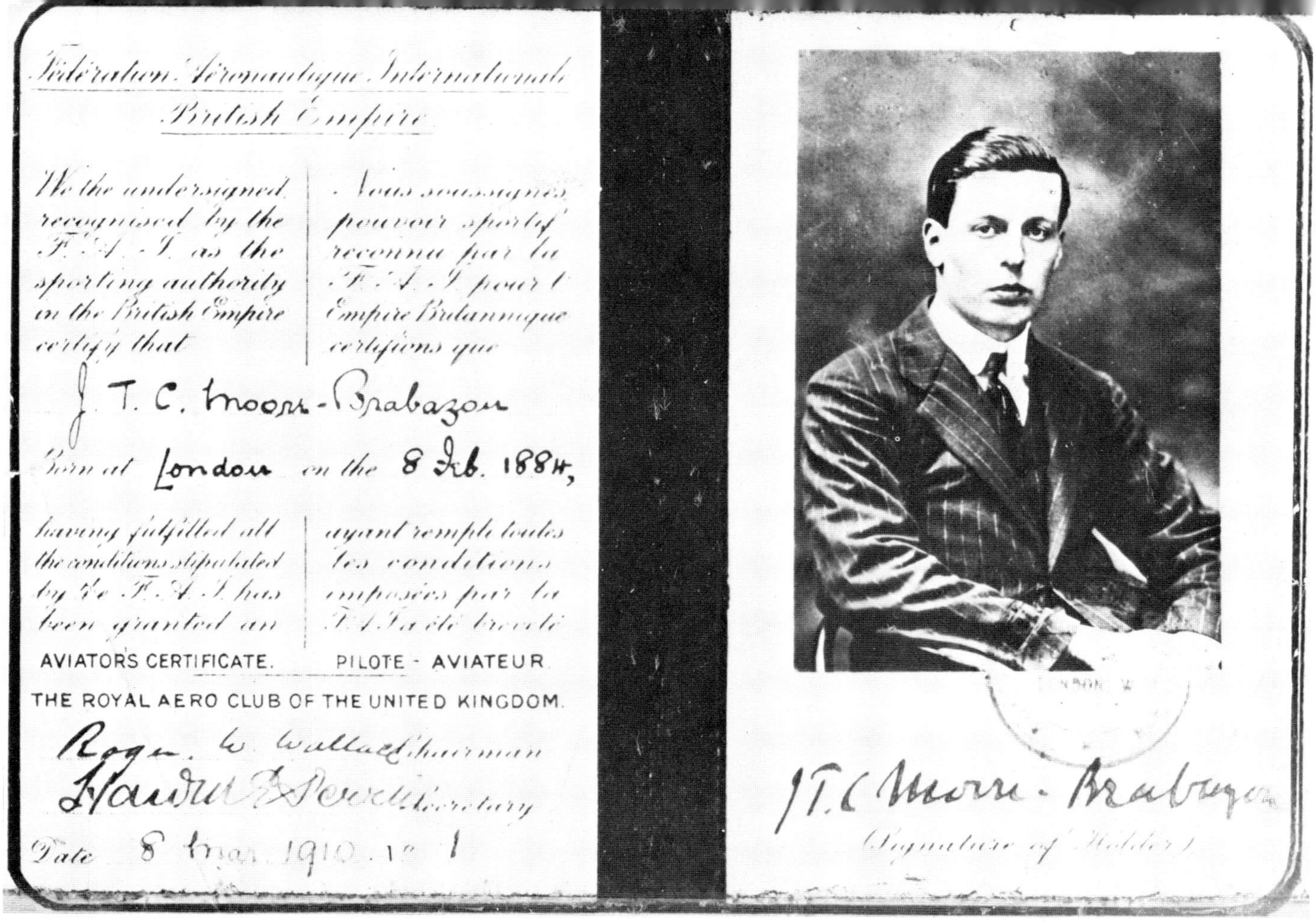

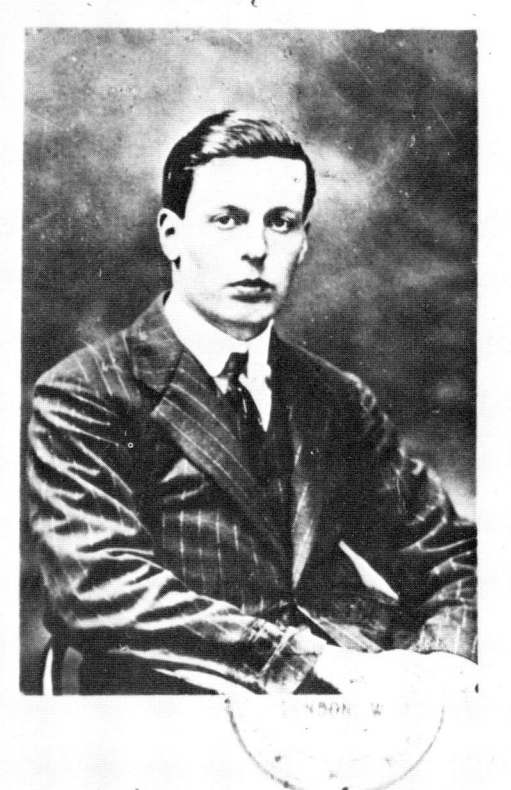

Fédération Aéronautique Internationale
British Empire

We the undersigned, recognised by the F. A. I. as the sporting authority in the British Empire certify that

Nous soussignés, pouvoir sportif reconnu par la F. A. I. pour l'Empire Britannique certifions que

J. T. C. Moore-Brabazon

Born at London on the 8 Feb. 1884,

having fulfilled all the conditions stipulated by the F. A. I. has been granted an AVIATOR'S CERTIFICATE.

ayant rempli toutes les conditions imposées par la F. A. I. a été breveté PILOTE - AVIATEUR.

THE ROYAL AERO CLUB OF THE UNITED KINGDOM.

Roger W. Wallace Chairman

Harold E. Perrin Secretary

Date 8 Mar. 1910 No 1

J. T. C. Moore-Brabazon

(Signature of Holder)

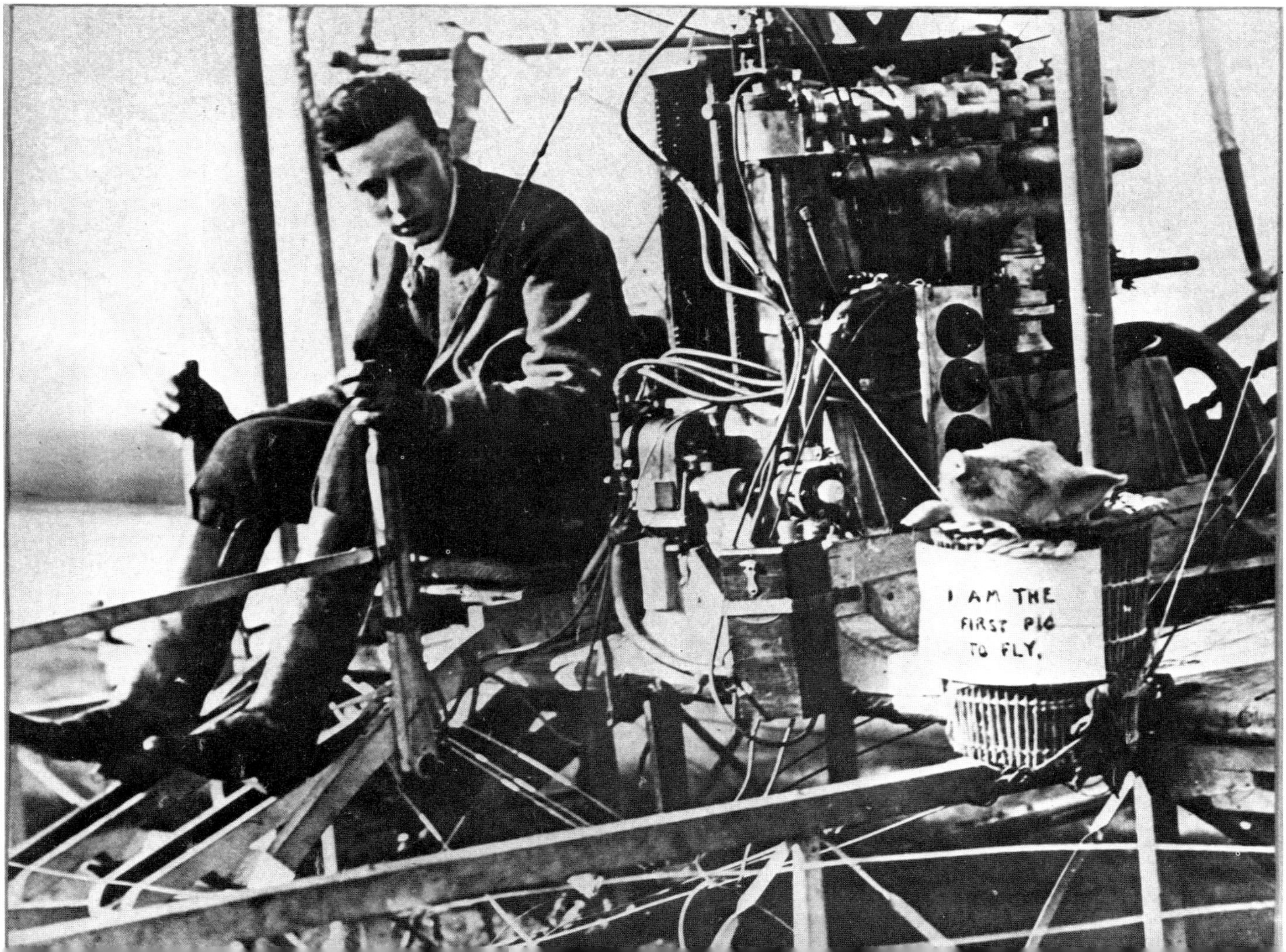
I AM THE
FIRST PIG
TO FLY.

Into action

Right: *British Avro 504 aircraft carry out the first strategic bombing raid in history on the Friedrichshaven Zeppelin sheds, November 21, 1914.*

When war did come there were no warplanes. Both sides sent aircraft to the fronts, but they were not designed as fighting machines. They were for use as spotter planes, to tell the soldiers down below what the enemy was up to, the sort of work that needed slow, reliable aeroplanes.

Germany seems to have had the strongest air force, with about 260 serviceable planes. The 1918 issue of *Jane's All the World's Aircraft* says of the British Royal Flying Corps: "The maximum number of aeroplanes capable of taking the air on one day did not exceed 30, which may be taken as representing the effective strength of the RFC at the outbreak of war."

But, with the Royal Naval Air Service's planes and about 155 belonging to the French, the Allies were able to bring their numbers up to something like 220.

One RFC officer is said to have remarked that pilots went into action equipped more as sportsmen than soldiers. And for a time, until men learned how to adapt the new "wonder of the world" into a means of destroying other men, it was a sportsmen's war . . . almost gentlemanly.

No one had ever fought in the air before. Pilots on both sides were still pioneers who, in the way of all pioneers, respected each other. They were fired at by friend and foe alike because no one had thought, at that early stage of the war, to put national markings on service aeroplanes.

Speeds were around the 75 mph mark, like that of the British BE 2 which could carry two men and a camera. The German Taube, a swept-wing monoplane, was four miles an hour slower, and Farmans, Blériots and Voisins were still in use.

Few aircraft had radios. Signalling was done mainly by Very light and note-dropping. And if a pilot was forced down behind the enemy's lines, or had to land in the sea, he could always send a message with his carrier pigeon.

Armaments were usually the pilot's revolver or the observer's rifle – though bricks are known to have been used – and the early bombs were hand dropped.

Pilots often knew where an enemy patrol would be at certain times each day, and it was not unknown for them to exchange a wave of farewell as each turned for home at the end of their duties.

But as speeds increased, and the fighter plane began to emerge, the impersonal instrument of the machine-gun probably made it easier for gentlemanly combat to give way to serious aerial warfare.

Before this happened, the enemy was killed with courtesy.

On July 21, 1915, a Voisin of No. 4 Squadron went out on patrol to Bapaume armed with a Lewis gun, six drums of ammunition, two revolvers and a rifle. The plane never returned from the mission, but a note was dropped over the British lines from a German aircraft to say that the Voisin had been shot down, the observer killed and the pilot taken prisoner.

The note concluded: "The German pilots have the highest praise for their opponent who died in an honourable fight."

One of the first fighter planes, the Vickers Gun Bus. The pusher propeller was used so that the nose gunner could fire forward and have a good field of view.

Sometimes, when a distinguished airman was shot down and killed, wreaths were dropped over his lines by the victors in his honour. In the air a pilot frequently knew who his opponent was because of the bold personal insignias which were painted on the sides of the planes.

From this it is easy to see why combat in the air during the First World War has so often been likened to the jousting of medieval knights in armour.

The Germans formed squadrons of highly trained pilots, giving them a virtual roving commission to go and fight where they were most needed. The men of these squadrons flew brightly coloured planes which, according to *Jane's*, "rivalled the rainbow in brilliancy".

The most famous of the groups, commanded by a Prussian cavalry captain, Baron Manfred von Richthofen, became known as Richthofen's Circus. Richthofen – called the Red Baron by Allied pilots because he flew a blood-red Fokker DR I triplane – proved to be the most successful "ace" of the war. He was credited with 80 victories before being killed in an air battle with British single-seaters in April 1918.

Sweeping from end to end of the Allies' lines in Flanders and France, the circuses were respected by their opponents as worthy fighters. There is something of this special atmosphere of respect, which undoubtedly existed among the men who fought in the air at the time, in the meeting between the German Werner Voss and the young A. P. F. Rhys-Davids – little more than a boy at 20 – a British second lieutenant.

Rhys-Davids had left school – Eton as it happens – at 16 and gone straight into the Royal Flying Corps. Voss, described as a "distinguished airman" who had brought down 49 Allied machines, was therefore an ace.

During the Third Battle of Ypres in September 1917, Rhys-Davids was in a patrol of SE 5s which crossed the lines at Bixschoote flying at 8,000 ft. They were about to tackle six Albatros Scouts when they saw another British SE being attacked by a German triplane.

Diving to the rescue Rhys-Davids and his flight commander got on the tail of the triplane. The flight commander, Major James McCudden, a veteran at 23, a VC and himself an ace with a score of 54, gave a first-hand account of the action:

"The German pilot saw us and turned in a most disconcertingly quick manner. . . . By now the German triplane was in the middle of our formation, and its handling was wonderful to behold. The pilot seemed to be firing at all of us simultaneously, and although I got behind him a second time I could hardly stay there for a second. . . .

"I now got a good opportunity as he was coming towards me nose on, and slightly underneath, and had apparently not seen me. I dropped my nose, got him well in my sight and pressed both triggers. As soon as I fired, up came his nose at me and I heard clack-clack-clack-clack, as his bullets passed close to me and through my wings. I

distinctly noticed the red-yellow flashes from his parallel Spandau guns. As he flashed by me I caught a glimpse of a black head in the triplane with no hat on at all."

McCudden was then diverted by the arrival of a red-nosed Albatros which tried to protect the triplane's tail.

But he was able to see that Rhys-Davids was having a low-level running fight with the triplane, and a second later it had hit the ground and exploded.

McCudden said: "As long as I live, I shall never forget my admiration for that German pilot, who, single-handed, fought seven of us and also put some bullets through all of our machines . . . the bravest German airman whom it has been my privilege to see fight."

It was discovered that the German had been Voss. "Rhys-Davids," said McCudden, "came in for a shower of congratulations, and no one deserved them better; but, as the boy himself said to me, 'Oh, if I only could have brought him down alive,' and his remark was in agreement with my own thoughts."

One month later Rhys-Davids was shot down and killed himself. They may have been "knights of the air", fighting with bullets instead of lances, and in aeroplanes instead of on chargers . . . but blood still took the shine from their armour.

By this time, of course, the fighting machine had really arrived. The slow spotter planes, at the mercy of air attacks by faster aircraft, had to be protected. The fighters built to do this began to fly in formations, and engage the enemy high above the spotters, who could then get on with photographing the other side's positions and movements.

The trouble with aeroplanes at the start of the war was that they could not be aimed at a target.

An aircraft's own propeller was in the way of a forward-firing gun, and it was no good trying to shoot down an enemy machine if you were going to shoot off your own propeller in the process.

So, for a time, guns had to be mounted so that they could be fired outwards, at an angle that would make sure the bullets cleared the disc of the spinning propeller blades.

One answer to the problem was to have a pusher propeller at the back of the aircraft. The gunner could then sit at the front and have a wide field of fire.

Right: Breakthrough in aerial warfare: Roland Garros's arrangement for a deflector device that would allow guns to be fired through the propeller disc. The small deflector channels can be seen near the "bend" in the propeller.

Above: *Bombers begin to emerge: Handley Page 0/400s prepare for a raid at a Royal Naval Air Service airfield near Dunkirk on April 20, 1918. The 0/400s operated mainly at night and their twin 360 hp engines gave them a speed of 98 mph and a range of 370 miles. Armament was 1,800 lb of bombs and up to five machine-guns.*

Facing page: *The Fokker Scourge: front view of the Fokker Eindecker fitted with Anthony Fokker's answer to Garros's deflector gear. The three machine-guns can be seen above the engine cowling pointing forward.*

Above: *Sensation at the front: the Sopwith Triplane which inspired Anthony Fokker to build the Dr.1. So great was the speed of development in those days that the plane was passed by Sopwith's experimental department in May 1916 and by the middle of the following month the Triplane was fighting in France.*

Right: *Anthony Fokker, the man with a genius for producing first-class aircraft. He is seen here (left) with a First World War fighter pilot named Hermann Goering, who was later to command the German Luftwaffe.*

The Vickers FB 5 – the "Gun-Bus" – was one of the first fighter planes of this type. They were very effective during 1914 and 1915, but they were slow – 70 to 80 mph – and cumbersome machines.

The breakthrough came in 1915. Roland Garros, the Frenchman who conquered the Mediterranean, fitted steel plates to the propeller blades of his Morane-Saulnier so that he could fire a gun forward and, if a bullet did happen to hit the whirling airscrew, it would be deflected without doing any damage.

Though it was an imperfect device, and presumably wasteful with ammunition, it had a startling effect.

The German pilots took little notice at first when they saw the Morane flying straight towards them, until it suddenly started firing at them THROUGH the propeller. By then it was too late and Garros claimed another victory.

Germany's James Bonds of the day were ordered to find out how Garros's mysterious secret weapon worked. But the spies failed.

Eventually the invention dropped into the Germans' laps. It happened as Garros was flying over the enemy lines in search of more victims. Engine failure forced him down and he and the plane were captured.

His device – triangular steel wedges with grooves in for the bullets to glance along – was studied carefully. The Germans sent for the Dutchman Anthony Fokker to reproduce the system for their own machines.

Instead of copying it Fokker improved it. "The obvious thing to do," he said, "was to make the propeller fire the gun." And he did, with an arrangement of small levers that allowed bullets to pass through the blades at safe intervals.

The Germans insisted that Fokker tested the device himself in an actual fight. With the new weapon fitted to one of his monoplanes, Fokker took off to look for something to shoot at. His opportunity came when he sighted a French Farman two-seater.

As he closed in on the unsuspecting plane, Fokker thought of the "deadly accurate stream of lead" he could fire at the Farman. He knew the French crew had seen him, and he also knew they would have no reason to fear bullets coming through his propeller.

Now he was right on the Farman's tail. "It would be just like shooting a sitting rabbit," thought Fokker. "The pilot can't shoot back at me because of his pusher propeller."

Suddenly Fokker decided "the whole job could go to hell". He had no wish to kill Frenchmen for Germans. The Germans could do their own killing. And Fokker veered away from the Farman and turned for home.

The Germans were not so squeamish. Fokker's E IV Eindecker monoplanes were fitted with the "interrupter" device and soon became the scourge of the air, giving Germany superiority in the skies for several months.

They became so much of a menace that on one occasion early in 1916 a dozen pilots were ordered to escort a single BE 2 reconnaissance plane.

The eventual answer to the Fokker scourge came from

Geoffrey de Havilland's DH 2 single-seaters. The planes, new versions of the old pusher propeller design, could fly at speeds approaching 90 mph and their easy manœuvrability proved a match for the Eindeckers.

Help had come from the little French Nieuport Scouts. They had been fitted with a gun on top of the wings so that it could be fired over the propeller. On the early types the arrangement created so much extra drag that, when the gun was being fired, the aircraft often lost speed and "sank". This was overcome by triggering the gun with a cable.

It was only a matter of time before the Allies had captured a plane carrying Fokker's interrupter mechanism. It happened in the spring of 1916, and the weapon was improved still more by being made to work on a gear system instead of levers. Later it was hydraulically operated.

From then on air supremacy seesawed between the two sides. It became a designer's battle – principally between the Sopwiths and the Fokkers, planes that distinguished themselves in both world wars – with one side gaining the upper hand and then the other.

By the autumn of 1916 the DH 2s had been outclassed by the new Albatroses, which were faster – their speed topped the 100 mph mark – and they had twin machine-guns.

Success in the air meant speed and the ability to manœuvre – turn, climb and dive – out of trouble. Naturally, not all the aircraft that were designed, and there were some 250 different types, had every one of these qualities. But in the search for the best combination some very fine planes were produced.

Just as the Albatros was giving the Germans the edge again, along came an unconventional little fighter to tip the balance back in favour of the Allies. The plane, regarded by the German pilots as the best fighter opposing them at the time, was the Sopwith Triplane.

The nimble little craft, which had three wings instead of the usual two, caused a sensation at the front. The "Red Baron" was apparently so impressed that he took Anthony Fokker to a forward position so that he could take a look at the triplanes in action, hoping no doubt that the Dutchman would be able to come up with something to equal the new Allied threat.

And he did. Fokker told his chief designer, Reinhold Platz, about what he had seen and asked him to get on with producing a triplane. It was all very casual. No technical drawings or details. Fokker just said he wanted a triplane, and Platz went ahead. That was the way it used to happen in those days.

Tommy Sopwith, now Sir Thomas, described the process like this: "Development was so fast. We literally thought of and designed and flew the aeroplanes in a space of about six or eight weeks. Now it takes approximately the same number of years.

"In those days all you had to do was to rough out a scheme on the back of an envelope, show it to those who were going to do the job, and they then started right away without needing anything else."

Right: *The Tin Donkey of 1915. Junkers applied his new form of wing construction to this aircraft and used an all-metal skin. At the time the plane was too heavy, but it was to pave the way for the modern airliner.*

Below: *Years ahead of its time, the Deperdussin of 1912. Highly streamlined with a stressed wooden skin it became the first aircraft to top 100 mph, but did not bring a big step forward in design.*

But by the time the Fokker triplanes were in service they had to contend with the more advanced Allied designs, the Sopwith Camel, SE 5as and the French Spads.

But Fokker was not beaten. In the spring of 1918 another new fighter of his went into service with the star German squadrons – the D VII, considered by many to be the finest fighter plane of the war.

The German authorities held a competition in late 1917 to try and find an aircraft to match the Allied fighters. Of the 31 planes that took part the D VII was received with unanimous enthusiasm.

It beat all-comers in the mock combats by its ability to manœuvre at high altitude, a quality that was to make it a formidable foe. Although of conventional biplane design, the D VII had thick, spar-strengthened wings – which gave support rather like a pole, thrust through the sleeves of a scarecrow's coat, holds its "arms" out straight.

Allied pilots who met it in the air were startled by the D VII's trick of "hanging on its prop" – the propeller apparently holding it up while the pilot pivoted the plane round on it, spraying his opponent with bullets.

The Dutchman and his designer Platz had produced yet another menace between them. But it didn't save Germany from defeat.

Fokker was still only 28 at the time. His D VII was so highly regarded that the Armistice ordered Germany's fighter machines to be handed over, and stated "especially the D VII type".

For Fokker this meant the destruction of years of work, and the loss of a huge investment. His genius for producing first-class aircraft had made him a rich man and most of his money was in Germany.

He described the order as a knock-out blow. "Its thoroughness," he said, "stunned me for a few days – then I tried to find a way to circumvent such disaster."

As had so often happened before, when Fokker was faced with a challenge he had proved more than equal to it. And this was no exception. He hid more than 220 planes and 400 engines in out-of-the-way barns and disused cellars. These, together with his fortune, were smuggled back to Holland in six trains with the help of heavily bribed officials.

After the war was over Fokker revealed that the planes he had built to shoot the Allies out of the skies could have been shooting Germans down instead. He claimed that the British had sent him an offer of £2,000,000 to return to Holland and build aeroplanes for them.

But the message had fallen into the hands of the Kaiser's secret service agents and Fokker never received it.

Alarmed, his "hosts" had then compelled him to become a naturalised German citizen.

And there was a final irony for the Allies. Fokker also claimed that he had gone to the British before 1914 and offered them his plans for fighter aircraft . . . and they had turned him down.

One reason for rapid changes of fortune in the air was that new designs were always falling into the enemy's hands. We have seen how both the Garros and Fokker gun-firing devices were copied after capture. Both sides were able to learn other secrets of each other's planes in the same way.

On the morning of June 28, 1916, the *Daily Mail* told the story, "How the Huns got our newest aeroplane."

Lord Montagu had indignantly revealed in the Lords the previous day "a blunder which made the Germans a present of a brand-new aeroplane of our latest and best type".

His Lordship said that an FE fitted with a 250 hp engine (and therefore almost certainly an FE 2d, a pusher biplane fighter-bomber) had left the factory at Farnborough on May 31, and within three hours, had been delivered intact to the Germans at Lille aerodrome.

The pilot had never flown to France before, and didn't know the geography of the country he had been expected to fly over. On June 2 a German radio message had informed the British that the plane, which had up till then apparently disappeared, was in their hands and would be "most useful".

Lord Curzon had replied in the House that such incidents had happened before and would happen again. "But they are not confined to one side or the other," he said. They happened to the Germans just the same.

Jane's records that the German Gotha bomber "somewhat resembles the Handley Page (0/400) and doubtless owes its detail improvements to the aeroplane presented by us to the Germans with involuntary generosity on January 2nd, 1917".

With this kind of tit-for-tat going on few developments could remain secret for long. But how much development was there?

It is often assumed that because there had been a war progress in aviation must automatically have been rapid. This is a view which is not shared by all the experts.

Remember what Sir Thomas Sopwith said? "Development was so fast. . . ." But was it? There might be a clue in something else that Sir Thomas said. He is quoted in the book *The Adventure of Man's Flight* as saying: "Until about the middle of the war there was no stressing at all. Everything was built entirely by eye. That's why there were so many structural failures. We didn't start to stress aeroplanes at all seriously until the Camel in 1917."

Stressing. This method of building aircraft had been known about since 1912. It was first employed by the Deperdussin firm of France. They built a little monoplane that proved to be something like 15 years ahead of its time.

The plane had a very modern look about it, compared with the braced and strung biplanes of the day, because of its streamlined shape. It was the first step from the Blériot monoplanes towards the low-wing monoplanes in use today.

Its streamlining was possible because of the stressed skin – or monocoque construction. Monocoque comes from the Greek word *monos* – single – and the French word *coque* – shell.

The skin of the Deperdussin's fuselage was moulded in

two shell-like halves and fitted together. No conventional framework was necessary in the pure monocoque design, the skin bearing all, or most, of the strains of flight. Later, when metal aircraft became common, extra stiffening members were introduced.

The monocoque Deperdussin was made of wood and designed by M. L. Béchereau. It became the first plane to fly at over 100 mph when, in September 1912, Jules Vedrines piloted it to a new world speed record of 105 mph at Chicago. A year later it pushed the record up to 124·5 mph at Rheims. Marcel Prévost was the pilot on that occasion. Both records were set up with Gnome engines.

In spite of its impressive performances the Deperdussin did not result in a big step forward in aircraft design at the time.

Most aeroplanes until well into the thirties were biplanes, with wood or metal frames covered in fabric. It was a tried and trusted design, traditional, strong and slow. But this was just what was wanted, especially at the beginning of the war.

One authority on aviation, Mr. C. G. Grey, once editor of *Aeroplane* magazine, believed that the war actually retarded genuine progress by ten years. And Lord Brabazon said, "On reflection, I very much doubt whether, on the commercial side, it did the whole movement any good."

Both recognised the value of increased scientific research which the war undoubtedly stimulated, and the spur it gave to production methods. But both were equally critical of the amount of energy devoted to building bigger and more powerful engines regardless of expense.

Brabazon pointed out that production costs, upkeep, economic fuel consumption and endurance were not of great importance to the designers of military machines.

Grey believed that the concentration on power resulted in the normal development of the aeroplane being neglected. He thought that if the experiments being undertaken throughout the world at the start of the war had been allowed to continue, stimulated by the annual air shows in Paris, London and Berlin, good commercial aircraft would have appeared within six years.

Probably the greatest move forward in aviation to come from the war was the development by the German, Hugo Junkers, of the cantilevered wing allied to the all-metal monoplane.

Junkers had experimented with the new form of wing construction as far back as 1910. The strength came from within, from spars or trusses, instead of from the outside through struts and wire bracing.

In 1915 Junkers produced the J 1, all-metal, and a monoplane with the thick cantilevered wings set midway between the top and bottom of the fuselage. But the German High Command showed little enthusiasm for it. Its heavy steel construction made it sluggish in flight, and earned it the nickname of the Tin Donkey.

Two years later came the J 4, a successful biplane. This was made mostly of light alloy and went into quantity

Above: *Just how big the aeroplane had grown can be seen from the people standing beneath the wing of this Handley Page V/1500 bomber. Only three of these giants were ready for action when the First World War ended, but they would have been able to bomb Berlin from England. They convinced the RAF that strategic bombing could win wars and led to the development of the Second World War Halifax and Lancasters.*

Left: *The first real passenger airliner, the Junkers F 13 transport. It had a corrugated metal skin and cantilevered wings. It went into service in 1919 and for ten years was the major airliner in Europe.*

production as a ground-attack fighter. The lessons Junkers learned in the extensive use of light metal were applied to bettering further monoplanes.

His series, with the distinctive corrugated duralumin skins, eventually led to the first real passenger airliner, the F 13 transport of 1919.

In spite of the criticisms that there was not enough real development, the war certainly boosted the production of aircraft. In Britain at the start of the war there were just 12 firms manufacturing aeroplanes, three specialising in sea-planes.

But as the importance of air power came to be realised, all sorts of trades were recruited to help push up pro-duction – even farm implement manufacturers and piano-makers.

The Air Ministry's *Short History of the Royal Air Force* of 1929 says: "England started the war with few aeroplanes and an insignificant aircraft industry. It finished the war with the most formidable air force ever contemplated."

But if it hadn't been for France it is doubtful whether this would have been the case. French planes and engines enabled Britain to survive the first part of the war, and gave a breathing space for the home aircraft industry to be built up.

From the 50 planes a month that were delivered during the first year of the war, production increased to a stagger-ing capability of 3,500 a month during the year up to the Armistice.

It was in this year, on April 1 – All Fools' Day – that the Royal Air Force was formed as a separate service. Even then there were still some "fools" around who doubted that the aeroplane could be much use except as the eyes of the Army.

It was still being debated whether the Allies were not "wasting their aerial units by employing any part of them on other duties than that of giving tactical assistance to the troops in the field".

The Germans certainly seemed to have little doubt about the usefulness of offensive air campaigns. They were using Gothas and Zeppelins to attack targets in England.

Bombers had grown since the Avro 504, the light single-engined 82 mph plane that made the first strategic strike in history.

Four of the naval machines had set out from the French airfield at Belmont on November 21, 1914, to fly the 125 miles to bomb the Zeppelin sheds at Friedrichshafen in southern Germany. Three of them reached the objective and one was shot down.

Exactly four years later, in November 1918, as the Armistice was signed, giant Handley Page V/1500s – a new heavy bomber with four 375 hp engines which the RAF called the "super" Handley Page – was ready to bomb Berlin direct from English bases.

The Wrights thought they had invented a way of making war impossible. But the aeroplane had hardly begun to reach its full capacity for destruction.

Converted warplanes began the first passenger service in Europe in 1919. This De Havilland DH Airco 18 was run by the pioneer Aircraft Transport & Travel company. Passengers sometimes got hot-water bottles to clutch during a flight.

The aeroplane conquers the world

The aeroplane was a plaything no longer. It had ceased to be the toy of rich sportsmen.

Flying had become a deadly serious business. The war had seen to that. For four years men had been deliberately killing each other with aeroplanes and the time had come to do something useful and worthwhile with them.

The end of the war meant that there were lots of aeroplanes with nothing to do. The armed forces were ready to sell them, at little more than their value as scrap, to anyone who wanted them.

And there were plenty of wartime pilots without jobs who did want them. But how do you earn a living with a symbol of terror? How do you convince people who yesterday were running in fear from aeroplanes that today they can make life easier?

The answer was to make aeroplanes and flying glamorous. So the aviators set out to conquer the world.

There were fat prizes to be won by those who dared enough. The London *Daily Mail*'s 1913 offer of £10,000 for the first non-stop Atlantic flight was still unclaimed, and an American hotel millionaire, Raymond Orteig, put up 25,000 dollars for the first pilot to make the flight from New York to Paris non-stop.

But there were also men to whom prizes meant nothing. They just believed in the future of aviation.

Converted warplanes opened up the first passenger airline services in Europe in 1919. The defeated Germans were first, laying on a service between Berlin, Leipzig and Weimar only three months after the Armistice was signed.

Ex-bombers, operated by the British and the French, began flying regularly between London and Paris. The flights grew from trips organised by the RAF to ferry VIPs from London to Army Headquarters in France.

In Holland, Anthony Fokker was collecting the planes and engines he had daringly smuggled out of Germany and setting up in business again.

In that first year of the pioneer airlines 5,000 people sampled the unique, often uncomfortable and frequently alarming experience of flying. Compared with the smooth, almost silent luxury of jet flight today with its comfortable reclining seats and attentive air hostesses, a flight in those days was still very much an adventure.

Top: *Lieutenant-Commander Albert Read taxis the NC-4 into Lisbon harbour after the first attempt to fly the Atlantic. The NC-4 was the only plane, out of the three that set out from Newfoundland, to get across. Read later flew on to Plymouth.*

Above: *About to overshadow the American transatlantic effort, the Vickers Vimy bomber of Alcock and Brown being prepared for take-off at St. John's Newfoundland.*

Crew and passengers had to suffer open cockpits. The seats they were provided with were cane and their feet rested – not on deep pile carpets, but wooden duck-boards. It was often an achievement to arrive at your destination at all.

Passengers were supplied with a long leather coat, helmet and goggles. If it was a really cold day they might also get a hot-water bottle to clutch during the flight.

Pilots found their way across country by flying close to prominent railway lines or main roads. And sometimes they endured the embarrassment of having to watch while, far below, a train or a car overtook them.

But mostly passengers entered into the spirit of things and proved to be pretty adaptable in emergencies.

One pilot, flying from London to Paris, was looking down at the French countryside idly watching a bus on the road below when he suddenly realised that one of his aircraft's engines was on fire.

"We put down at once in a field," he said, "and got everyone out, including their luggage, before the whole aeroplane went up in flames."

By this time the bus had caught them up and everyone, passengers and crew, climbed aboard and went to Paris in it.

Another pilot, flying from London to Cologne in Germany, took nearly a week to make the trip. He was delayed by having to make forced landings all over the place. Airliners were so slow then that, at the first sign of trouble, a landing could be made in any convenient field.

Throughout the entire chapter of mishaps his passengers never left the plane. It was all part of the fun to stick with it and, anyway, it was also quite something in those days to be able to say: "I have just flown to Cologne."

In America the eager, adventurous wartime fliers were earning a living by flying the mail and barnstorming round the country in aerial circuses. Both occupations, though legal, were extremely hazardous.

Another, and illegal, way of earning a few dollars was by flying consignments of "bootleg" liquor.

It was the Roaring Twenties, and prohibition was in force in the United States. Alcohol was forbidden. Those who wanted to drink could get their supplies from the "moonshiners" who made liquor in secret.

The pilots who flew it out from the hidden stills in the country districts had an existence that was just as perilous as that of the mailmen or the barnstormers.

Government revenue agents were always on the look-out for the moonshiners, who assumed that any strange aeroplane they saw flying about was a "revenooer" spy and usually blasted away at it with both barrels of their shotguns.

Being shot at became so routine that pilots didn't pay too much attention when they saw the little white puffs of smoke down in the woods, other than thinking that it meant they would have an extra chore to do on the aeroplane when they landed – patch up the bullet-holes in it.

The mail was flown in worn-out biplanes left over from the war, usually DH 4s and Curtiss Jennies. There were few aids to help the pilots battle through savage weather. It cost a lot of money to light an airfield for a night landing and not enough people thought it worthwhile to send their letters by air.

The flying circuses were made up of groups of young whizz-kids who flew from town to town putting on shows of stunt flying and aerobatics. They hoped that their death-defying antics would attract a crowd of people who could then be persuaded to pay for joy-rides in their noisy, smelly, draughty, rattletraps of machines.

One of these young men was known as "Daredevil" Charles Lindbergh. They called him "Daredevil" because of his breathtaking wing-walking acts. Lindbergh had experienced many brushes with death, both during his days as a barnstormer and while flying the mail.

By surviving them all he earned himself another nickname – "Lucky" – and it was during one of his lonely mail flights that Lindbergh thought of trading on his luck as no man had ever dreamed of before.

He was chugging along on the St. Louis–Chicago run, thinking about how out of date his old DH 4 was, when he first had the idea of putting on a demonstration of what an aeroplane really could do. He would show all those businessmen who only thought of aviation in terms of the flying fools of the aerial circuses. He would show the world.

What he needed was a plane . . . just a big fuel tank with an engine. It would be able to stay up for days.

Top: *The Handley Page W8F. This is a later version of the W8 airliner which was fitted with an extra motor. It was the first three-engined aircraft to be used by Imperial Airways.*

Above: *Stopover in the desert: Passengers from the Armstrong Whitworth Argosy "City of Coventry" wait for their airliner to be refuelled at an airfield on the Cairo-Khartoum sector of the Central Africa run. These three-engined aircraft helped to cut out unnecessary forced landings in this kind of barren area where the locals could not always be relied on to be friendly.*

Left: *The Douglas World Cruisers: Lined up before their attempt to fly round the world, the four aircraft are made ready for their six months trip.*

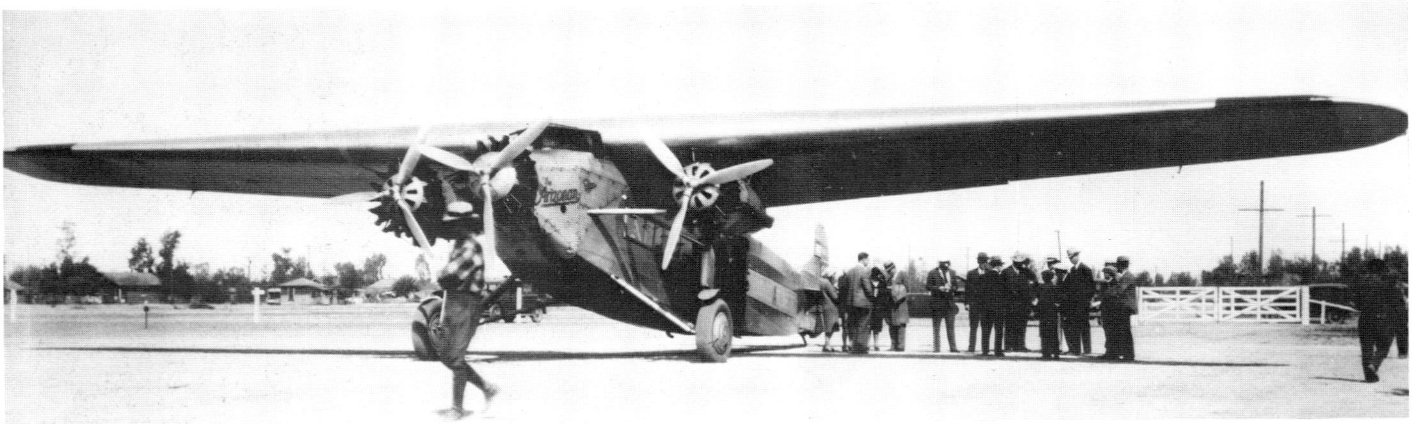

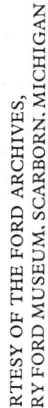

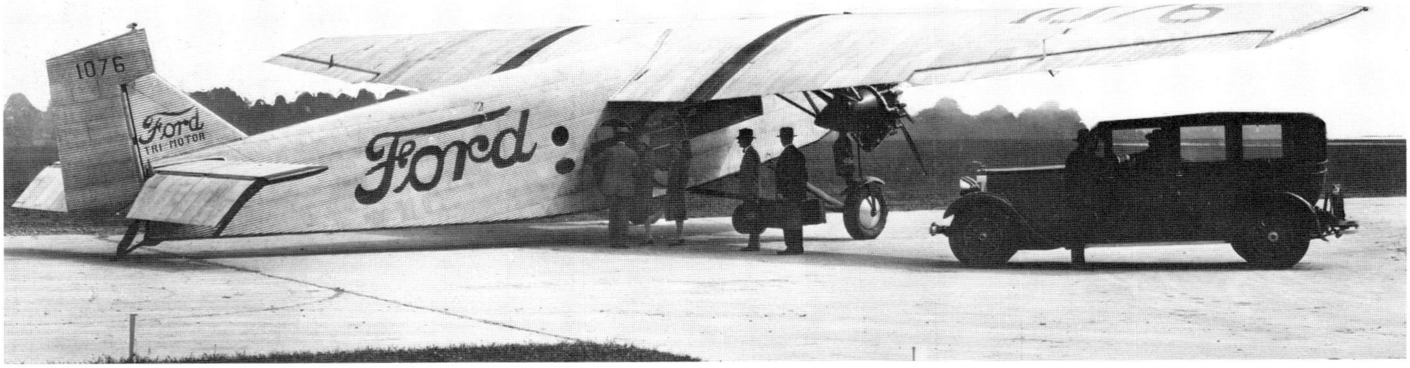

COURTESY OF THE FORD ARCHIVES, HENRY FORD MUSEUM, SCARBORN, MICHIGAN

Top: *Fokker put three engines into his high-wing monoplanes and the airliner of the future began to take shape. This is one of the later famous Fokker trimotors, the F-10.*

Above: *The Fokker shape emerges in America and Henry Ford, pioneer of the family motor-car, produces the Ford Trimotor. Known as the Tin Goose it became the United States' first successful airliner. It had three 300 hp engines and a top speed of 134 mph.*

Below: *The new shape helped Charles Lindbergh to find the plane that he wanted for his attempt to fly the Atlantic solo. Ryan Airlines built him the* Spirit of St. Louis *and, with all his bills paid, Lindbergh here pilots it over San Diego before setting out on his record flight to St. Louis.*

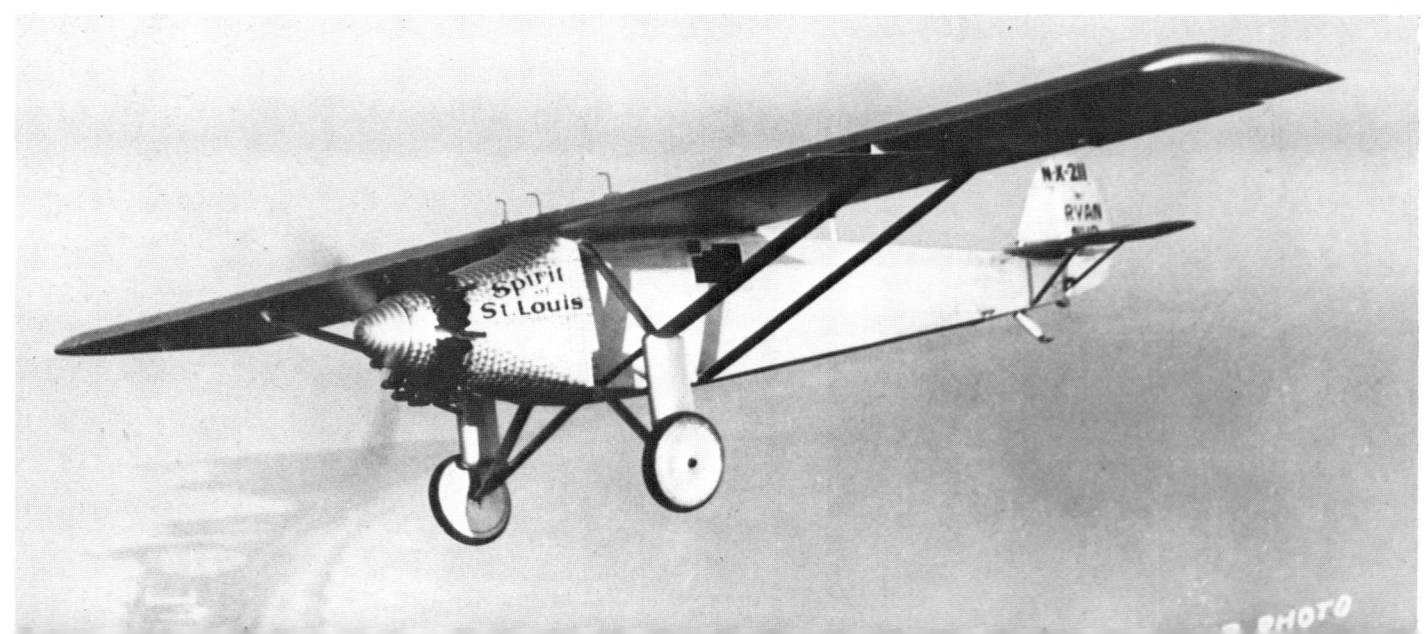

Right: *The proud Lindbergh fondly clutches the propeller of the Spirit of St. Louis.*

Below: *Just before taking off from San Diego for St. Louis, Lindbergh posed for this historic photo. H. J. van der Linde, later Ryan Aeronautical Company factory manager, is on top of the plane, fuelling it through funnel. Others are, left to right, O. R. McNeel, welding foreman; George Hammond, student mechanic pilot; Lindbergh; Donald Hall, Chief Engineer, and the late A. J. Edwards, sales manager of Ryan Airlines.*

It could even be flown from New York to Paris without stopping. Perhaps he was mad, but the trip couldn't be any more dangerous than flying the mail in winter.

The 25,000-dollar Orteig prize would easily cover expenses. If the New York–Paris flight could be done there would be no limit to the future of the aeroplane.

These were the thoughts that passed through Lindbergh's mind. But first there had to be a plane that could make the flight. It would have to be a lot different to his old DH 4.

Meanwhile, there was a lot of glory left for the biplane to capture. The Atlantic was the big challenge, and America decided to show off its big new Curtiss flying boats by attempting the crossing in May 1919.

Three of the big four-engined planes left Newfoundland on the 16th to fly to England by way of the Azores and Portugal. Just in case anything went wrong the United States Navy stationed no fewer than 39 ships along the route.

And things did go wrong. The aircraft became separated when they ran into fog. Then one of them, the NC (Navy Curtiss)-1 made a forced landing 200 miles short of the Azores, and though the crew were picked up, the plane had to be abandoned.

The NC-3 also came down in the sea. It was so rough that the commander, John H. Towers, could not take off again, but he managed to taxi his damaged plane the 200 miles to the Azores.

The third plane, the NC-4 commanded by Lieutenant-Commander Albert C. Read, survived the fog and flew on to Horta in the Azores safely. The 1,380-mile flight was made at an average speed of 75 mph. From Horta Read flew on to Lisbon and finally to Plymouth, arriving in England on May 31.

The American attempt was completely overshadowed within a fortnight by two Britons, Captain John Alcock, who was 27, and the 33-year-old Lieutenant Arthur Whitten Brown.

Undeterred by the news that a six-week drought in Britain had broken and rough weather was waiting for them over the ocean, they took off from St. John's, Newfoundland, on June 14 in a converted Vickers Vimy bomber. Their destination was Ireland.

A little over 16 hours later an excited London policeman jumped on to a passing bus to inform the startled passengers that Alcock and Brown had flown the Atlantic.

It was, Alcock said later, "a terrible journey". Soon after take-off Brown watched helplessly as the propeller on the generator that supplied power to their radio broke loose, carrying away one of the bracing wires with it.

The roar of the twin 360 hp engines and the howling of the slipstream made normal talking impossible. So Brown had to give Alcock the bad news by way of a message written on a page torn from his notebook.

The rough weather they were expecting was there all right. For most of the 1,880-mile flight it was so bad that they could see neither sky nor water. This made it extremely

Above left: *The low-wing monoplane emerges: The final configuration of Boeing's Monomail.*

Above: *Prelude to a revolution: The B-9 bomber into which Boeings put all the experience they had gained with the Monomail. The plane brought together stressing, improved construction and smooth skins.*

difficult for Brown to navigate and Alcock to keep the plane straight and level.

For hours they were alone in a blanket of freezing fog which covered the Vimy in ice. Brown had to climb out of his cockpit to clear away snow from the glass on the fuel-supply gauge.

Suddenly Alcock noticed that the note of the engines was rising to a scream. He was diving straight down towards the angry Atlantic.

For 4,000 ft he fought to bring the big plane under control. Lower and lower it dived . . . until, just a few feet above the waves, he forced the nose up again. He did it so violently that the Vimy almost looped.

The one favourable thing about the flight was the tail wind that followed them all the way. At last they were over the islands off the Galway coast and Alcock was circling round the masts of the Clifden radio station looking for a place to land.

He spotted a stretch of smooth-looking green turf. It turned out to be a bog and, after running along the ground for a short way, the Vimy's wheels sank, tipping the plane up on its nose. Soon, men from the radio station who had heard the plane circling overhead, were running to help – some of them still in pyjamas.

The flight won Alcock and Brown the *Mail*'s £10,000 prize, and knighthoods.

There were other men of other nationalities who were ready to test the capabilities of the aeroplane: two Australian

brothers, Ross and Keith Smith, flew another Vimy from Britain to Australia, covering the 11,294 miles in 27 days. Two Italian biplanes flew from Rome to Tokyo; yet another Vimy was used on the first flight from Britain to Cape Town, South Africa.

During this period, between the end of war and 1920, three things happened which were to be of profound importance in the development of the aeroplane.

Junkers produced the F 13, the first plane specially designed as a commercial airliner. It was a single-engined, cantilever, low-wing monoplane with the characteristic corrugated metal skin.

Another German, Professor Adolph K. Rohrbach, built a four-engined monoplane called the Zeppelin-Staaken E.4250 which could carry 18 passengers. This plane also had a metal skin, but it was smooth.

And Anthony Fokker, using his experience in building warplanes for the Germans, built his F 11. This had a fabric-covered fuselage over a welded steel tube frame and a thick cantilever wing placed above the fuselage. It was a style that was to set a fashion for high-wing monoplanes during the next ten years.

But more important was the fact that a large part of the strength of the wing came from its plywood skin, which carried some of the stresses of flight.

Eventually the three designs – the Junkers low wing, the Rohrbach smooth skin and the Fokker stressing, which was first used successfully in the 1912 Deperdussin, were to

Above: *The plane the US Army chose instead of the Boeing, the Martin B-10. This is the B-10 B, the largest model of the series. Its wing-span was 70 ft, length 45 ft, speed 212 mph and its engines were two Wright R-1820-33 of 740 hp.*

Above right: *The first classic modern airliner, the Boeing 247. It had a top speed of 200 mph and a ceiling of 25,400 ft, could carry ten passengers, two pilots and a stewardess as well as mail and baggage.*

come together and bring about the birth of the classic, streamlined modern aeroplanes that we know today.

Flying in America was having a lean time. People in high places had no faith in the value of military aviation.

The assistant chief of the Army Air Service in Washington, General Billy Mitchell – whose outspoken criticism of official indifference was finally to get him court-martialled – organised a series of spectacular flights to arouse public support for air power.

The most ambitious was the flight round the world by four Douglas World Cruisers, specially built biplanes with interchangeable wheels and floats so that they could use land or sea bases on their journey.

The four single-engined planes left Santa Monica, California, at five-minute intervals on St. Patrick's Day, 1924, a 25,553-mile flight ahead of each two-man crew.

One of them crashed into a mountain in Alaska, but the others flew on over Japan, China, Burma, India, Turkey and Europe to England. Another was forced down in the Atlantic on the next stage of the flight, but the remaining Cruisers carried on over Iceland, Greenland and finally back to America. The round trip took them nearly six months.

The aeroplane was really spreading its wings. And the idea of air travel was beginning to catch on. This meant specially designed airliners but, although the movement towards commercial monoplanes had begun in Germany, the British stayed faithful to the biplane.

One of the earliest airliners was the twin-engined Handley Page W/8. Unfortunately there had been little improvement in the reliability of engines and aircraft of this type usually found themselves unable to fly on if one motor failed in flight.

Since the success of an airline depended on its ability to get its passengers where they wanted to go, something had to be done to cut out unnecessary forced landings. It was specially important when flying over the more wilder parts of the globe, such as the Middle East desert regions, where travellers from an aeroplane in trouble could never count on the locals not to be hostile.

The obvious solution was to fit three engines, and this resulted in the Armstrong Whitworth Argosy and the DH 66 Hercules going into service on Britain's Empire routes.

Junkers put three engines into his G 24 in 1925 and Fokker fitted them to a high-wing monoplane the same year, the first of the famous Fokker Trimotors.

The following year the shape emerged in America when William B. Stout combined the Junkers construction with the Fokker design. The plane – which became known as the Tin Goose – proved to be America's first successful all-metal transport. Henry Ford, pioneer of the family motor-car, bought Stout's company and put the plane into production as the Ford Trimotor. He also encouraged American airline operators to think of carrying passengers instead of just mail or freight.

The monoplane was beginning to come into its own and establish itself over the biplane. The trimotors were to make

The complete modern airliner, the DC-1 in its TWA markings.

more spectacular achievements possible – like the American, Lieutenant-Commander Richard Byrd's polar flights in 1926 and 1929 – and inspire the production of other planes with the new, high-wing shape.

As the Europeans changed the shape of the aeroplane, the Americans streamlined it – another factor in the progress towards a revolution in design that was only just around the corner.

In 1927 the worth of good streamlining was demonstrated by John K. Northrop in his Lockheed Vega. He made the fuselage of moulded plywood and used the Fokker type of plywood structure for the high wings. The plane was able to cruise at 135 mph when speeds of only 100 mph were being achieved by other aircraft.

The new developments made it possible for Charles Lindbergh to find the aeroplane he had been looking for.

Lindbergh was almost 25 with four years of flying behind him and an unknown captain in the Missouri National Guard. He was convinced that the time had come to face "the essential problem of how to use man's creation [of the aeroplane] for the benefit of man himself".

The sort of plane he wanted was going to be expensive, and he had little money. So he made a rough list of what he thought he would need and set off in search of people to back him.

He was a man who hated to do things just to make an impression, and thought it a bit of a waste of money to buy himself a new outfit of clothes when he went to see the

Top: *Finally, the incredible DC-3 – the first plane that could make money just by hauling passengers. It has proved to be a unique aeroplane and has been referred to as the finest piece of machinery ever built.*

Above: *The DC-2 and the 100th Douglas transport, completed on June 5, 1935. It had taken Douglas 54 weeks to produce 100 of the aircraft, and it was one of these planes that came in second in the MacRobertson England to Australia air race in 1934.*

Right: *James Doolittle, then a Lieutenant, standing on the float of the R3C-2, the Curtiss biplane in which he won the 1925 Schneider Trophy. It was the last biplane to win the cup before monoplanes began to take over.*

Wright Corporation to try and get hold of one of the new Bellanca monoplanes.

The people he approached were horrified at his intention to attempt the New York–Paris flight alone and in a single-engined plane. They thought it was too much of a risk.

But Lindbergh insisted that the plane he flew must have only one engine. To have more, he argued, would merely increase the chances of engine failure, and he would rather have extra fuel than an extra man.

Finally a group of St. Louis businessmen agreed to help Lindbergh. With their backing, and 2,000 dollars of his own savings, he contacted numerous well-known manufacturers to see if they would build him a plane. One after another they either turned him down flat or wanted to impose conditions that he found impossible to accept.

But he had heard of a small and almost unknown company called Ryan Airlines, of San Diego in California, who were building high-wing monoplanes for mail carrying.

Lindbergh found the Ryan Company, which had a small factory near a fish cannery, enthusiastic about his ideas. They even offered to throw in extras – such as a metal propeller and the best instruments – at cost price.

A new engine, the Wright J-5C Whirlwind, a 220 hp, air-cooled power unit, had just been developed. It was proving extremely reliable. Three of them had been used in Byrd's Fokker for the North Pole flight in 1926, and Lindbergh was confident that one could carry him safely to Paris.

Ryan said they could build him his plane, with the engine, for 10,580 dollars. And what is more, they promised to have it ready for him in 60 days.

There was no time to lose. Other more famous flyers had their eyes on the 25,000-dollar Orteig prize.

The Frenchman René Fonk was to attempt the crossing in a Sikorsky trimotor; his countrymen Charles Nungesser and François Coli were preparing to fly from Paris to New York; a new Fokker was being built for Byrd; and two US Navy men, Commander Noel Davis and Lieutenant Stanton Wooster, were testing a trimotor biplane.

These men were reputed to be spending 100,000 dollars on their projects, nearly ten times more than Lindbergh could afford. But one by one his rivals met disaster.

Fonk crashed on take-off, and two members of his crew died; Byrd's Fokker crashed during a test flight; Davis and Wooster were killed in another crash; and Nungesser and Coli disappeared while actually over the Atlantic.

It was no wonder that the newspapers gave Lindbergh a new nickname – the Flying Fool – for thinking of making the trip in a single-engined plane alone.

Out at the Ryan factory all other work practically stopped so that as many people as possible could concentrate on getting Lindbergh's plane finished. And, as promised, just 60 days after work began Lindbergh test flew the aircraft over San Diego Bay. Its registration was NX 211 – N was the international code letter for America, and X stood for experimental. Lindbergh christened the plane the *Spirit of St. Louis*.

On May 10, 1927, with all his bills paid and tests completed, Lindbergh left San Diego for St. Louis. He made the non-stop flight in 14 hours 25 minutes, a new record from the Pacific coast. It made him an instant celebrity when he arrived in New York two days later.

The week he spent there, making final checks on his plane and waiting for favourable weather conditions over the Atlantic, was chaotic. Reporters, photographers and sightseers were everywhere.

He needed publicity, but hated the way some newspapers particularly the tabloids – manipulated stories about him. When he and his mother refused to embrace for the benefit of the Press cameras, photographers took pictures of two other people embracing and faked a shot for their newspapers by superimposing the faces of Lindbergh and his mother to make a composite picture.

Later he wrote: "Accuracy, I've learned, is secondary to circulation – a thing to be sacrificed, when occasion arises, to a degree depending on the standards of each paper."

Accuracy was sacred to him. In the air it meant the difference between life or death to a pilot.

Early on the morning of May 20 Lindbergh opened the throttle of the *Spirit of St. Louis* and began his take-off run over the soft, rain-soaked ground of Roosevelt Field, New York. He had no view forward because the plane had been fitted with a big fuel tank in the front part of the fuselage. In place of a windscreen he had a periscope.

Left: *The German contribution to low-wing airliner design of the period, the Junkers JU 52, here showing a fine example of corrugated skin construction. It could carry 15 passengers and was also used as a bomber.*

Right: *It couldn't happen today – an aircraft landing in the heart of London. This Short Calcutta flying boat City of Alexandria is pictured at anchor on the River Thames opposite the Houses of Parliament. By the beginning of the 1930s these aircraft were flying on the Empire routes carrying 15 passengers at a cruising speed of 90 mph.*

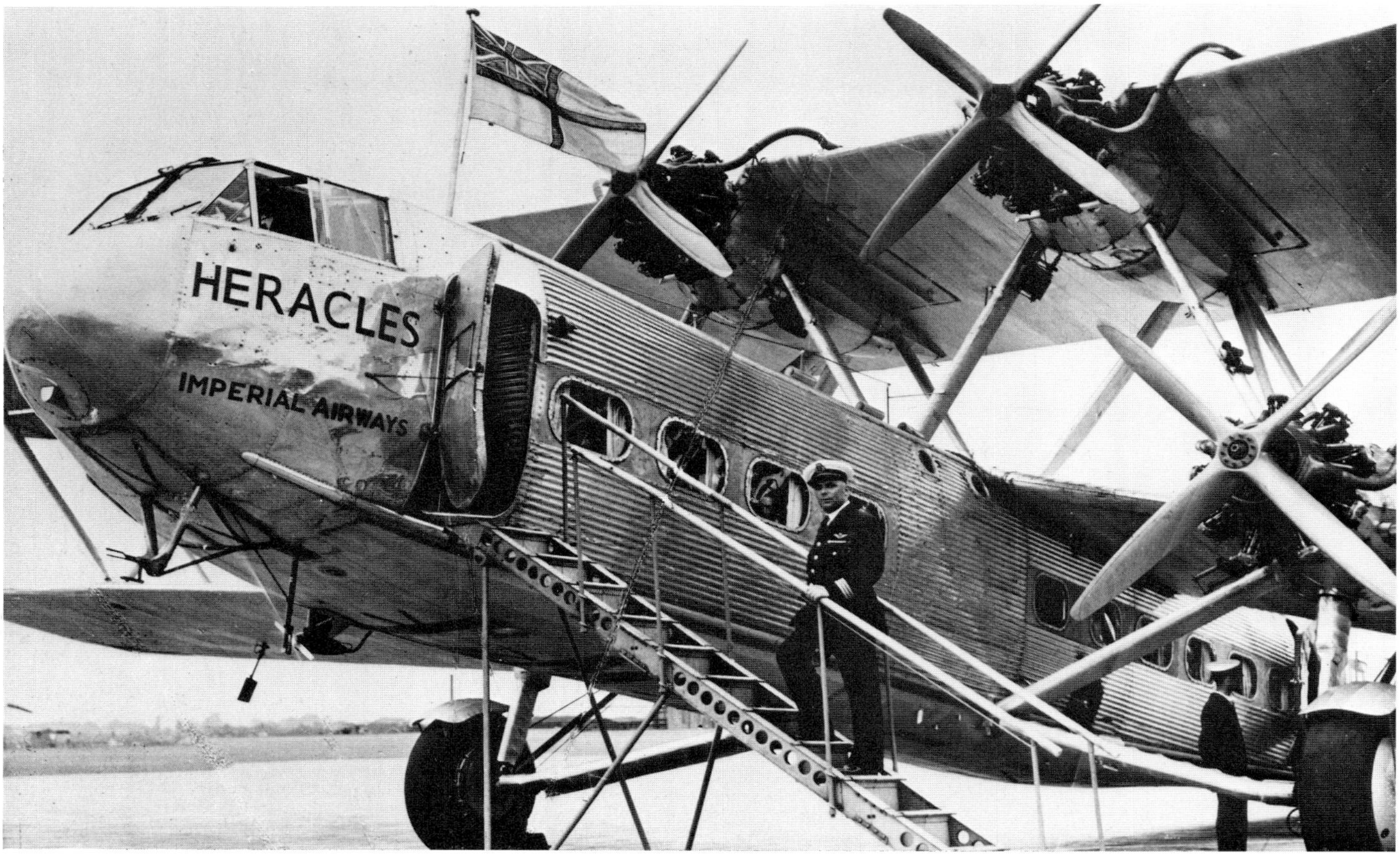
HERACLES
IMPERIAL AIRWAYS

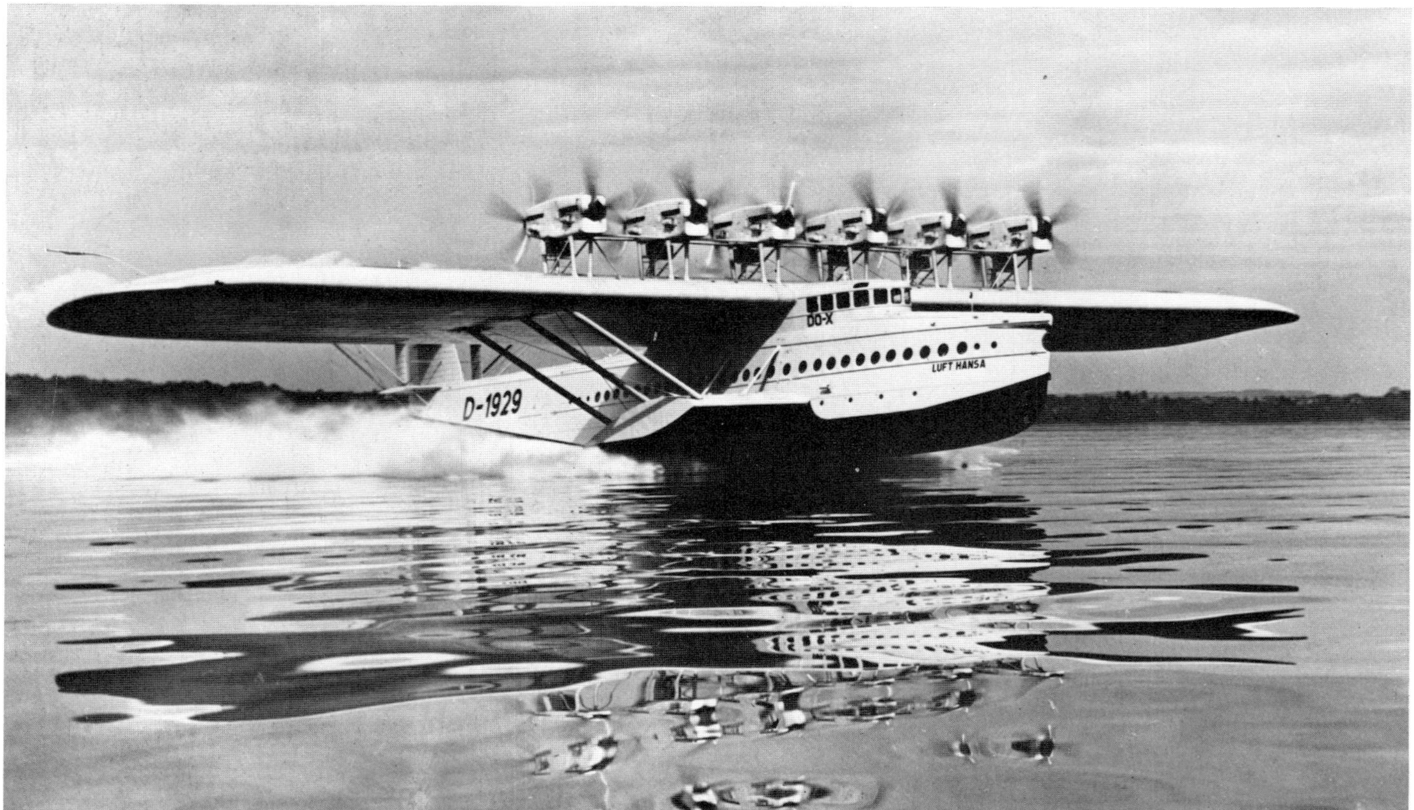
DO-X
LUFT HANSA
D-1929

The plane cleared the telephone wires at the end of the field by 20 ft and Lindbergh, followed by several newspaper planes crammed with photographers, set course for the long flight to Paris 3,600 miles away.

One by one the escorting aircraft turned back leaving him alone amidst the wastes of water and sky. He had been ruthless about keeping the weight of the plane down, refusing to carry a radio because they were not reliable enough, and even cutting out unneeded areas from his navigational charts to save extra ounces.

Now he noticed he had picked up some weight he hadn't bargained for – lumps of mud on his wings thrown up by the wheels during take-off. But there was nothing he could do, he couldn't reach out and scrape it off. And soon there were other things to think about.

Storms, ice, fog, a cloudburst and . . . just as big an enemy . . . tiredness. Hour after hour the *Spirit of St. Louis* droned on. To fight off the overwhelming desire to sleep he cupped his hand into the slipstream to direct the icy blast on to his face. When things seemed to be going well, he forced himself to think about what could go wrong. Being afraid is one sure way of staying awake.

At other times he used his fingers to prise his eyelids open.

It was in the twenty-sixth hour of his flight that he saw his first living thing in that vast expanse of ocean – a porpoise. In the twenty-seventh hour he saw some birds and he thought how lucky they were to be able

Left: *The HP 42. One of the most elegant and dignified airliners ever built but, according to Anthony Fokker, it has a "built-in head wind" because it was slow. In ten years of flying the HPs covered ten million miles without a fatality.*

Below left: *The giant Dornier Do X flying boat takes off in a flurry of spray. Built in 1929 as an experiment the 12-engined monster proved that large flying boats were possible and crossed the Atlantic at the beginning of the 1930s.*

Below: *Routes across the Pacific ocean to Asia were pioneered by the Boeing and Martin flying boats. This Martin China Clipper is riding at anchor under the palms. Its owners, Pan American, opened up a service to the Orient on November 22, 1935.*

Above: *One attempt to make long distance flight possible was the Mayo composite aircraft built by Shorts. The "pick-a-back" idea was developed for the north Atlantic experimental mail service and consisted of the large, lower flying boat which was lightly loaded and the smaller, upper plane which was carried on its back. The small plane was flown out over the ocean with a full load of cargo and fuel and, when within range of its destination, it was launched in mid-air and the larger plane returned home. In July 1938 the pair pictured, Mercury and Maia, carried out the first commercial crossing of the Atlantic in this way.*

Below: *Europe was catching up with America and producing four-engined types of its own. The Focke-Wulf Fw 200 Condor of Lufthansa was intended for transatlantic service and in 1938 one of them flew from Berlin to New York in under 20 hours. The Condor had four 720 hp engines, a speed of 233 mph, a range of 4,000 miles and was capable of carrying 26 passengers.*

to rest on the water.

And then . . . a boat, and more. Fishing-boats. The sight of them brought him sharply awake. Europe could not be far away.

Lindbergh spotted a fisherman's head sticking out from a porthole in one of the boats. He circled and, gliding down to within 50 ft of the water, slid back his cabin window and shouted: "Which way is Ireland?"

He had spoken to people on the ground this way before and had usually received some signal in reply. But this time there was none. The fisherman just stared. So Lindbergh gave up and flew on.

Then, through a curtain of rain, the faint smudge of the Irish coast. He calculated his position as he flew in over the beautiful green fields. He was exactly on course . . . and two hours ahead of schedule. In his excitement, and his delight at seeing the people run out of their cottages to wave to him, he lost all sense of direction.

He suddenly realised he had turned completely round and was heading back out over the Atlantic. Quickly he banked the *Spirit of St. Louis* round on to his course again. On over England, the county of Cornwall. Plymouth slid by on the left and he was over the Channel.

As he approached the coast of Normandy, with success in sight, he began to worry because he had forgotten to get a visa to permit him to land in France. And he also began to think about what he would have to buy when he reached Paris. He hadn't even packed a toothbrush.

Soon his elation overcame his minor worries. He considered flying the rest of the way round the world. It would be, he thought, beneath the dignity of the *Spirit of St. Louis* to be sent back home to America by boat.

In the thirty-third hour of his flight he became aware that it was past supper time and he had eaten nothing since taking off from New York. He pulled out a sandwich from the brown paper bag of them he had brought. Then he remembered his canteen of water.

Throughout the flight he had been rationing himself, taking only careful sips in case he was forced down in the Atlantic. Now, with Paris less than an hour away, he could drink all the water he wanted.

After all the dangers, the terrible hours of loneliness, Lindbergh's obsession with perfection still showed through. He stopped himself throwing a sandwich paper into the fields below. He did not want a litter of waste paper to be his first contact with France.

And he thought about the wonderful plane that had brought him so many perilous miles. It had faltered only once. The engine had coughed and spluttered briefly when the nose fuel tank ran dry, as had been planned. But it had picked up again immediately when he switched on the fuel supply from his other tanks.

They had depended on each other, he and the *Spirit of St. Louis*. The flight had been made, not by "I" or "It", thought Lindbergh, but "We". They had done it together.

He picked up the flashing beacons of the London to

The airlines were thinking of intercontinental flights with aircraft that had pressurised cabins so that passengers could breath easily though flying very high. The first of the pressurised airliners was the Boeing Stratoliner, the United States' first four-engined plane to operate regularly on domestic routes.

Paris airway, and it was only a few minutes before the glow of Paris appeared on the horizon. He found the Eiffel Tower and circled round it, then turned north-east searching for Le Bourget airport.

But where was it? It wasn't on his maps, and no one in America had known exactly where it was. But, they had told him: "It's a big airport. You can't miss it."

Through the darkness he picked out the hangars of the airfield, and the thousands of tiny lights along one side of it.

The wheels of the *Spirit of St. Louis* gently touched earth again and, as Lindbergh turned the plane to taxi towards the floodlights, he saw that the whole field in front of him was alive, covered with thousands of running figures.

He brought the plane to a halt and opened the door to climb out. Dozens of hands grabbed him and he found himself being carried shoulder high. Hundreds of people were shouting his name. Souvenir hunters began to strip the very fabric from his plane, even stealing his engine and navigation log books.

Fitzhugh Green, writing in Lindbergh's book *We – Pilot and Plane*, described the reception in Europe as possibly "the greatest torrent of mass emotion ever witnessed in human history".

It was roughly the same as Beatlemania – probably even greater than the fantastic greetings given to the Beatles by their fans in the 1960s.

That night at Le Bourget they had to call out the Army. Thousands of people who had been following Lindbergh's progress in the newspapers, all converged on the airport for his arrival. The crowd broke through the steel fences, sweeping soldiers and policemen aside in their enthusiasm.

At last an American reporter helped Lindbergh to escape by putting on his flying helmet and diverting the attention of the adoring crowds.

The headlines of the world screamed out the news:

LINDBERGH LANDS IN PARIS: CITY GOES WILD
– *Chicago Sunday Tribune.*
GREAT EPIC OF THE AIR: FLYING FOOL'S TRIUMPH
– *News of the World.*
'FLYING FOOL' YESTERDAY: HERO TODAY
– *Daily Mirror.*
NEW YORK TO PARIS IN LESS THAN $1\frac{1}{2}$ DAYS
– *Daily Telegraph.*

"Lucky" Lindbergh's gamble had paid off. His daring and belief in the aeroplane had created, in the words of the American Ambassador to Paris, Myron T. Herrick, "one of history's 'supreme moments'."

Lindbergh was deluged with fan mail, business offers and requests to write and make public appearances. To one offer of a million-dollar contract he said: "You must remember this expedition was not organised to make money but to advance aviation."

And when asked what good he thought the flight had done he answered that he believed it was the forerunner of a great air service . . . to bring people nearer together in

understanding and friendship than they had ever been before.

It did not escape Lindbergh's notice that the Europeans were encouraging passenger airlines at a time when, in America, operators were mainly concerned with carrying the mail.

He urged his countrymen to build airports at every town and city to speed the development of passenger flights. America had a great natural advantage over the small European countries. It was vast, and aircraft were not restricted by having to cross international frontiers. This, coupled with the natural disposition of Americans to travel, helped put the United States ahead of the field in commercial aviation.

The year after Lindbergh's flight, Squadron-leader Charles Kingsford Smith, an Australian, conquered the Pacific. He flew a Fokker F VII with a crew of three from Oakland, California, to Australia by way of Hawaii and Fiji.

And in Germany a rocket-propelled plane was tested. The seeds that were one day to bear the fruit of the jet and the spaceship had taken root.

American designers were studying a remarkable lecture given in the United States by Dr. Rohrbach. His ideas on stressed-skin construction for wings, which consisted of a flat box-shape with a separate rounded section at the leading edge and a tapering section making up the trailing edge, led Boeings to build the Monomail.

It was a single-engined, low-wing monoplane with the added streamlining of an engine cowling and a retractable undercarriage. Boeings' experience with the Monorail was put into their B-9 bomber of 1931 but, instead of a single engine, they fitted this plane with two engines, one in each wing leading edge.

The Junkers low wings, Fokker's stressing and Rohrbach's improved construction, together with his smooth, metal skins, had at last come together. The revolution in aircraft design was about to take place.

The B-9, with its top speed of 186 mph, was faster than the fighter planes of the time. But it was rejected by the Army in favour of the Martin B-10 bomber which had an even better performance – 200 mph – and enclosed cockpits.

So Boeings turned the B-9 into an airliner, the 247. It was the first of the classic type, and a plane that, in its most refined form, really lacked only one thing – flaps.

The 247 was a low-wing, all-metal, stressed-skin monoplane. It was highly streamlined with a retractable undercarriage and good cowlings round its twin 550 hp Pratt and Whitney Wasp radial engines. The engines were also fitted with superchargers – devices which force in air, enabling engines to go faster and planes to fly higher where the atmosphere is thinner.

It was designed to fly on when one engine failed, which meant greater safety for passengers. The 247 also had variable-pitch propellers – the "twist" of the blades could be altered to give the best performance for take-off and

In Britain Armstrong Whitworth built the Ensign, a 40-seater high wing monoplane.

cruise – and it was fitted with de-icing equipment and an automatic pilot.

The plane appeared at a time when great progress was being made in the production of better instruments, such as the artificial horizon and the turn and bank indicator, which meant pilots no longer depended on being able to see the ground in order to fly straight and level.

James H. Doolittle, who was to become a top commander in the Second World War, had made the first completely "blind" flight in a plane with a hooded cockpit in 1929.

Now, with instruments like the altimeter and the rate of climb indicator and two-way radio coming into general use, flying was shedding its old pioneering image.

The 247 carried only ten passengers, three fewer than the Fords. But its cruising speed of 155 mph meant that it could fly coast-to-coast in the New York to Los Angeles run in 20 hours, four fewer than the trimotors were taking.

It was first introduced in 1933. But a year earlier a company called United Airlines had recognised the 247's possibilities and ordered 60 of them straight off the drawing-board, ensuring that it would be the only airline for some time to have the new plane.

Other airlines naturally feared that United would take a lot of their passengers away. They would have to have 247s – or something equally as good – to stay in business. Competition was about to play a part in the creation of another airliner that was to prove itself not only better than the 247, but probably the greatest airliner the world has yet known.

Transcontinental and Western Airlines – later to become Trans World Airlines – tried to buy some of the new Boeings, but they were told they could not have any until United's order was complete. So they contacted the other big aircraft companies in the hope of finding one that could build them a plane to match the 247.

TWA had in mind an all-metal trimotor that could carry 12 passengers. One of the letters detailing the sort of aircraft they wanted arrived at the Douglas company, a firm which had been specialising in making small military planes. The idea of building the sort of transport TWA were after was something new for Douglas, but they decided to try.

They met the challenge of the 247 with the first Douglas Commercial – the DC-1.

The trimotor idea was dropped. Boeings had proved that two engines of the right sort were enough, and Douglas had the even more powerful 710 hp Wright Cyclones. They also had better engine cowlings, and flaps.

Only one DC-1 was built because tests showed that though it was faster than the 247, and able to carry more people, it could be improved still further. Douglas lengthened the plane to take 14 people, added still more powerful engines and put it into production as the DC-2.

The complete, modern airliner had arrived. Outside America people were doubtful about the claims made for the new planes. But in 1934 their superiority was proved dramatically when a 247 and a DC-2 were entered in the MacRobertson England to Australia race.

The DC-2, belonging to the Dutch airline KLM, came in second to a de Havilland Comet, a specially designed twin-engined monoplane which was the ancestor of the Second World War Mosquito. The Boeing was third and another Comet was fourth.

But the DCs could be improved even more. American Airways wanted a "sleeper" transport to fly overnight from New York to California while passengers slept in bunks instead of sitting in seats. In adapting the DC-2 to take the sleeping berths Douglas came up with a new, bigger plane, the famous DC-3.

The DST – Douglas Sleeper Transport night plane – had seven upper and seven lower berths, with a separate private cabin for honeymoon couples. The "day plane" version, which became the DC-3, was capable of carrying up to 32 tourist-class passengers.

Powered by two 900 hp Cyclones the new plane left the ground for the first time on December 17, 1935 – the thirty-second anniversary of the Wrights' first flight.

It was an immediate success. Coast-to-coast flying times were slashed and airlines began to make profits. American Airlines' president, C. R. Smith, said of the DC-3: "It was the first airplane that could make money just by hauling passengers."

A unique aeroplane had been produced. It was safe, fast and strong. By 1939 the DC-3 was flying 90 per cent of the world's airline business. Over 13,000 were built, a total that is far greater than for any other airliner,

and many of them are still flying today.

It was known by a variety of names and designations. The Army called it the C-47, the Navy knew it as the R4D. In England it was the Dakota, in Japan the L-2D and in Russia the Li-2.

The DC-3 played a vital role in the Second World War as the Allies' standard transport and many stories and books have been told and written about its exploits during active service.

One DC-3 was making a flight from Hong Kong to Chungking in 1941 when it was forced down because of a Japanese air raid.

The Japanese bombers attacked it as it stood helpless on the ground at Suifu. When the raid was over the plane was seen to have had one wing blasted off.

A replacement was sent for. But the only one available was from a DC-2 which was five feet shorter than a DC-3 wing and designed to carry loads thousands of pounds lighter. It was flown the 900 miles from Hong Kong and fitted to the stricken plane which then made a perfect flight back to its base, becoming known as the DC-2½.

Other stories tell of a 21-seater version taking off with 74 people on board, and of DC-3s continuing to fly after losing large sections of wing or tail.

The plane has turned out to be virtually irreplaceable. Its appearance, with the 247, influenced the Europeans to bring out designs to compete with it, but none of them were really successful.

Above: *Another four-engined British airliner that was being planned before the new war came was the Fairey FC 1.*

Right: *The Lockheed Electra. It was a plane like this that Amelia Earhart mysteriously disappeared during her attempt to fly round the world in 1937. The Electra had a retractable undercarriage, two 450 hp engines, a top speed of 210 mph and a range of 810 miles.*

Facing page: *Wiley Post, the one-eyed pilot who became the first man to conquer the world alone in an aeroplane. He did it in this aircraft, the Winnie Mae, in July 1933 and it took him seven days.*

At the same time as the DCs and Boeings appeared on the scene Junkers built the Ju 52. It was an old-fashioned trimotor, a low-wing monoplane with the traditional corrugated skin, but it continued in airline and military service up until 1945. To try and match the new American airliners Junkers brought out the Ju 86. This was based on the 247, but it had twin tail fins and later became better known as a bomber. The Heinkel 111 also owed a lot to the American planes, as did the British Bristol 142, forerunner of the Blenheim bomber.

The monoplane had now become the dominant shape, though biplanes were to continue flying until well into the 1940s. The success of the new airliners only confirmed the superiority of monoplanes which had been consistently winning the international seaplane speed races for the Schneider Trophy.

A French aviation enthusiast, Jacques Schneider, donated the trophy and the first contest, in 1913, was won by the French. A Deperdussin monoplane with a 160 hp Gnome engine covered the 172-mile course at an average speed of 45·75 mph.

The next seven winners were all biplanes and the contests developed into a three-cornered battle between Italy, America and Britain.

The last biplane to win was the American Curtiss R3C-2 in 1925. It was flown by James Doolittle and was probably the last word in biplane design, beautifully streamlined and sleek. Doolittle's speed was 232·6 mph and the plane had a 600 hp engine.

After 1925 the biplane never got a look-in. An Italian Macchi M 39 powered by an 800 hp Fiat engine won in 1926 at a speed of 246·4 mph.

The next three races were taken by the British Supermarines to win the trophy outright. The final race, in 1931, was won by Flight-Lieutenant J. N. Boothman at an average speed of 340·08 mph. His plane, the Supermarine S 6B had a Rolls-Royce engine of 2,300 hp.

His speed and the size of the engine is some indication of how aircraft had developed since the first Schneider Trophy race 18 years before. The designer of the Supermarines, R. J. Mitchell, later used the experience gained from the races to produce the Spitfire fighter.

Then, in 1934, an Italian Macchi-Castoldi MC 72 pushed up the air speed record to 440·675 mph with a 2,800 Fiat engine.

Britain had been developing her long-range Empire routes ever since Sir Alan Cobham's series of survey flights in the 1920s and 1930s. He had opened up air routes to the Middle East, India, Australia and South Africa and had also helped to pioneer refuelling in the air.

Still clinging to biplanes Britain introduced the elegant and dignified Handley Page 42s in 1931. There were two types, a 38-seater for use on European routes, and a 24-seater for use on the tropical routes.

The giant four-engined planes had a top wing-span of 130 ft, making them not far off the size of today's Boeing 707s.

Passengers flew in cabins very similar to the super luxury railway carriages of the day with thickly padded armchairs, shaded lights and curtains at the windows. There were uniformed stewards to serve in-flight meals which were eaten from fine china.

The HP 42s stayed in service for ten years, flying over 10,000,000 miles without a fatality. But they were slow. They had a struggle to reach their cruising speed of 100 mph, and Anthony Fokker described them as planes with a "built-in head wind".

But the introduction of the monoplane airliners, the lack of good airfields on the Empire routes and the amount of water that had to be crossed led to the equally luxurious Short flying boats in 1936.

They had promenade decks and lounges that converted into bedrooms at night. The Southampton to Sydney flight took nearly ten days with stopovers at first-class hotels on the way.

The Germans had built a big flying boat, the Dornier Do X, one of which once made a flight with 169 people on board. It had 12 engines, a wing-span of 157 ft and weighed 55 tons.

Competition was on for the transatlantic services. The Do X made the round trip to America and back from Germany at the beginning of the 1930s. But there was rivalry, not only from the Short Empire boats, but from Pan American's Boeing Clippers and the Martin flying boats which had set up services across the Pacific to Asia.

The airlines were beginning to think of regular flights between the great continents. Such flights would need bigger and more powerful aeroplanes than the Douglases, the Boeings or the equally good but smaller Lockheed Electras that were operating so successfully on internal routes.

What was needed was a four-engined airliner capable of flying Atlantic distances with a cabin that was pressurised. Pressurising allowed an airliner to fly higher in smoother air where passengers in an unpressurised plane would not be able to breathe properly because of the lack of oxygen.

This was to be the next stage in the development of transport aeroplanes and the first was the Boeing 307 Stratoliner which went into service in 1940.

By this time Europe was beginning to catch up with the Americans. Germany's first four-engined types, the Ju 90 and the Focke-Wulf Fw Condor, had appeared. In Britain the Armstrong Whitworth Ensign, a 40-seater, high-wing monoplane, was flying and de Havilland had produced an advanced design in the Albatross. Two other four-engined planes, the Fairey FC 1 and the Short S 32 were also planned.

While all this technical progress was being made the adventurers had not faded from the headlines. And the men were not having things all to themselves either . . . women were equally determined to show that they were just as capable of setting up records for long-distance and endurance flights.

Harriet Quimby, an American, had flown the English Channel only three years after Blériot in 1912, and in a Blériot monoplane, too.

The two most famous women pilots were Amelia Earhart, another American, and Britain's Amy Johnson. Both of them became world heroines.

Amelia Earhart was the first woman to fly the Atlantic – though as a passenger – in a Fokker trimotor seaplane in 1928. Four years later she became the first woman to fly the Atlantic solo and in 1935 flew a Lockheed Vega across the Pacific from Honolulu to California.

In 1937 she set out in a Lockheed Electra to fly round the world, but the plane disappeared over the South Pacific and her fate is still a mystery.

Amy Johnson was an ex-typist. She was the first English-woman to fly solo to Australia, making the trip in 1930 in 19 days. But her career ended as tragically as Amelia Earhart's when, on January 5, 1941, the plane she was ferrying for the Air Transport Auxiliary crashed into the Thames estuary and she was killed.

And so, through the bravery, skill and daring of the men and women of many nations, the aeroplane finally conquered the world.

The man who first conquered the world alone in an aeroplane was Wiley Post, a colourful American with only one eye. Piloting a modified Lockheed Vega he completed the solo round trip from New York in just over seven days in 1933.

That same year a man with piercing eyes and a small black moustache came to power in Germany. His name: Adolf Hitler. His symbol was the swastika – the crooked cross. And, at the end of the decade, he plunged the world into a new war – the biggest and most destructive war in human history.

From out of the chaos the aeroplane was to emerge, not only as the most decisive weapon of war, but in a completely new form.

Scramble...for peace!

An aeroplane ended the Second World War at 8.16 on the morning of August 6, 1945.

That was the time that the most terrible weapon ever used in war – the atomic bomb – exploded over the Japanese city of Hiroshima. A single aeroplane dropped a single bomb and unleashed hell on earth. The city ceased to exist. So did nearly 80,000 human beings.

Japan did not surrender for over a week, and a second atomic bomb was used against another city, Nagasaki. But the war really ended on that beautiful summer morning when man first let loose on his fellow men the basic power of the universe.

Special Bombing Mission No. 13

The Atomic Age had been born three weeks earlier. The infant's first cry was heard 250 miles away from where the birth took place, at 5.30 am in the New Mexico desert 50 miles from the American Air Force base at Alamogordo.

The name is strangely like Armageddon – the mythical site where, according to the Bible, the final battle on Earth between good and evil will be fought before the Day of Judgment.

An international team of scientists created the atomic "child" which was christened the Manhattan Project. From the start the parents knew they were bringing a monster into the world.

In the early days of the project – which began in earnest in 1939 – there was fear that an atomic explosion might cause a gigantic chain reaction which would set fire to the atmosphere and the oceans and consume the whole Earth.

No one knew exactly what would happen, except that whatever did would be utterly dreadful.

Because of this some scientists did not want an atomic bomb to be used on people without warning. They wanted the Japanese to be given either the chance to surrender or be shown through some demonstration the awful destruction they faced.

But to the men who had to actually decide if and how the bomb should be used, President Harry S. Truman of the United States and Winston Churchill of war-battered Britain, there seemed to be two things to consider:

Would an atomic bomb end the six-year-old war?

Would it make an invasion of Japan unnecessary and therefore save more lives – on both sides – than would be lost in an atomic raid?

If there were any doubts in their minds at the time they would have been banished on March 9, 1945.

That night 334 American aircraft rained fire bombs down on Tokyo, Japan's capital city. It was the most destructive military action in history. Over 15 square miles of the city were left in ruins and there were more casualties than in an atom bomb raid.

If so many people could be killed during a "normal" bombing, why should there be any hesitation over the use of an atomic weapon?

A special squadron, the 509th, was formed to drop the

atomic bomb. It was made up of the finest aircrew in the US Air Force and put under the command of Paul Tibbets, a 29-year-old colonel.

The squadron was equipped with 15 B-29 Superfortresses, new long-range heavy bombers. The planes had four 2,200 hp engines, were pressurised so that they could bomb from great heights, and had the first reversible-pitch propellers which helped to slow them down when they landed.

All armament, except the tail guns, was stripped from the planes. This was to make them as light as possible so that they could use all of their 368 mph top speed to make a quick getaway from an atomic blast.

The 509th was based on the tiny Pacific island of Tinian, part of the Mariana group which had been seized from the Japanese. It was only 1,500 miles from Japan's home islands.

The atomic operation was surrounded with the utmost secrecy. Only a very few people knew what it was all leading up to. And to help keep it as secret as possible two code names were used: Centreboard, for the operation itself, and Little Boy for the bomb.

No single flight was ever planned so carefully or so far in advance. Months before an atomic bomb even existed the planes of the 509th were carrying out "dummy runs" with their single practice bombs that the crews called "pumpkins".

But there were no fairy godmothers around to use these pumpkins to bring about any happy endings. The only resemblance Operation Centreboard had to a fairy story was that Japan had been picked to play the part of a Cinderella who was doomed to sit among the ashes of her own cities.

Slowly but surely the Special Bombing Mission with the fateful number 13 took shape.

Three cities were chosen as possible targets: Kokura, Nagasaki and the "primary objective" . . . Hiroshima. There would be only one bomb, and it must not miss. It therefore could not be trusted even to the new miracle "electric eye" called radar, it had to be dropped visually.

Day after day bomb-aimers and navigators studied aerial photographs of the target cities until they knew them as well as their own back yards. For a bomb-aimer to drop the bomb visually he had to be able to see the target, and that meant good weather was essential.

There were to be seven planes on Mission No. 13. Three were to leave early to report on the weather conditions over each of the three targets and, depending on which was the clearest, the city to be bombed would be decided in the air.

One plane would carry the bomb – Tibbets's B-29, which he named the *Enola Gay* after his mother. He would be escorted by two other planes packed with instruments and cameras to record what happened when the bomb exploded.

The last aircraft would fly to Iwo Jima, an island just short of the halfway mark between Tinian and Japan. This was to be a spare which would have the bomb transferred

Above: *Little Boy, the first atomic bomb detonated in war, which was dropped by Tibbets and his crew from their aircraft the* Enola Gay *on the city of Hiroshima. It weighed five tons and had the force of 20,000 tons of high explosive.*

Above: *"We won the war today":* Enola Gay *lands back at Tinian Island after the atomic bomb mission.*

Right: *8.16 am on the morning of August 6, 1945: Little Boy explodes over Hiroshima and the giant mushroom cloud hangs 40,000 ft in the air. Below, a city has vanished.*

Left: *War from the air: Tokyo in flames after a raid by B-29 Superfortresses in May 1945. Two months earlier, in the most destructive military action in history, 334 American planes destroyed over 15 square miles of the city.*

Bird of peace: the DC-9 modern jet airliner capable of flying close to the speed of sound. Its rear-mounted engines create a quiet passenger cabin and produce the beautiful "clean" line of today's big jets.

Facing page: To the rescue: the hovering aeroplane – a helicopter – which can operate in areas which other forms of transport would find impossible. Here a Bell 47 of the Los Angeles Sheriff's Aero Detail waits for a stretcher patient to be loaded aboard.

Below: Armed jet: A Provost standing ready for take-off from the snow-covered runway of a British Aircraft Corporation airfield in the north of England. This aircraft is one of several supplied to the Sudanese Air Force.

Above: *The Spitfire: The plane that helped to outfight the Luftwaffe during the Battle of Britain and one of the most formidable fighting machines in the world at the time. But the first design, in 1934, was a failure. Sir Robert McLean, the head of Vickers, informed the Air Ministry that a new plane – a "real killer fighter" sketched out by Reginal Mitchell – would be developed and, under no circumstances, would anyone be allowed to interfere with the designer. The result was the Spitfire we know with eight guns mounted in the wings. Nearly 20,500 were built plus over 2,500 Seafires – the Naval version – and they fought on every front in the war. The one in the picture is a Mk XI.*

Above: *A piece of aerial artillery: The JU 87 Stuka dive bomber, Hitler's lumbering terror weapon, which was hopelessly outclassed when it came to fight in the air.*

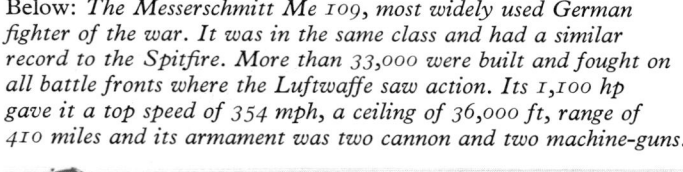

Below: *The Messerschmitt Me 109, most widely used German fighter of the war. It was in the same class and had a similar record to the Spitfire. More than 33,000 were built and fought on all battle fronts where the Luftwaffe saw action. Its 1,100 hp gave it a top speed of 354 mph, a ceiling of 36,000 ft, range of 410 miles and its armament was two cannon and two machine-guns.*

Above: *The means of victory, the bomber. The Avro Lancaster is believed by some to have been the most successful heavy bomber of the war. Like the Spitfire, it was also born out of failure. When the twin-engined Manchester bomber was hit by troubles it was decided to alter the design and fit four engines. It resulted in the finest British bomber of the Second World War and one of the most successful aircraft ever built. Between 1942 and the end of the war Lancasters dropped over 608,000 tons of bombs and took part in the epic Dambusters' raid in May 1943 when aircraft of 617 Squadron breached vital German dams with specially designed bombs. The Lancaster had a 101 ft wing-span, four 1,460 hp engines, a top speed of 287 mph, could carry 22,000 lb of bombs and was armed with ten guns.*

Above: *German bombers heading for England during the German preparations for Operation Sealion. These are Heinkell IIIs and the picture is a still from the United Artists film* Battle of Britain.

Left: *Even after the Battle of Britain was over the Luftwaffe continued to bomb important British cities. Two Dornier 17s fly over the dockland of East London, the fires their bombs have started beneath them.*

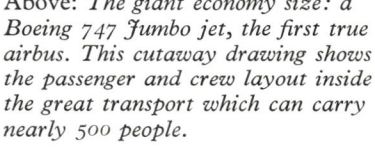

Above: *The giant economy size: a Boeing 747 Jumbo jet, the first true airbus. This cutaway drawing shows the passenger and crew layout inside the great transport which can carry nearly 500 people.*

Left: *Inside a Jumbo; the extra space allows luxury touches.*

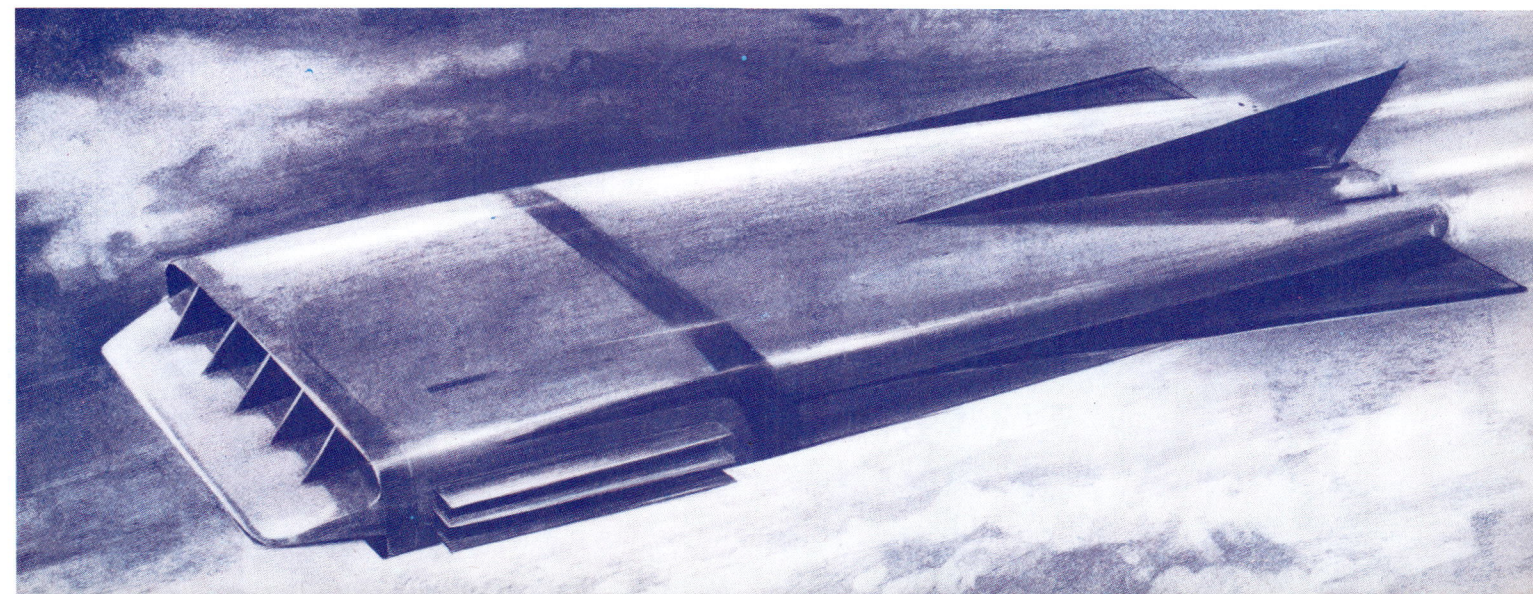

Superjet: the Anglo-French Concorde supersonic transport. The aircraft has the "slender" shape of the immediate future. Its 1,450 mph – twice the speed of sound – will make day-trips between Europe and America possible.

A look at the future: Lockheed's design for a Mach 7 hypersonic airliner, the "son" of the SST. It uses a "blend" of fuselage and control surfaces into a wing shape in which the entire nose section is given over to the propulsion inlet system. Passengers would be housed in the central cabin with the ramjet airflow diverted round it to discharge nozzles at the rear. This airstream could be deflected to give vertical take-off and landing. The small fin provides stability and control.

to it if anything went seriously wrong with the *Enola Gay* while it was in the air.

Towards the end of July the Allies gave the Japanese an ultimatum: surrender unconditionally, or face "prompt and utter destruction". No mention was made of the atomic bomb.

There was no response. Japan had had her chance.

Some Kind of Nightmare

August 6th, 1.37 am: The three weather planes, *Straight Flush*, *Full House* and *Jabbit III*, rose above Tinian and headed out across the Pacific towards Japan.

Just over an hour later Colonel Paul Tibbets rolled the *Enola Gay* to the end of the runway. To his right, *The Great Artiste*. To his left, a plane with no name – just the number 91.

The control tower called up Tibbets: "Dimples 82 [the flight call sign] you are clear for take-off."

Those words could have signalled the moment of greatest peril for the whole mission – but for a navy scientist, Captain William Parsons. If the *Enola Gay* had crashed on take-off with the only existing live atomic bomb on board, the entire operation, including half of Tinian island and the men who had been training for months to drop the bomb, would have been wiped out.

An atomic explosion is caused by two lumps of material

Left: *Japan's Mitsubishi Zero was one of the finest fighter planes of the war. At the time of the Pearl Harbor attack it had the reputation of being the best carrier-borne fighter in the world. The Zero was a single-seater with a 1,020 hp engine and a top speed of nearly 350 mph. It was armed with two machine-guns and two cannon. Sometimes it also carried two 132 lb bombs for use in air-to-air attacks – the bombs were dropped on enemy aircraft from above.*

Below left: *Day of infamy: On the morning of December 7, 1941, Japanese aircraft attacked Pearl Harbor, Hawaii. The great ball of fire is the armaments magazine of the USS Shaw exploding. The attack came without warning and the Japanese pilots met almost no opposition.*

Below: *Pearl Harbor burns; The attack lasted just over an hour and in that time all eight American battleships in the harbour were sunk or damaged and nearly 250 aircraft were destroyed. The Japanese lost 29 planes.*

called uranium 235 being forced together. That day this was to be done by a small explosive charge being fired within the bomb to shoot one piece of U-235 at the other like a bullet.

Parsons decided not to insert the charge into the bomb until the *Enola Gay* was safely airborne. In that way, even if there was a crash, the bomb would not be lost. Parsons spent hours in the *Enola Gay*'s bomb bay practising the delicate operation of fitting the charge into the bomb to make it live.

2.45 am: Dimples 82 lifted her wheels off Tinian's runway and climbed away into the night sky. Soon Tibbets was joined by his two escorts, and the *Enola Gay*, *The Great*

Artiste and No. 91 slipped easily into a big "V" formation for the long flight into history.

The spare plane, the *Top Secret*, was on its way to Iwo Jima to perform its stand-by role and William Parsons was crouched over the five tons of shining metal in the belly of the *Enola Gay*. Carefully he eased home the firing charge. Little Boy now had a heart. It was live. And Mission No. 13 was on its way.

Tibbets decided it was time to let the rest of his crew in on the secret of what they were carrying. He said to Sergeant Bob Caron, the tail gunner: "Say, Bob, you figured out what we're doing yet?"

"Is it some kind of chemist's nightmare?" Caron said.

"No, not exactly," said Tibbets. "How about a physicist's nightmare?" asked Caron.

"Yeah," answered Tibbets. "That's about it."

Suddenly, in Caron's mind, the last piece of the jigsaw snapped into place: "Hey, Colonel," he said, "are we splitting the atom today?"

The *Top Secret* touched down on Iwo Jima and the pilot, Captain Charles McKnight, taxied the plane up behind a special loading pit from where the bomb could be transferred straight into the aircraft. He did not leave his controls.

7.09 am: Major Claude Eatherly's *Straight Flush* approached the outskirts of Hiroshima. At the same time the *Full House* was over Nagasaki and *Jabbit III* was over Kokura.

The air-raid warning sirens sounded in Hiroshima as Eatherly flew across the city. The area was ringed by cloud, but the town itself was clear.

7.25 am: Eatherly's wireless operator tapped out the message: "Y2.Q2.B2.C1". Two hundred miles away over the Pacific it was decoded by Tibbets in the *Enola Gay*. The message told him that conditions were right over the main target and it advised him: "Bomb Primary."

The other weather planes also reported clear targets, but Nagasaki and Kokura did not matter now. The *Straight Flush* flew back across Hiroshima and headed for home, leaving behind a doomed city.

8.09 am: Tibbets identified his target. To protect the crew's eyes from the atomic flash each man had a pair of close-fitting dark goggles. The only colour they would admit was purple. Tibbets now ordered his men to put on the goggles and wait for a radio tone signal to begin in their earphones. When they heard the sound – which indicated that the automatic bomb release was operating – the men were to pull down the goggles over their eyes.

The *Enola Gay* was flying westward at 31,000 ft. Speed: 285 mph. Suddenly Lieutenant Morris Jeppson, who had been looking after the bomb's checking equipment during the flight, picked up his parachute and buckled it on. Then he hooked up his oxygen mask to an emergency supply bottle.

He was thinking that the bomb blast might blow in the windows of the plane and depressurise it. He did not want to be caught without any oxygen to breathe if that happened. Several members of the crew watched his performance uneasily, but no one moved to copy him.

8.11 am: The target was 17 miles ahead and, as the *Enola Gay* began the bombing run, the two escort planes dropped back to be ready with their recording instruments.

The minutes were ticking by . . . but in the *Enola Gay* time seemed to be standing still. The men who had come to do this awful thing could not quite believe, somehow, that it was actually happening. Everything seemed so unreal.

Major Tom Ferebee, the bomb-aimer, hunched over his bomb-sight and watched Hiroshima slip by beneath him. The city looked like a giant hand with its fingers outstretched. The spaces between the fingers were the branches of the Ota River, and he was searching for his aiming-point – a bridge over the widest branch.

8.14 am: He saw it. With just over a minute to go, Ferebee started the automatic device that would end with the bomb being released from the plane.

8.15 am: Seventeen seconds left. Now he switched on the radio warning tone and each man in the *Enola Gay* pulled down his goggles.

Back on Iwo Jima, McKnight also heard the tone in his earphones. Still sitting at the controls of the *Top Secret*, he called outside to his waiting crew that the bomb was about to be dropped.

At that moment the *Enola Gay*'s bomb-bay doors sprang open. Ferebee's finger was on the button that would release the bomb if it failed to fall automatically. But, looking back through the transparent nose of the plane, he saw Little Boy drop into space – awkwardly at first – then right itself and plunge on down.

The tone signal ended abruptly in an eerie silence. The silence would last 43 seconds . . .

. . . Down in the city people had just finished breakfast. There had already been one air-raid warning that morning, two hours earlier – when Eatherly's plane had flown over to check the weather – and nothing had happened. So it was not surprising that not much attention was paid to the new intruder. A man sitting on the steps of the Sumitomo Bank did not even bother to look up. . . .

8.16 am: Little Boy reached its detonation height – 1,850 ft above the city. There was a giant blue-white flash. It was like an enormous photographic flash bulb going off. Then, in an instant of time too small to measure, a great ball of fire 1,800 ft across with a temperature at its centre of 100 million degrees Centigrade.

The man outside the bank just vanished . . . but his shadow was "photographed" on to the granite steps – the area surrounding it was bleached out – by the fierce flash. The impression did not begin to fade for more than 20 years.

In the instant that Little Boy released its fury – a force equal to 20,000 tons of ordinary high explosive – Hiroshima became a desert.

After the flash came the fantastic heat: people near the point of the explosion – "ground zero" – were burned crisp without knowing what had hit them. Bare skin two miles away was seared and roof tiles on the houses melted.

After the heat came the blast: it destroyed every building within an area of five square miles. A column of white smoke climbed 40,000 ft above the city and fanned out at the top into a great mushroom shape. At its base a mass of black, boiling dust with rivers of grey smoke rushing towards the centre.

After the blast came the rain: it was a strange rain – black – with drops as big as marbles. The moisture in the air, vaporised and forced upwards by the heat of the atomic explosion, had collected the dust from the pulverised build-ings on the way. Eventually it reached a cold altitude, condensed, and fell back to earth again.

After the rain came the wind: the air which had been pushed outwards by the blast now rushed back with the force of a tornado, tearing up trees, filling the Ota River with giant waves and spreading the fires that were already raging throughout Hiroshima.

As soon as Little Boy had left the *Enola Gay*, the plane, five tons lighter, leaped upwards. Tibbets put the nose down and poured on all the power to get as far away from the bomb as he could.

Hauling the *Enola Gay* round in a 150-degree turn, which made the machine's metal scream in protest, he was about

Facing page: *A giant among aircraft, the B-17 Flying Fortress. It earned its name because it was originally designed as a coastal defence weapon, but it went on to lead the USAAF's daylight offensive in Europe, dropping over 640,000 tons of bombs.*

Below: *The Wellington medium bomber. This aircraft employed a construction known as geodetic – a basket-like framework covered in fabric. It was devised by airship pioneer Barnes Wallis. Though an efficient design it was an expensive form of building aircraft and has never been used on a commercial plane. The Wellington carried a crew of six, had two 1,145 hp engines, a top speed of 247 mph and could carry 4,000 lb of bombs.*

eight miles away when the bomb went off. Three shock waves, travelling at 12 miles a second, slapped hard at the aircraft and then Tibbets turned back towards Hiroshima to take a look at the damage.

"What a mess!" It was the awe-struck Caron. They had all taken off their dark goggles, and they could see the blossoming mushroom cloud on top of what seemed to be an angry, boiling pot of tar.

One of them thought that Ferebee had missed the target completely and dropped the bomb in open country – there was nothing of the city to be seen.

"My God," said Captain Robert Lewis, the co-pilot, "what *have* we done?"

Tibbets flashed a message to the scientists and service chiefs waiting on Tinian island: "Results good. No fighters. No flak." Then the *Enola Gay* collected her escorts and, like three birds of prey that had shared a well-hunted kill, they flew home.

When Jeppson walked into his tent after landing he found an old navy friend waiting for him who asked: "What have you been up to?"

"We just won the war today," said Jeppson.

★

Shattered Dreams

The war ended in the air, and it had begun in the air, on September 1, 1939, when Hitler's bombers struck at Poland as his troops and tanks swept across the border.

It is often described as the start of the "greatest war in history". It wasn't. It was the start of the WORST war in history. Nearly 55,000,000 people died, almost seven times the number killed in the First World War.

Wilbur and Orville Wright's dream of the aeroplane forcing peace upon the world was finally shattered. It had taken a hard knock in 1914 and crumbled still further throughout the 1930s. Several "little wars" had broken out, in Spain, Ethiopia and China, giving Germany, Italy and Japan the chance to test the power of their new air forces.

When the "big war" came the aeroplane was in a highly advanced stage. In no other war the world had known had there been such a devastating weapon to fight with.

Francesco de Lana had prophesied 300 years before that whole cities would be "destroyed from a great height" . . . and they were. Octave Chanute had also seen it all coming when he said: "No part of the field will be safe, no matter how distant from the actual scene of conflict" . . . nor, in the end, was it.

But it was not only Wilbur and Orville's dream that was to end in ruins. Adolf Hitler had a dream as well – of building his Third Reich into a German empire that would last for a thousand years. The aeroplane was to shatter this dream, too.

In Hitler's hands the flying machine, once the symbol of man's freedom, became the tool of his enslavement, one of what Winston Churchill called "the lights of perverted science" that heralded a new Dark Age.

Top: *An American B-24 Liberator flies over a towering column of smoke after its bombs had set the oil refinery on fire during a raid on Ploesti. It was after suffering heavy losses in the Ploesti attacks that the Americans realised the value of fighter escorts for their bombers. The Liberator – more of these bombers were built than any other American Aircraft during the war – had four 1,200 hp engines, a top speed of 290 mph, a range of 2,100 miles, ten machine guns and it could carry 8,800 lb of bombs.*

Above: *The highly successful German fighter, the Focke-Wulf 190, which was particularly good at high-altitude combat. This put it into the front line of Germany's defence against Allied bombing raids. Its 1,770 hp engine gave it a top speed of nearly 450 mph, a ceiling of 37,000 ft and a range of 530 miles. Armament: two cannon, two machine-guns.*

The P-47 Thunderbolt which was widely used as an escort for the heavy bombers after its range had been increased with extra fuel tanks. They were also used as ground-attack planes. Its 2,300 hp engine gave it a top speed of 428 mph, it could climb to 42,000 ft and had eight machine-guns.

There proved to be only one answer to the threat of the aeroplane – and that was the aeroplane itself.

In 1935 Hitler announced that, in defiance of the military restrictions placed on Germany after the First World War, he had an air force – the Luftwaffe – that was equal to Britain's and nearly as strong as France's. The Führer was not telling the truth, but he shocked the British and the French into a frantic rearmament drive.

The decisions taken at this time were the ones that were to win the war for the Allies and lose it for Germany.

Though nothing can ever detract from the skill and courage of The Few, the 1,000 pilots of RAF Fighter Command who, in 1940, won the Battle of Britain over the harvest fields of England against the vastly superior numbers of the Luftwaffe, the foundations for that victory, and the ones that followed, were laid many years before.

Lord Trenchard, the RAF's first chief, began to lay those foundations when he planned for the future after the First World War. He fought for an independent service and placed a high value on training for his aircrews for when better aircraft came long. For in 1934 the RAF was still a force of old-fashioned wooden biplanes.

Hitler panicked France into ordering hundreds more out-of-date aircraft. But Britain decided on new types and by 1939 the metal monoplane was the backbone of the RAF.

In spite of this, by September 3, the day Britain's Prime Minister, Neville Chamberlain, announced that the nation was once again at war with Germany, Hitler's boast had become reality. The Luftwaffe could put nearly 4,000 planes into the air, almost twice as many as the RAF could.

Yet the Führer's air force had a built-in weakness. It was an instrument of land power, committed to the support of the army on the ground.

Its tactical role had been decided as a result of Germany's experiences in the Spanish Civil War and the success of the Junkers 87 Stuka dive-bomber.

The Stuka was a terror weapon. Its kinked wings and claw-like undercarriage gave it a fearsome appearance as it dived almost vertically on to its target. Sometimes the Stukas were fitted with screaming sirens designed to confuse and panic the defenders on the ground.

But the Ju 87 was really little more than a piece of aerial artillery. It had a short range and a speed of only 245 mph, which made it as slow as the RAF's Gladiator biplanes. When it came to fighting in its own element, the air, it proved easy prey for the faster British fighters and had to be withdrawn from the Battle of Britain.

In making the Luftwaffe the "handmaid" of the army Germany, the country which had done so much for the advancement of aviation, completely failed to grasp the true meaning of air power.

Hitler – a corporal in the First World War – had based his thinking on near-1914–18 ideas. He had backed a loser.

British tactics were based on strategic air power – the power of the bomber. Winston Churchill, who took over from Chamberlain as Prime Minister on the eve of the Battle of Britain in May 1940, summed it up in a minute to his War Cabinet. He wrote: "Fighters are our salvation but bombers alone provide the means of victory."

It was Churchill who was on the winner.

The fighters that were to be the salvation, not only of Britain but of civilisation itself, were the Supermarine Spitfire and the Hawker Hurricane.

Neither plane was created with the idea of saving anything. The Spitfire was a direct descendant of the Schneider Trophy winners. So was the Hurricane, but it also had as ancestors the famous First World War Sopwith Camel and Triplane.

After Britain's wins in the Schneider Trophy seaplane races Air Chief Marshal Sir Hugh Dowding, later to become head of Fighter Command and leader of The Few, suggested that the pursuit of speed for its own sake should stop. Instead of building more planes for competitions, why not put the knowledge gained from the races to some good use?

Dowding's idea was to encourage manufacturers to develop two landplanes with the highest possible performance, but which could land at a speed slow enough for them to use any existing airfield.

Sir Sydney Camm's design, the Hurricane, and Reginald Mitchell's, the Spitfire, were chosen. They were no more than experiments in high speed, but with eight guns in their wings firing outside their propeller discs they became two of the most formidable fighting machines in the world.

The Hurricane first flew in 1935. At the start of the war it had a speed of just over 300 mph. The Spitfire, which made its maiden flight in 1936, was 50 mph faster. Many variants of the two planes were developed, including ground-attack, anti-tank, carrier and photo-reconnaissance versions.

By the end of the war the Spitfire XXII fighter-bomber could fly at 454 mph, which was slightly faster than Britain's first jet fighter, the Meteor 1, and it could climb 1,000 ft higher to 43,000 ft.

The Spitfire was highly respected by the men who had to fight against it. Reichmarshal Hermann Goering, the Luftwaffe's chief, discovered how much when he visited one of his fighter squadrons one day during the Battle of Britain. He told his men that they had the finest aircraft in the world. What more, he demanded, did they need to chase the British from the skies?

"I request," one of his pilots said, "that my unit be re-equipped with Spitfires."

The bombers that were to be the means of victory – the big four-engined Stirlings, Halifaxes and Lancasters which, in Churchill's words, were to "beat the life and soul out of Hitler" and reduce Germany to rubble – did not come along until later. In her peril Britain needed the fighters to meet the threat of invasion. The bombers had to wait.

Germany, located in the middle of the great land mass of Europe, decided that long-range heavy types were not necessary. The Nazis relied on their trusty Stukas and their light and medium bombers – Heinkel 111s, Dornier 17s and Ju 88s.

They smashed all resistance from the air ahead of Hitler's powerful mechanised ground forces. And the Führer swept victoriously across Europe. Within a few months Nazi jackboots had marched to the shores of the English Channel.

England stood alone and the rest of the world held its breath, expecting Britain to have its neck wrung like a helpless chicken. But there was nothing "chicken" about Britain, as Adolf Hitler and Hermann Goering were soon to discover.

"Hitler knows," said Churchill, "that he must break us on this island or lose the war." To break the British the Luftwaffe had to defeat the RAF. It had to win control of the air for Hitler to be able to launch his plan for the invasion of England – Operation Sealion. Goering thought it could be done in four days.

It seemed that easy. The might of the unbeaten German Air Force, 3,500 aircraft, stretched from Scandinavia in the north to the Bay of Biscay in the west. Behind the white cliffs of Dover the RAF had ready just 704 fighters, 620 of them Hurricanes and Spitfires, which Dowding had held on to when others would have committed them disastrously to the defence of France.

And he also had the "secret weapon" of radar. Radar had grown from the popular science-fiction idea of a death ray. Air force chiefs had actually discussed such a device to knock the German bombers out of the sky.

Left: *American output was a big factor in the Allies' strength in the air. This is a section of the Boeing factory where B-17s were being produced.*

Above: *The beginning of the end for the Nazis: American C-47s – the military version of the DC-3 – drop hundreds of paratroops in Southern France during the Allied invasion on August 15, 1944.*

But they were told by Robert Watson-Watt, a down-to-earth scientist at the National Physical Laboratory, that a "destroyer" ray was impossible. However, he went on, a "detector" ray was not.

He knew that radio waves "bounced" back to earth from layers of the higher atmosphere, and he devised equipment to prove that they could also be bounced back from aircraft.

The rays, picked up on a screen like a television set, could detect formations of approaching enemy planes, and ground controllers were able to work out how many there were and where they were heading. It meant that defending fighters no longer had to fly a system of permanent patrols. They could be kept on the ground and then directed to where they were most needed.

Later radar was applied to gun- and bomb-sights, helped night-fighter pilots "see" in the dark and in the detection of submarines at sea. Nowadays it is used for early warning against missile attack, weather forecasting, guiding modern airliners and it enabled the Apollo astronauts to make a safe landing on the Moon.

In 1940 it played a vital part in making a mockery of Goering's estimate of how long the Battle of Britain would last.

The Luftwaffe did not defeat the RAF in four days. It tried for three months – from the middle of July until the middle of October – and failed.

It was now that the Luftwaffe's weakness showed up. Without heavy bombers it was just not up to the job of terrorising Britain into submission. The Dorniers, Heinkels and Junkers were too light to be effective. The twin-engined Messerschmitt 110 fighter soon proved to be almost as big a disaster as the Stuka, and the only fighter in the same class as the Spitfire, the Me 109, was handicapped by having to protect the bombers.

Had Goering stuck to trying to wipe out Fighter Command's airfields he might have succeeded, for towards the end of August the constant attacks and sheer weight of numbers of the German planes began to swamp the RAF.

But the Reichmarshal kept switching to other targets – ports, factories, cities. The Luftwaffe wore itself out forcing the pace, while the British commanders held back, saving their striking power either by design or instinct, until they could deliver a knock-out blow.

Their hard-pressed pilots were often in action several times a day. Here is how one of them spent a Saturday during the battle:

He was up at 4.15 am. Three-quarters of an hour later his squadron was told to "scramble" – the order that sent fighter pilots racing for their aircraft to intercept incoming raiders.

On that first sortie they saw nothing. But by 8.30 they were back in the air and met four lots of Ju 88s with Me 109 escorts over the Channel. The squadron, flying at 15,000 ft, was able to get a crack at the bombers before the higher-flying 109s could interfere. Our pilot gave one of the Ju 88s a two-second burst of fire and watched it crash into the sea.

He throttled back his Spitfire so as not to overshoot the enemy formation and present its gunners with a sitting target. The 109s dived down to the rescue and suddenly he found one right on his tail. But it was going too fast and, as it went by, he got it in his sights and pressed his gun button. The 109 began to smoke and it, too, crashed into the sea. Then he flew home for breakfast.

But there was time only for a hot drink before the squadron was scrambled again. This time it met more 109s, and the clash developed into a dogfight – aircraft chasing each other about the sky in single combat. He followed one 109 all the way to the French coast before getting close enough to shoot at it, and it crash-dived into a field.

Four o'clock in the afternoon: yet another scramble. Over the Thames estuary the squadron ran into more Ju 88s and 109s. He was able to claim one more enemy fighter which broke up in a mass of flame and went into the river. Not one of the fights had lasted more than five minutes.

The battle reached a climax on September 15. It was a Sunday and Winston Churchill, perhaps sensing that it was to be a day of history, drove with his wife to No. 11 Group Headquarters at Uxbridge, north-west of London. They were greeted by Air Vice-Marshal Sir Keith Park, the New Zealander who commanded the group. Park said to the Prime Minister: "I don't know whether anything will happen today. At present all is quiet."

Within a quarter of an hour the Churchills had a ringside seat at what was probably the most important battle the free world had ever fought.

The radar picked up large numbers of aircraft building up over the French coast. There were so many that they took a long time to assemble, and the British fighters were ready for them when they arrived.

The Prime Minister kept his eyes on the operations room indicator board. It showed that, one after another, squadrons were being scrambled to meet a massive attack by 100 bombers and 400 fighters.

And, one after another, red bulbs began to glow on the board as each squadron went into action. Eventually Churchill noticed that every one was in the air.

"What other reserves have we?" he asked.

"There are none," said Park.

In the afternoon the Luftwaffe came again. Another 100 bombers, 300 fighters. And when the score was totted up at the end of the day the RAF claimed to have destroyed 183 German aircraft.

After the war the true figure was found to be 60, with RAF losses of 26. The totals for the entire battle were: German losses, 1,733 planes; British losses, 915.

It was a severe defeat for the Luftwaffe. It had failed to gain control of the air and, in October, Hitler scrapped Operation Sealion. The threat of invasion was past.

Churchill had warned that the survival of Christian civilisation would depend on the Battle of Britain. Now it was over and he said: "Never in the field of human conflict was so much owed by so many to so few."

That was how The Few – the RAF pilots who fought in the battle – got their name. They were not only Britons. They came from America, all over the Commonwealth and from the occupied countries of Europe.

Thanks to them, and the planes they had flown, the world had been saved from being crushed under the heel of Nazi tyranny. It was now time to fight back, to go over to the offensive and smash the enemy's ability to make war.

The Luftwaffe, driven to seek the cover of darkness, kept up nightly bombing attacks on London and other important British cities until the spring of 1941. Then Hitler turned on Russia.

And, in the Pacific, Japan turned on America.

In the early hours of December 7 a large Japanese aircraft carrier force lay 200 miles to the north of Pearl Harbor, the American air and naval base in the Hawaiian Islands.

At dawn a wave of bombers, escorted by the best carrier-borne fighters in the world at the time – Mitsubishi Zeros – roared out of the morning sky on the unsuspecting Americans.

They met almost no opposition. In one hour and five minutes all eight US battleships in the harbour had been sunk or damaged and 239 army and navy planes destroyed. For the loss of 29 aircraft Japan had crippled American power in the Pacific.

As President Franklin D. Roosevelt told the US Congress the following day, it was a date that would "live in infamy".

The Rising Sun of Japan spread across the Pacific as swiftly as the Swastika of Germany had cast its shadow across Europe. But where the Nazis had conquered with air and ground forces, the Japanese conquered with air and sea forces. Unchecked, they swarmed south to within striking distance of Australia and west to the gates of India.

American aid for Britain's lone fight against Nazism had been pouring across the Atlantic, but Pearl Harbor brought the United States into the shooting war.

Like Britain, America believed that the bomber was the key to victory and, in the Boeing B-17, had the most powerful bomber in the world.

First flown in 1935 it had four 1,200 hp engines, a top

Right: *The German answer to America's bombing power, the Me 264 four-engined bomber with which Hitler hoped to attack New York.*

Centre right: *A new type of flying machine: Germany's V-2 rocket "revenge weapon" which brought death and destruction to southern England as the war drew to a close. It came too late to save the Nazis from defeat, but it was the beginning of the race to the Moon.*

Foot of page: *The Heinkel 178, the aircraft that ushered in the jet age when it took off for the first time on August 27, 1939.*

speed of over 300 mph and a range of about 2,000 miles. It was originally designed as a defensive weapon to patrol America's coasts and meet any possible attacker well out at sea. For this reason it was called the "Flying Fortress".

Instead it became an offensive weapon and built up a reputation as "a giant among aircraft".

But, like the rest of the world, America had thought that Britain might be overrun by Hitler's armies. If this had happened the United States would have had to carry the war over the great oceans, something that could be done only by aircraft that could fly further than the Fortress.

Though the B-17 was good, it could not cross the Atlantic and bomb Europe or carry the offensive over the Pacific to meet the Japanese threat.

As a first step towards this, the Superfortress was born – the B-29 – a plane with twice the range and twice the power. The first was completed in 1942 and, though it did not go into action soon enough to be used against Germany, the B-29 finally forced Japan to surrender.

The first B-17s to join the mounting offensive against Germany arrived in England in the summer of 1942. The Americans believed in daylight attacks. Their bomb-aimers could be more precise about hitting their targets and therefore their raids would be more effective.

They also believed that if heavy bombers, like the B-17s and the B-24 Liberators, carried enough guns and flew in close formations they would be able to protect themselves against fighter attacks.

The RAF had learned early in the war that this was not so when twin-engined Wellingtons and Hampdens had been shot out of the skies like sitting ducks. This was because the Luftwaffe's Me 109s and 110s had developed an attack from the side and above – a blind spot for the bombers.

And close formation flying only gave the fighters a bigger target to shoot at. So the RAF had to bomb by night.

By the time the Americans were carrying out their high-altitude daylight raids over Europe the Luftwaffe's fighters, like the 450 mph Focke-Wulf 190 – which was very good at high-altitude combat – were heavily armed with cannon as well as machine-guns.

In August 1943 a force of 177 Liberators raided the German-held oilfields at Ploesti in Rumania. Fifty-four of them

Left: *One of the first combat jets, Germany's Me 262 which went into action in 1944. A single-seater, its jets gave nearly 2,000 lb of thrust enabling it to top the 500 mph mark. Armament: four cannon, 24 rockets.*

Below: *The Doolittle Raiders: America prepares to hit back at Japan. The flight deck of the US aircraft carrier* Hornet *crowded with B-25 Mitchell bombers which had been taken to within striking distance of their targets.*

Facing page: *In the Pacific, aeroplanes and the carriers they operated from took over from the battleship as the main weapon of war. A Grumman Hellcat, one of the fighters that helped win control of the air from the Japanese Zero, returns to the carrier* Lexington *after a mission. American Hellcats shot down over 5,000 enemy aircraft in the Pacific and were used as bombers as well as fighters.*

were shot down. And two raids against the ball-bearing factories at Schweinfurt in Germany cost nearly another 100 bombers.

After this the Americans at last realised that unescorted heavy bombers, no matter how well armed, could not protect themselves well enough in daylight.

Something had to be done. The bombers would have to be given fighter escorts. But little had been done to extend the range of single-seater fighters up to that time.

The answer was to give them extra fuel tanks so that they could fly further. The tanks were tear-drop shaped and fitted beneath the wings. They could then be dropped by the fighters when they were empty.

This vastly increased the range of fighters like the P-47 Thunderbolt, which was used extensively as an escort over Europe. And by 1944 the long-range P-51 Mustangs were able to stay with the bombers all the way to Berlin.

Soon Hitler's Reich was under non-stop attack, from the RAF by night and the Americans by day. Radio and radar aids to navigation and bomb-aiming made the raids more deadly. Bigger and bigger bombs made them heavier.

On May 30, 1942, over 1,000 RAF bombers took part in Operation Millennium against Cologne. It was the heaviest attack yet attempted in the history of air warfare. About one-third of the city was destroyed for the loss of 40 aircraft which did not return and another 116 which were too badly damaged to fly again.

No army on the ground could, in the space of a single night, have delivered such a blow at the price.

Germany was thrown on to the defensive. With half the Luftwaffe tied up fighting the Russians, the Germans found themselves in exactly the same position as the British had been in 1939–40. They desperately needed fighters.

A large part of the secret of the Allies' growing strength in the air was the huge number of planes being produced by American industry. In 1942 US factories rolled out 50,000 aircraft. Two years later output had nearly doubled.

During the six years of the Second World War over 700,000 planes were built – nearly twice as many as in all the 42 years of aviation since the Wrights had built their original Flyer in 1903 – and America was responsible for almost half of them, 300,000.

Above: *A Douglas Dauntless dive bomber zooms into the attack during an action in the Pacific. At the Battle of Midway Island Dauntlesses sank three Japanese carriers and helped to destroy a fourth. The planes were two-seaters with a single 1,000 hp engine, a top speed of 250 mph and a range of 1,345 miles.*

Facing page: *A Japanese torpedo bomber explodes in the air after being hit by a shell from an American aircraft carrier.*

Germany had no answer to the giant air armada that was pounding it to destruction day after day, night after night. America's aircraft factories were too far away to be attacked, though Hitler did think about trying it.

In 1942 came the first flight of a plane designed to reach New York, the Me 264 four-engined bomber. It was to have carried 4,000 lb of bombs and its range was to have been achieved at the expense of armament.

The plane had a tricycle undercarriage and one wheel on each main leg was dropped on take-off, presumably to save more weight.

But it never did the job it was intended for. By 1943 Germany's aircraft industry had gone over almost entirely to the production of fighters and the Luftwaffe was gradually being reduced to making only hit-and-run raids on Britain.

Throughout the whole of the war some 72,000 tons of German bombs fell on the British Isles. In reply Allied bombers dropped nearly 1,250,000 tons on Germany.

The only let-up in the air offensive came in the late spring of 1944. British and American bombers switched their attacks to railways, bridges and airfields in France to prepare the way for D-Day, the Allied landing on the beaches of Normandy on June 6.

With ground troops firmly established on the continent of Europe once more, the bombers went back to attacking Germany. And the attacks were so effective that the Luftwaffe's new fighters were destroyed, on the ground and in the air, almost as fast as they were delivered.

It was now that a new terror came out of the skies. It was brought by a new type of flying machine that, within a few years, would make the weapons of the most destructive war in the history of the world seem as puny as bows and arrows.

And it was to give man the power to destroy himself completely . . . or reach for the stars.

This new type of flying machine was the V-2 rocket, one of two *Vertelgunswaffen* – revenge weapons – with which Germany hoped to stave off its approaching doom. The other was the V-1 pilotless bomb, a small aeroplane which carried 1,870 lb of explosive in its warhead and flew at about 400 mph.

The V-1 made a noise like a motor cycle, and when its engine cut out it glided down on to its target. But the V-2's liquid-fuelled rocket engine gave it a speed of around 3,600 mph – well above the speed of sound – and it gave no warning of its approach. It weighed over 12 tons on take-off and carried a 2,000 lb warhead.

The V-1 and the V-2 were launched against the south of England in 1944 and 1945. It was the beginning of robot warfare. The V-weapons led to the giant intercontinental missiles of today which have now largely taken the place of the piloted aeroplane as the most decisive weapon of war.

At the same time as the V-weapons, a new type of aeroplane also appeared in the skies of Europe – the jet.

Britain and America had decided to improve existing aircraft designs because the war would not last long enough for new designs to be put into action.

It was the right policy for winning wars, for the jet and the other advances, the V-1 and the V-2, came too late to save Germany from disaster.

But it was from the losers, as it had been during the First World War, that the next stage in the development of the aeroplane came.

An Englishman designed the first practical jet engine. His name was Frank Whittle, a young RAF cadet, who realised that ordinary propeller-driven aeroplanes would soon reach their limits of speed and height.

He produced a completely new form of power unit. His engine called for air to be drawn in at the front, mixed with fuel, ignited and ejected at the rear in a powerful jet that would thrust an aircraft forward.

But he found little enthusiasm for his ideas in Britain and, while he worked to perfect his design throughout the 1930s, the Germans overtook him.

Dr. Hans von Ohain, who may have studied Whittle's plans when they were published in 1932, developed a similar engine and it powered the world's first jet plane, the Heinkel 178 which flew on August 27, 1939. A Whittle engine did not put an aircraft into the air until two years later.

The first combat jets, Britain's Meteor and Germany's Me 262, went into action in 1944. But not against each other. The jets had to wait for another war to break out, in Korea in 1950, before they met in the air.

It was the dawn of a new age for the aeroplane. Designs were to become simpler and cleaner. Speeds, now hovering around the 450 mph mark, were to be pushed up to 500 mph and beyond.

The first rocket-propelled plane – also German – the Me 163, which went into action in 1944, could reach nearly 600 mph. Speeds like this were to bring a whole new set of problems for aircraft designers.

But already those problems were being tackled. It was well known to German scientists that an aeroplane could fly better at high speeds if its wings, instead of being straight, were swept backwards. This knowledge was to change the shape of aircraft completely.

It may have been the birth of a new age for the aeroplane, but it was the death of the age of Nazism. Though the jet had arrived it was only a matter of time before the German war machine collapsed.

The Nazis had been thrown out of Russia and Africa. The Allied armies were advancing across Europe from the west after the landings in France and, with the surrender of Italy, from the south as well.

Hitler, the man who had written that he understood the importance of physical terror . . . the man who, when it all began, urged his generals: "Act brutally! Close your hearts to pity! Be harsh and remorseless!" . . . The man in whose name the most monstrous crimes in history had been committed, now learned what it felt like to have his own country overrun and see his own cities crumble to dust.

On April 10, 1945 a force of 1,300 American Fortresses and Liberators escorted by 850 fighters attacked what was left of the Luftwaffe. The raid was followed by another crippling blow six days later.

A total of 1,223 German aircraft were destroyed – a large number of them on the ground because the Allied strategic air offensive had seen to it that there was little fuel and few pilots left to fly them.

It was, for all practical purposes, the end for the Luftwaffe. The day that the second raid took place General Carl Spaatz, commander of the US Strategic Air Forces in Europe, announced that the air war was over – his bombers had no more targets to destroy.

It was also the end for Adolf Hitler.

Like a real-life Frankenstein he had created a monster – the war – a thousand times more hideous than the one made by the evil genius of fiction. And, like Frankenstein's creature did, Hitler's monster pursued its creator to destruction.

On April 30, 1945, in his underground bunker in Berlin, with Russian shells bursting in the heart of the city, Hitler shot himself. The man branded by Churchill as a "bloodthirsty guttersnipe" was dead.

One week later Germany surrendered unconditionally. After their capture Field-Marshal Karl von Rundstedt, who had led Germany's last stand – the Battle of the Bulge – in the Ardennes in December 1944, and Field-Marshal Albert Kesselring, commander of the Luftwaffe's Air Fleet II during the Battle of Britain, both said that air power had been the main cause of Germany's defeat.

Churchill's promise that the Japanese would be taught a lesson they would never forget was to take another year to fulfil.

The war in the Pacific was decided by a series of great sea battles in which aeroplanes, operating from aircraft carriers, took over as the main weapon from the battleship.

After Pearl Harbor America struck defiantly back at Japan on April 18, 1942, with a daring attack on Tokyo and other cities by the Doolittle Raiders.

The same James Doolittle who had made the first blind flight in 1929 led the mission. It was carried out by 16

The Vought F4U Corsair was regarded by many Japanese pilots
as the best Allied fighter. It first went into action in 1943 and was
capable of over 400 mph. An unusual feature of the aircraft was
its "kinked" wings.

B-25 Mitchell bombers which were taken to within striking distance of Japan by the carrier *Hornet*.

They were the only twin-engined bombers to fly into combat from the deck of a carrier.

The plan was to sail to within about 400 miles of their targets, but the *Hornet* was spotted by enemy ships and the Mitchells had to take off when they were 700 miles out.

In foul weather and with a heavy sea running the *Hornet*'s deck heaved as each plane, loaded with 2,000 lb of bombs and 1,141 gallons of fuel, staggered into the air. The B-25 normally needed a run three times the length of a carrier deck to get airborne and some of the aircraft almost fell into the sea.

Clipping the wave-tops to avoid being intercepted by enemy fighters the Mitchells reached their targets, dropped their bombs and then turned for China where they were to land.

But, because of the bad weather, darkness and the extra distance they had to fly, one by one the planes ran out of fuel. The crews either took to their parachutes or made crash landings.

The raid did little damage, but it boosted the flagging American spirits, and gave the Japanese something to think about.

A month later came the Battle of the Coral Sea off New Guinea. It was a victory for the Americans and the first naval battle in which the crews of the opposing ships never saw each other. The surface forces remained below the horizon while the action was fought from the air by carrier-based aircraft.

At Midway Island the Japanese suffered another setback when Douglas Dauntless dive-bombers sank three of their carriers and helped to finish off a fourth.

The tide had turned. Fighters like the 400 mph Vought F-4U Corsair, the Grumman Hellcat and the TBF Avenger torpedo-bomber began to regain control of the air from the Zero.

Huge and bloody battles took place for the Marianas, the Philippines and Iwo Jima. The Americans leap-frogged their way back across the Pacific. The islands they recaptured became air bases for heavy bombers to pound

The plane of death: Pilots who flew this aircraft, the Japanese Oka flying bomb, knew they would never return from a mission. It was a manned missile similar to the unmanned German V-1 and powered by a rocket engine. Thousands of young Kamikaze airmen – suicide pilots – sacrificed their lives by deliberately crashing Okas into Allied warships in a final, desperate attempt to save Japan from defeat. The Kamikazes also flew to their deaths in ordinary aircraft.

the next objective and finally for B-29s to operate against Japan itself.

In the jungles of Burma Allied troops pushed back the Japanese with the help of supplies dropped from the air. America's B-29 bomber bases in China were kept operating by the pilots who flew perilous supply missions from India over "The Hump" – the towering, uncharted Himalayan mountains.

By Allied agreement America had been left to develop the transport aircraft, and Douglas had produced a "big brother" for the DC-3, the four-engined DC-4. Sometimes very heavily laden, these planes battled through 100 mph winds, blinding snowstorms and over treacherous 16,000 ft mountain ranges to keep the war materials flowing.

By 1945 Japan was beaten, but surrender would have been the final dishonour. Fanatical young airmen volunteered to become Kamikazes – suicide pilots – to try and save their homeland from invasion. Over 5,000 of them sacrificed their lives by deliberately crashing their planes into Allied warships.

And it was all in vain.

Out of the summer sky came the *Enola Gay*, to teach Japan – and the world – the lesson it would never forget.

The war was over, but the real scramble . . . for peace . . . was only just beginning.

Through the barrier

Above: *The fastest aeroplane to fly, the 5,000 mph X-16, about to leave its B-52 mother plane for a high-altitude flight.*

The small, barrel-shaped plane had been in the air for 17 minutes. Now, its wheels touched down on the tarmac of an RAF airfield "somewhere in Lincolnshire" and soon it had been rolled into a hangar away from prying eyes.

For it was still wartime. The date: May 15, 1941. The place: Cranwell. After the flight the group of people who had been watching retired to the officers' mess and, for a long time, one pilot could be seen sitting in a chair with a puzzled frown on his face.

It had been a strange plane. There had been something odd about it and he couldn't think what it was.

Suddenly the expression on his face changed from a frown to utter astonishment. He shot up straight in his chair and said: "My God! chaps. I must be going round the bend – it hadn't got a propeller."

The plane without a propeller was the Gloster-Whittle E.28/39, Britain's first jet. Its flight brought triumph to Frank Whittle's dedicated struggle to produce a practical jet engine after 13 years of hard work.

Gerry Sayer, Gloster's chief test pilot, had taken the E.28 down Cranwell's long runway and, soaring to 25,000 ft, had reached a speed of 370 mph. It was well above the top speed of the Spitfire at the time.

Below: *The plane without a propeller: the Gloster Whittle E.28/39, the aircraft that crowned Frank Whittle's work on the jet engine.*

Later a demonstration flight was arranged for Winston Churchill at Hatfield, near London. To make sure that the E.28 would not be mistaken for an enemy aircraft and shot down by patrolling RAF fighters, it was provided with an escort of two Spitfires and a Typhoon.

The four aircraft were to meet over the airfield and the three fighters were to stay with the little jet to protect it.

But though the E.28 was kept down to a cruising speed it left its escorts far behind and, after the rendezvous over Hatfield, they never saw it again during the whole of the flight.

It had landed again and been put away in a hangar before the first of the escorting Spitfires arrived back in a screaming power dive.

Something sensational had happened to the aeroplane.

Soon after the E.28's first flight a Whittle engine was sent to the United States so that America could develop a jet, too. Whittle followed in secret to assist the American engineers.

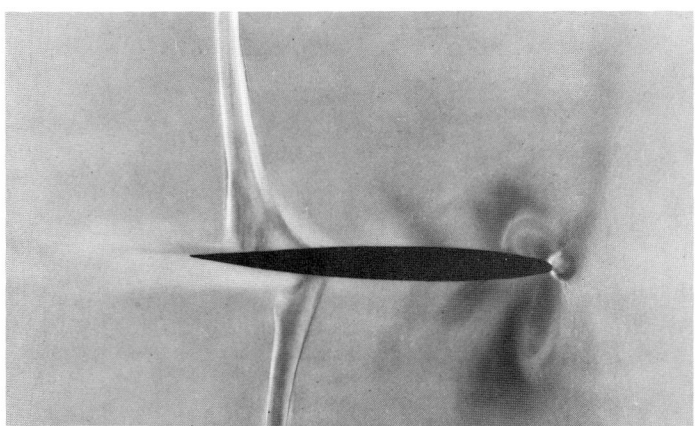

Above left: *These photographs of a wing cross section in a wind tunnel show how pressure waves build up as an aircraft flies up to the speed of sound. Mach 0·7: The general airflow is still below the speed of sound, but the dark line above the centre of the wing is the start of a pressure wave.*

Left: *Mach 0·9: Approaching the barrier. With the increase in speed shock waves have formed at the top and bottom of the wing surface and moved back towards the trailing edge. The turbulence in the wake of the upper wave has affected the flow over the rear part of the wing and makes the aircraft difficult to control. This would cause the pilot to feel as though his plane was being buffeted.*

Left: *Mach 1: The Concorde model in the wind tunnel has passed the speed of sound and the perpendicular shock waves have bent back. They will stay stuck to the surfaces of the aircraft as long as it is travelling supersonically. There is no more buffeting and the waves spread out and reach the ground to be heard as the sonic boom.*

Below: *One of the many ideas to come out of Germany was the leading edge flap, seen operating here as this Boeing 727 touches down. Leading edge flaps were used in addition to the normal trailing edge flaps to improve the behaviour of swept wings at low speeds.*

Left: *Towards the ideal aeroplane, the Bell X-5. It was the first plane to be able to adjust its wings in flight.*

Left: *The fastest gun in the West, the F-111. It is the only swing-wing design to have seen active service. For low-speed flight, take-off and landing its wings swing right forward . . .*

. . . for high-speed flight the wings swing right back to form a delta shape.

Left: *Charles Yeager's experimental Bell X-1, the aircraft that first broke through the barrier of sound. It was rocket-powered and Yeager called it* Glamorous Glennis.

He was shadowed everywhere by protecting FBI agents and was asked to use a false name at his hotel. He chose "Whiteley", but kept forgetting how to spell it which lent a slightly comic "cloak and dagger" air to his visit.

The wartime development of the piston engine had pushed the speed of propeller-driven aircraft up and up. The jet brought even more speed.

But pilots of conventional, straight-winged aeroplanes had discovered an invisible barrier in the sky. In very fast dives they found their planes being shaken and buffeted violently. Some had even broken up as if torn to pieces by a giant hand. Others had just gone out of control and crashed.

The aeroplane had reached a new frontier. Some people believed it had also reached its limit, that the invisible barrier could never be crossed.

But, like Mount Everest, or the Moon, it was there and, sooner or later, human beings would have to pit themselves against it.

The barrier was found to rise up in front of an aeroplane as it approached the speed of sound – 760 mph at sea level, less in the thinner air higher up. Because of this discovery the new challenge was called the Sound Barrier.

In flight an aircraft pushes aside the air, setting up pressure waves which spread out, like the wake of a ship, from all its surfaces.

At subsonic speeds – those below the speed of sound – the air is easily able to move out of the way of an oncoming plane. But at supersonic speeds – those above the speed of sound – the air waves cannot move out of the way because the aircraft is moving as fast as they are.

So they pile up against each other to form high-pressure shock waves. When they reach the ground they produce the familiar sonic boom and they also cause the buffeting and loss of control, difficulties which are called compressibility problems.

Wings are the first parts of a plane to go supersonic because air is speeded up by their curved top surfaces. Shock waves grip controls, set up very high drag and cause the smooth, lifting airflow which clings to the wing – the boundary layer – to come unstuck.

In all high-speed aircraft today there is an instrument called a Machmeter. It is named after the Austrian supersonics pioneer Ernst Mach and tells a pilot how fast he is travelling compared to the speed of sound.

Sonic speed is defined as Mach 1. The supersonic range stretches from Mach 1 to Mach 5 and above this is the hypersonic range.

Though the Germans overtook Whittle and flew the Heinkel 178 two years before the E.28, he found, when he examined their engines after the war, that his jets were better. He came to the conclusion that the Allied bombing blockade had denied the Germans top-grade metals and that they had been so eager to put jet planes into the air that they had not developed their engines well enough.

The real German genius lay in design, and here they undoubtedly did lead the world. Their prolonged studies of high-speed flight had made it possible for them to make a start on solving compressibility problems. And when the war ended they were well on the way to tearing down that barrier in the sky.

Supersonic flow was nothing new to Professor Ludwig Prandtl. He had studied it in steam-turbine engines as far back as 1906. He was one of Germany's most brilliant scientists and he created a school of research at the Aeronautical Laboratory of Göttingen.

It was two of his pupils, the Professors Adolph Busemann and Albert Betz, who discovered during the 1930s that supersonic drag could be cut down by sweeping back an aircraft's wings.

With enough sweep-back, flow over the leading edge of a wing stays subsonic even though the aircraft it is attached to is flying at supersonic speed.

But sweep-back was not the only idea that came out of Germany. During the war the German scientists were also working on the development of:

The delta wing. This is triangular shaped and, extended right back along the fuselage of an aeroplane, it does away with the need for a tailplane. It also gives better low-speed handling and is the wing shape adopted for the first supersonic airliners.

Leading-edge flaps. These are small flaps used on the front edge of the wing in addition to the normal large flaps on the trailing edge. Their value, once again, is in improving the way a swept wing behaves at low speeds during landing and take-off.

Variable sweep-back. This is the swinging wing, known today as "variable geometry". It is an attempt to combine the best of both worlds, thin wings that can be swung forward for low-speed flight and swung right back for operations at high speed.

The idea was being discussed as far back as 1918. During his Wilbur Wright Memorial Lecture to the Royal Aeronautical Society, Dr. W. F. Durand, chairman of the American Advisory Committee for Aeronautics, said: "The ideal aeroplane should be able to change its wing area in accordance with the conditions and circumstances of flight."

Dr. Alexander Lippisch began experimenting with variable sweep in Germany in 1941, but turned to the delta wing instead.

Then, in England just after the war, Dr. Barnes Wallis, designer of airships, bombs and planes, made further studies of it for his hypersonic, all-wing, tailless airliner, the Swallow.

The first plane to be able to adjust its wings in flight was the experimental Bell X-5 which was completed in America in 1951.

France, Russia and America have all produced swing-wing designs and they have been described as the weapons of the future. But only one has so far seen active service, the American Mach 2·5 F-111.

It was called the "fastest gun in the West" when it went

Above: *Britain's Fairey Delta 2 which created a new world air-speed record of 1,132 mph in 1956. The aircraft was also used for research into the problems of high-speed flight when Concorde – the Anglo-French supersonic transport – was being planned.*

Right: *The latest of Russia's Mig family, the Mig 23 Foxbat, which is able to fly at 1,800 mph. It is a single-seat, twin-jet interceptor, strike – reconnaissance aircraft.*

into action in Vietnam in March 1968. But almost as soon as it began operations three of the first eight aircraft were lost, a poor performance for what was supposed to be the world's most advanced tactical fighter, and the planes were quickly withdrawn from combat.

One of the main drawbacks with swing-wing aircraft seems to be their great weight, which cuts down performance. Weight was one of the reasons why America's supersonic airliner was changed from a swing-wing to a fixed-wing design, throwing the United States years behind in the race to capture a share of the market in supersonic passengers.

Until the "bugs" in swing-wing aircraft are finally ironed out we shall have to do without Dr. Durand's "ideal aeroplane".

But, back to the sound barrier.

In 1944 work began in America on an experimental plane to discover just what did happen at and – if possible – beyond the new frontier.

The plane, the Bell X-1, was fitted with a rocket motor because pure jets were still not powerful enough to push an aircraft past the speed of sound in level flight. It also had straight wings. The value of swept wings was either unknown or not recognised outside Germany at the time.

By 1947 man was ready to hurl himself at the barrier. The dangers were known. A year earlier Geoffrey de Havilland, son of the famous early pioneer, had been killed when his DH 108, the first British experimental plane with swept wings, broke up at or near the speed of sound.

So when Charles Yeager, a 25-year-old fighter pilot climbed into the bullet-nosed Bell X-1 on October 14 it may have crossed his mind that he could be about to fly to his own death.

A B-29 "mother" plane carried the X-1 over Muroc Dry Lake, California, and released it at 25,000 ft. When Yeager felt himself fall free from the big bomber above him he levelled out the X-1 and fired his rocket motor.

The falling sensation ceased and the plane streaked to 37,000 ft. Yeager's Machmeter needle flickered to Mach 0·97 and he felt himself being buffeted and hammered by the built-up shock waves. Suddenly it all stopped. The meter had jumped to Mach 1·05. He was through the barrier.

Later he said that he was disappointed that breaking the sound barrier was such a tame affair. He hadn't told anyone but the night before making the flight he had cracked some ribs at a ranch party. His injured ribs hurt him as he pulled hard on the lever to close the X-1's cockpit door. That moment had been the most painful part of the whole operation.

Yeager's conquest of the sound barrier proved that, instead of being limited, properly designed aircraft with enough strength to withstand supersonic pressures could go on to reach undreamt of speeds.

American, British and Russian engineers who entered Germany after the war was over were amazed at the progress made by the "enemy" scientists, and the lessons they learned were used as a basis for the second generation of jets.

These, the first swept-wing fighters like the American Sabre and the Russian Mig-15, appeared in the same year as the X-1's dramatic flight.

The performance of jet engines improved rapidly and soon air-speed records were being shattered with alarming regularity.

In September 1948 a Sabre set a new record of 670·981 mph. By June 1956, less than eight years later, a British Fairey Delta 2 had almost doubled that figure by flying at 1,132 mph.

The aeroplane had entered the supersonic age.

The most up-to-date strike and fighter aircraft now fly at more than twice the speed of sound every day. The latest of the Russians' Mig family, the Mig-23 Foxbat, has flown at over 1,800 mph and the fastest military plane in service, the Americans' Lockheed SR-71, can fly at 2,000 mph.

Aircraft like these mean that planes such as Britain's 1,000 mph-plus interceptor, the Lightning, and the American F-104 Starfighter, which can fly faster than sound straight up, are already out of date.

We are now entering the hypersonic speed range with manned aircraft and to study this the Americans have built the X-15 rocket plane.

It is the fastest aeroplane yet to take to the air and made its first flight in 1959 after being launched from beneath the wing of a B-52 jet bomber.

An improved version has made possible speeds of Mach 8 – about 5,400 mph – and heights of nearly 100 miles. This is the region of near space where satellites orbit the earth.

The X-15 is a combination of aircraft and spacecraft, the first of the aerospace planes of the future. During its ten years of experimental operations it has provided much valuable knowledge of the heating problems at high speeds and the control problems at high altitudes.

Some of the X-15 research missions have been flown by Neil Armstrong, the first man to set foot on the Moon.

The aircraft is the forerunner of many advanced techniques. One of them will be the further development of manned lifting bodies like the Northrop HL-10 and the Ryan X-24. These are wingless, egg-shaped craft likely to provide cheap space travel in years to come.

At the moment multi-stage rockets like the Saturn V are necessary to lift a small manned module into space, each stage breaking away to be abandoned after its motors have boosted the spacecraft clear of the earth.

This is a very expensive form of space flight. One Saturn V costs as much as a dozen B-52s and most of it becomes just space "junk" shortly after a launch.

When the Apollo command module returns to earth a complicated recovery task force has to be waiting to pick it up after it has re-entered the atmosphere and parachuted down into the sea.

But a manned lifting body would be thrust into space by cheap, disposable booster rockets. On the return trip the pilot would make a controlled re-entry and land on an airfield runway. Then, just like any ordinary aeroplane, the craft could be used for other flights.

Before these things can happen even more research has to be done. The knowledge gained from the flights of the X-15 is now being directed towards the creation of a much more advanced experimental plane to fly at about Mach 12 which should be ready, perhaps, before 1980.

Though we have come so far since that wintry day at Kill Devil Hills, reached fantastic speeds, climbed to fantastic heights – we are still pioneering.

Full Circle

When the Second World War ended it soon became plain that men were not going to be able to live happily ever after with each other.

The victorious Allies were divided by a clash of basic beliefs. Instead of being united in a newly won peace the world was split in two – the East, led by Communist Russia, and the West, led by America.

Ever since, the two great power blocks of nations have flexed their muscles and hurled insults at each other. There has been lots of pushing and shoving. Occasionally the fists have flown. But always things have stopped short of an all-out third world war.

The reason: fear!

Left: *The Lockheed SR-71 is the world's fastest military aircraft and capable of a speed of 2,000 mph.*

Above: *Britain's 1,000 mph plus fighter, the Lightning. Its wings are so thin and so swept that, in this picture they are almost invisible.*

Above: *The supersonic look of the F-104 Starfighter. Its wings are razor sharp and stubby and set well back. The nose is needle sharp. All these features help to reduce drag at high speed and enables the F-104 to fly faster than sound straight up.*

Left: *An X-15, a combination of aircraft and spacecraft, is winched up under the massive wing of a B-52 mother plane before a flight.*

Below left: *The X-15 is dropped into space for another experimental flight in near space at a speed of up to Mach 8. The knowledge gained from the X-15 will eventually lead to even faster aircraft able to operate in the hypersonic speed range.*

In 1949 Russia exploded an atomic device. Each side now had the means to make a Hiroshima of Washington, a Nagasaki of Moscow.

And, within three years, an even more terrible weapon was to be produced. The hydrogen bomb. It was to be so powerful that the type of bomb that had destroyed Hiroshima would be used merely as a "match" to set it off.

The first lot of pushing and shoving came from the Communists. After the war, Germany was divided into four sections, French, British, Russian and American. Berlin, deep in the Russian zone, was split into two with one half being governed by the Western powers, the other by the Russians.

In 1948 Russia blockaded the city, cutting off all land traffic in an effort to force the West to abandon the German capital.

The challenge was met by the aeroplane. A short time earlier fleets of Allied aircraft had been flying missions to Berlin to destroy it. They now began flying missions of mercy to keep the city alive.

Using three 20-mile-wide air corridors the big transports kept the 2,000,000 Berliners supplied with food, fuel, medical equipment and the thousand and one other things they needed for normal, everyday living for over a year.

Every few minutes, day and night, in all weathers, the planes landed, unloaded and took off again for another round trip. They delivered more than 2,000,000 tons of supplies to the beleagured city.

Embarassed by the resolve of the West, the Russians finally lifted the blockade. Through the Berlin airlift the aeroplane had put a stop to Communism's first post-war step towards its vowed ambition – world domination. And it had done it without the use of military force.

But it wasn't long before the fists were flying. In Korea, a small Asian country bounded by Communist states to the north-west of Japan, which few people in the West had ever heard of.

Like Germany it was also a divided country and, on June 25, 1950, the Communists in the North invaded the independent republic in the South.

Apart from bringing the first air battles between the new jet fighters, Korea served to ram home the lesson of the Second World War . . . that air power was vital.

Chinese Communists entered the fight from bases in Manchuria, to the north, and though United Nations aircraft – mainly American – were able to gain command of the skies over the battlefields, they were unable to strike at the source of the Communists' strength for fear of touching off a third world war.

It resulted in stalemate between the two sides. Neither was able to achieve a decisive victory and an armistice was signed in July 1953.

The two incidents – Berlin and Korea – made the Western powers realise that they would have to be constantly alert and strong enough to meet any new threat wherever it might occur.

The rush to be ready began an arms race that has pushed forward the development of the aeroplane at ever-increasing speed.

America took the lead in the race on November 1, 1952, by exploding a full-scale hydrogen bomb on the tiny Pacific island of Elugelab.

Elugelab disappeared. In its place a crater one mile wide and 175 ft deep was blasted out of the ocean bed. The bomb's mushroom cloud rose 25 miles high and spread itself 100 miles wide.

The explosion was so immense that a new unit of measurement had to be invented – the megaton. It described a force equal to 1,000,000 tons of ordinary high explosive. The Elugelab bomb was a three-megaton device – it was equal to the combined weight of all the bombs dropped on Germany and Japan during the Second World War. It was 150 times more powerful than the Hiroshima bomb.

And it was only the beginning.

Less than a year after Elugelab the Russians announced that they, too, had a hydrogen bomb, even more powerful than the Americans'. The balance of terror had been restored.

Now, any "bully" nation with just a few H-bombs could, in one surprise attack, completely destroy all opposition and rule the rest of the world by fear.

Atomic bombs had been used twice. What was to stop a nation that was evil enough yielding to the temptation to strike first with the new monsters of destruction?

One thing. The fear that any nuclear attack would be returned . . . instantly.

For this to be a reality there had to be aircraft with, not just a long range, not just an intercontinental range, but a global range. They had to be able to reach any target on earth, anytime.

On February 26, 1949, the Superfortress *Lucky Lady II* tucked up her wheels and left the runway at Carswell Air Force Base, Texas. At the controls, Captain James Gallagher.

On March 2 – 94 hours and 1 minute later – Gallagher settled the *Lucky Lady II* back on to the same runway after the first non-stop flight round the world. The plane had covered 27,500 miles, refuelled five times in the air and, at the halfway mark, dropped a load of bombs on a pre-selected target.

The flight was not merely one more milestone in the history of the aeroplane. It proved that global ranges were possible and demonstrated that no one and nothing on this planet could ever hope to escape if man should go to war again.

The *Lucky Lady II* was an improved version of the B-29, the aeroplane that had ended the war with a single blow in 1945. Now, only a few years later, she was an old lady.

Her round-the-world flight was the piston-engined, propeller-driven bomber going out in a blaze of glory. The *Lucky Lady II* and her kind was about to hand over her duties to the new jet bombers.

The nuclear bomb and the jet engine had revolutionised warfare. There was no longer any need for large fleets of bombers when one plane, armed with an atomic or hydrogen bomb, could cause more damage than a 1,000-bomber raid.

And the Great Powers set about rebuilding their air forces, re-equipping them with completely new offensive aircraft.

American designers were quick to take advantage of the ideas they had picked up from the Germans and produced the first swept-wing bomber, the B-47 Stratojet, in 1947.

Its first flight was, significantly, on December 17 – exactly 44 years to the day after the Wrights' first flight at Kill Devil Hills – and it has been described as "one of the world's truly revolutionary aeroplanes".

The Stratojet had six engines and a speed of more than 600 mph. For the manufacturers, Boeing, it was an important "double" achievement. The B-47's high speed made it as fast as any fighter, just as the Boeing B-9 bomber of 1931 had been before it.

And, like the B-9, it was to set a pattern for the civil and military designs that were to follow.

The engines – one outboard and two inboard on each wing – were hung in pods, another feature adapted from the Germans who had used it on their Ju 287 bomber.

Pod-mounted engines were easier to get at to repair and acted as balances against wing flutter, so reducing the weight of the wing. The use of underslung podded engines is now standard practice on the big American jets.

The B-47 was only a medium bomber, with a range of about 3,000 miles. By the beginning of the 1950s really giant jet bombers were in the air.

In August 1954 the round-the-clock-ready wing of America's air force, Strategic Air Command, began to get the first of the B-47's replacement, the B-52 Stratofortress.

The plane was probably the pinnacle of long-range, strategic heavy bomber design. It had a wing-span of 185 ft and a length of 156 ft 6 in. Its eight jets gave it a range of 12,500 miles and a top speed of 660 mph.

The B-52's performance was outstanding from the start. Three of the big planes landed at March Air Force Base, California, in January 1957 after a non-stop round-the-world flight which took them 45 hours and 19 minutes – half the time it had taken the *Lucky Lady II*.

And the Stratofortress could carry a bomb load of 50 megatons. In one bomber an explosive force more than 16 times greater than that heaped on Japan and Germany during the Second World War.

Soon it was the turn of bombers, too, to break through the sound barrier. In 1956 the world's first operational supersonic strategic bomber, the delta-winged B-58 Hustler, was in the air.

Into it was built a new aerodynamic design "gimmick" called the "area rule" concept discovered in the laboratories of the National Advisory Committee for Aeronautics.

Wind-tunnel experiments had shown that drag could be

Above: *Towards cheap space travel: the X-24 manned lifting body. Craft like these will, in the not too distant future, be boosted into space and be able to return to earth like an ordinary aircraft. The technique means that they can be used over and over again, cutting out the wasteful multi-stage rocket of today.*

Above: *The Boeing B-50, a developed version of the Second World War B-29 Superfortress. One of these aircraft, the* Lucky Lady, *made the first non-stop flight round the world in 1949.*

Upper right: *Exactly 44 years after the first flight at Kill Devil Hills came the first flight of another "revolutionary" aeroplane, the B-47 Stratojet. It put modern bombers in the same speed range as jet fighters just as Boeing's B-9 had done in the 1930s.*

Right: *For their jet designs the Americans adopted the German method of podded engines slung under the wings. This Ju 287 bomber has two podded engines in the wings and two attached to the fuselage near the nose. The French used fuselage mounted engines – but at the rear – when they built the first short-range jet transport, the Caravelle.*

cut down even more in supersonic aircraft by giving them a longer nose and a fuselage with a pinched-in "waist". Aircraft built like this became known as "flying Coke bottles" because their shape was similar to the outline of a Coca-Cola bottle.

But it was not only the shape of the aeroplane that was changing. As the jet planes grew bigger and faster the way they were built had to be changed as well.

Smooth skins that would not buckle under the strains of high-speed flight became much more important. Supersonic aircraft must be light and very strong.

Now, instead of being shaped out of sheet alloy, many forms are finely sculpted from thick slabs of metal and new "sandwich" materials are widely used. Sandwich panelling – thin sheets containing a honeycomb of reinforced plastic or aluminium – is so airy that it can be seen through and though weighing only one-fifth as much as solid sheeting it is just as strong and rigid.

The equivalent of half an acre of this material was built into the XB-70 Valkyrie, America's Mach 3 bomber that was originally intended to replace the B-52s and Hustlers.

Very fast aircraft are also fitted with power-operated control surfaces because great force is required to change the attitude of a plane in the fierce grip of supersonic pressure waves.

Progress towards a nuclear bomber force was slower in Britain than it was in America. A straight-winged tactical bomber, the Canberra, appeared in 1949 and turned out to be one of the most successful of the early designs. It was built in America as the Martin B-57 and many of the 600 mph twin jets are still in service today.

Britain's first swept-wing big jet bomber was the Valiant of 1951.

It was the forerunner of a trio of aircraft which together made up the V-bomber force, so called because all their names began with a "V". The other two, the Victor and the Vulcan, both flew a year after the Valiant but were more advanced designs.

The Victor had crescent wings – sweep-back was reduced towards the wing-tips – and the Vulcan had delta wings. All of them possessed near-sonic speeds – faster than the B-47, but they did not have the great range of the B-52.

The V-bombers were a break from the German and American practice of podded engines. Their power units were placed in the wing roots, which helped to cut down drag but made the wing structure more complicated because the strengthening spars had to be built round the engines. This same form of engine mounting was used on the Comet, the world's first jet passenger transport.

And the three planes are good examples of how tailplanes were shifted with the coming of the jet engine.

The Valiant's tailplane was situated halfway up the fin so that it would be clear of the searing blast of the exhaust outlets in the trailing edges of its wings. The Victor had a "T"-tail – the tailplane sat right on top of the fin – which is now common practice on rear-engined jet airliners. And

Left: *Gigantic B-52 Stratofortresses – perhaps the pinnacle of bomber design – in action over Vietnam. The B-52 is 156 ft long with a wing-span of 185 ft. Its speed is 660 mph and its range 12,500 miles. Armed with nuclear weapons it can deliver an explosive force 16 times greater than all the Allied bombs dropped on Germany and Japan during the Second World War.*

Above: *The first supersonic bomber, the B-58 Hustler. Its delta-wing shape can be clearly seen, its speed is nearly 1,500 mph, and it carries its nuclear weapons in the elongated pod under the fuselage.*

Below left: *The aerodynamic design "gimmick" called the "area rule" – which gave aircraft a "Coke bottle" shape – can be seen in the nipped-in waists of these Grumman Tigers. The area rule concept helped to cut down drag at high speeds.*

the delta-winged Vulcan had no tailplane at all.

The "other side" – Russia – was also producing nuclear jet bombers. At the same time as the Boeing production lines were beginning to roll out the big B-52s for Strategic Air Command, two Soviet bombers made their first public appearances over Moscow. They were the twin-jet Tupolev Tu-16 Badger medium bomber and the Myasischev Mya Bison, a four-jet long-range bomber.

They were not remarkable or advanced planes, but they were effective weapons produced by a nation which, up to that time, had not even been in the same street as America or Britain when it came to jet invention.

But the Russians had an aerial "ace" up their sleeves.

It was 1955. The new generation of warplanes had arrived. The B-52 was flying. The RAF had taken delivery of its first Valiants.

These were the planes that were going to keep the peace. With their nuclear bomb loads they were intended to make the Communists think twice before putting into practice any of their fancy ideas about taking over the world.

America had set up radar tracking stations in Turkey, right on the doorstep of Russia, to make sure they knew every move the "enemy" made. It was at one of these stations that a tiny blip was picked up on one of the glowing green scanner screens.

That blip told the Americans that the Russians had launched a long-range missile from a site on the Black Sea coast. And the Soviet Union's Air Chief Marshal Pavel

The XB-70 Valkyrie, America's experimental Mach 3 bomber, which made extensive use of sandwich materials – light, honeycomb panelling which cuts down weight. The strange looking Valkyrie has been used for research into America's supersonic transport programme. It was switched to this role when missiles took over from bombers as the United States' main striking weapon.

Zhigarev announced that Russian long-range bombers were to be replaced by ICBMs – intercontinental ballistic missiles.

Air Chief Marshal Zhigarev had pronounced the death sentence on the manned strategic bomber as the most effective weapon of war.

On the collapse of Germany, Russia and America had "grabbed" the best brains behind the V-1 and V-2 weapons. The German scientists, who had been on the point of developing a rocket that could cross the oceans when their laboratories were overrun by the Allied armies, continued their research for their new masters.

The art of rocketry progressed swiftly in Russia and Zhigarev's announcement, which heralded a revolution in the conduct of warfare, was to have a profound effect on the future of the aeroplane.

Three things influenced the Russian decision to abandon the manned bomber as its first line of attack:

The high cost of developing and producing complicated nuclear jet bombers. . . .

The large airfields they needed to operate from, which had to be manned by enormous ground staffs, were easy targets. . . .

And missiles could easily be concealed. . . .

Two years after that blip appeared on the American radar screen a Russian rocket put Sputnik 1 – man's first satellite – into earth orbit. The flying machine had reached out to the borders of space.

And in 1960 a Russian missile knocked an American U-2 spy plane out of the sky as it flew 68,000 ft over the centre of the Soviet Union. It demonstrated that the Russians not only had effective offensive missiles, but defensive ones as well and could probably shoot down any attacking force of high-flying nuclear bombers.

Four years later America, too, committed itself to the age of the robot weapon of war. Defence Secretary Robert McNamara announced to the US House of Representatives Armed Services Committee that "most aiming points in the Soviet target system can best be attacked by missiles . . .". From now on, he said, long-range bombers would be used in follow-up attack.

The strategic bomber had had its day.

Missiles are now supreme.

Whole families of them have been developed by both sides, from small shoulder-launched field missiles, similar to the anti-tank bazooka of the Second World War, to giant hypersonic ICBMs that can be launched from beneath the ground or beneath the sea. Capable of speeds up to 15,000 mph they can reach any target on Earth within a few minutes.

For some years it has been possible to launch hydrogen bombs from orbiting satellites. There seems to be no reason why they could not be put up on permanent space patrol and, if war ever did come again, they could be "called down" at the push of a button and computer-directed to their targets.

One of these weapons, called FOBS – the fractional orbital bombardment system – could destroy Britain in a single blow. The device, rocket launched into a low orbit, can carry up to ten separate H-bomb warheads – a total nuclear load equal to 25,000,000 tons of high explosive and 1,250 times more powerful than the Hiroshima bomb.

The warheads, "scattered" in space, can seek out a target each. Such a weapon aimed at Britain would be able to wipe out every major city in the country.

These are the truly monstrous means of destruction that have displaced the bomber. And fighters, too, have ceased to fight. They are now merely high-speed, manned missile-launching platforms.

But it would be wrong to suppose, from all this, that the piloted military aircraft has ceased to be of any use in war at all.

The missile has brought aerial warfare full circle.

It has forced the aeroplane back into its original role as a tactical weapon for the support of ground operations – the role it had when it was first used in a major war back in 1914.

And to meet the combat needs of the world's air forces during the 1970s and 1980s, which could include full-scale nuclear war or more limited "brushfire" conflicts such as Korea and Vietnam, yet another new generation of aeroplanes is emerging.

These will be multi-purpose aircraft which will appear in bomber, interceptor, strike and reconnaissance versions and be able to make very short or vertical take-offs.

The first of them might have been Britain's TSR 2. Development of the plane began in the late 1950s and it has been described as the "flying miracle . . . perhaps the most brilliant military aircraft yet conceived".

After flying one of the prototypes the TSR 2's chief test pilot said that it was far ahead of anything else in the world, "the smoothest supersonic aeroplane I ever flew".

It was designed to fly at 800 mph below treetop height, hugging the contours of the earth and automatically guided by a computer-controlled radar system. In theory this would have enabled it to have reached its target undetected by flying under enemy electronic defences.

But the British decided that such a complicated aircraft was too expensive and it was scrapped – some say "murdered" – in 1965 in favour of the American F-111 after £200,000,000 had been spent on the project.

In that same year the Russians displayed a system of low-level anti-aircraft missile defence which added weight to the arguments of those who wanted to kill off the TSR 2. Other critics pointed out that if it could deliver nuclear bombs then it was basically evil and should be destroyed anyway.

The plane was an indication of how costly a complex modern combat plane had become.

To get round the problem of the high price of producing advanced designs the smaller, not-so-well-off countries of Europe are now "clubbing" together to build the planes they need for their mutual defence.

International co-operation like this has resulted in the Anglo-French Jaguar, a lightweight, high-performance aircraft that is due to enter service in the 1970s.

The Jaguar is intended for use as an advanced trainer, tactical support and reconnaissance plane. Its twin turbo-fan engines will give it a speed in the Mach 2 range.

Great emphasis has been placed on a simple design so that it can operate from unprepared airstrips and aircraft carriers and, as a weapons platform, it is stabilised by computer.

A European partnership, begun by Britain, West Germany, Italy and the Netherlands, is also developing a MRCA – multi-role combat aircraft – for further in the

Top: *First of the V bombers, the swept-wing Valiant. British designers preferred to place the Valiant's four jets in the wing roots instead of podding them like the Americans.*

Above: *The delta-winged Vulcan which was also used as a flying test bed for Concorde's Olympus engine.*

Right: *A Victor trails its braking parachute and shows off its crescent wings.*

future which will almost certainly be supersonic with swinging wings.

And America has plans for an AMSA – advanced manned strategic aircraft – which is likely to be bigger than the F-111 but smaller than the B-52. Also employing a swinging wing, the AMSA is expected to have a top speed of Mach 2·5 and an unrefuelled range of up to 10,000 miles.

All these aircraft are the machines of destruction, but the research that has gone into developing them has produced a huge "fall-out" of knowledge that has been of immense benefit to civil aviation.

Advanced techniques discovered by building warplanes have been used to make bigger, better, faster, more comfortable and safer airliners and helped to bring about the great air services that Charles Lindbergh believed would, in time, bring the people of the world nearer together in understanding and friendship.

The Shiny Set

The frozen beach at Kill Devil Hills, jerked abruptly awake by the chatter of the Flyer's tiny engine on that momentous morning when the Wrights made their first flight, fell silent again after 12 seconds.

It all happened less than a lifetime ago, but now there is probably never a single moment in any day when the whine of a jet's whirling fan blades cannot be heard somewhere in the world – never a single second when an aeroplane is not flying.

From the 5,000 passengers a year carried by the pioneer civil airlines in 1919 the figure had topped the 2,500,000 mark by the outbreak of the Second World War.

At the end of the war, in 1945, the number leaped to 9,000,000. One year later it had doubled and it has gone on rising until now the civil airlines of the Western world are carrying more than 300,000,000 passengers every year. The Russians and the Chinese, for some reason, do not reveal their annual figures.

The war completely changed people's attitude towards flying. An enormous aircraft industry had been created and airfields built all over the world. Thousands of military and civilian officials had become familiar with air travel which they came to accept as part of everyday life.

Flying was no longer the pastime of madmen with little regard for their own skins or those of others.

Transatlantic flights had been commonplace since the early 1940s. The Americans began shipping aircraft to Britain by sea to help the war effort, but they had been taking up to three months to arrive. So it was decided to get them to England quicker by flying them over under their own power by way of Newfoundland, Greenland, Iceland and Scotland.

But though the jet engine revolutionised the design of military aircraft the civil airliner stayed on a plateau.

For 25 years, until the big commercial jetliners appeared in 1958, passenger transport planes remained basically DC-3s. They were simply "stretched" so that they could carry more people and given four engines which produced higher speeds and longer ranges.

The typical four-engined, propeller-driven monoplane airliners of the 1940s and 1950s became known as the DC-4 generation because the DC-3's big brother set the pattern for them.

And the men who flew them, a new breed of "glamour boys" with smart, gold-ringed uniforms whose crews included pretty hostesses and whose work took them to all the romantic cities of the world, were nicknamed the "Shiny Set" by the service fliers who had a more deadly job to do.

In America, where air traffic is equal to that of the rest of the world put together, the demand was for aircraft with longer and longer ranges. The competition resulted in the stretching process becoming a seesaw affair as each manufacturer strove to outdo his rivals.

The DC-4 of 1942 had a cruising speed of 200 mph and a range of 1,000 miles. Three years later its range had been doubled.

But by then the Lockheed Constellation, a pressurised airliner with triple tail fins, had appeared with a cruising speed of 270 mph and a range of over 2,000 miles. And Boeing produced the double-decker Stratocruiser based on the Superfortress bomber. This had a speed of nearly 300 mph and a range of 3,000 miles.

Passenger-carrying capacity of the DC-4 generation was nearing the 100 mark.

Above: *Three V bombers together: They illustrate how tailplanes shifted with the coming of the jet. The Victor (left) has a T-tail. The Vulcan (centre) has no tailplane at all because of its delta wings. The Valiant (right) has its tailplane half-way up the fin.*

Top right: *Armament for modern warfare: A French Mirage 5 ground-attack aircraft with air-to-ground, air-to-air missiles, rockets, bombs and ordinary ammunition.*

Right: *TSR 2 "the flying miracle": It might have been the first of the new generation of multi-purpose planes but a year after its first flight it was scrapped as too expensive.*

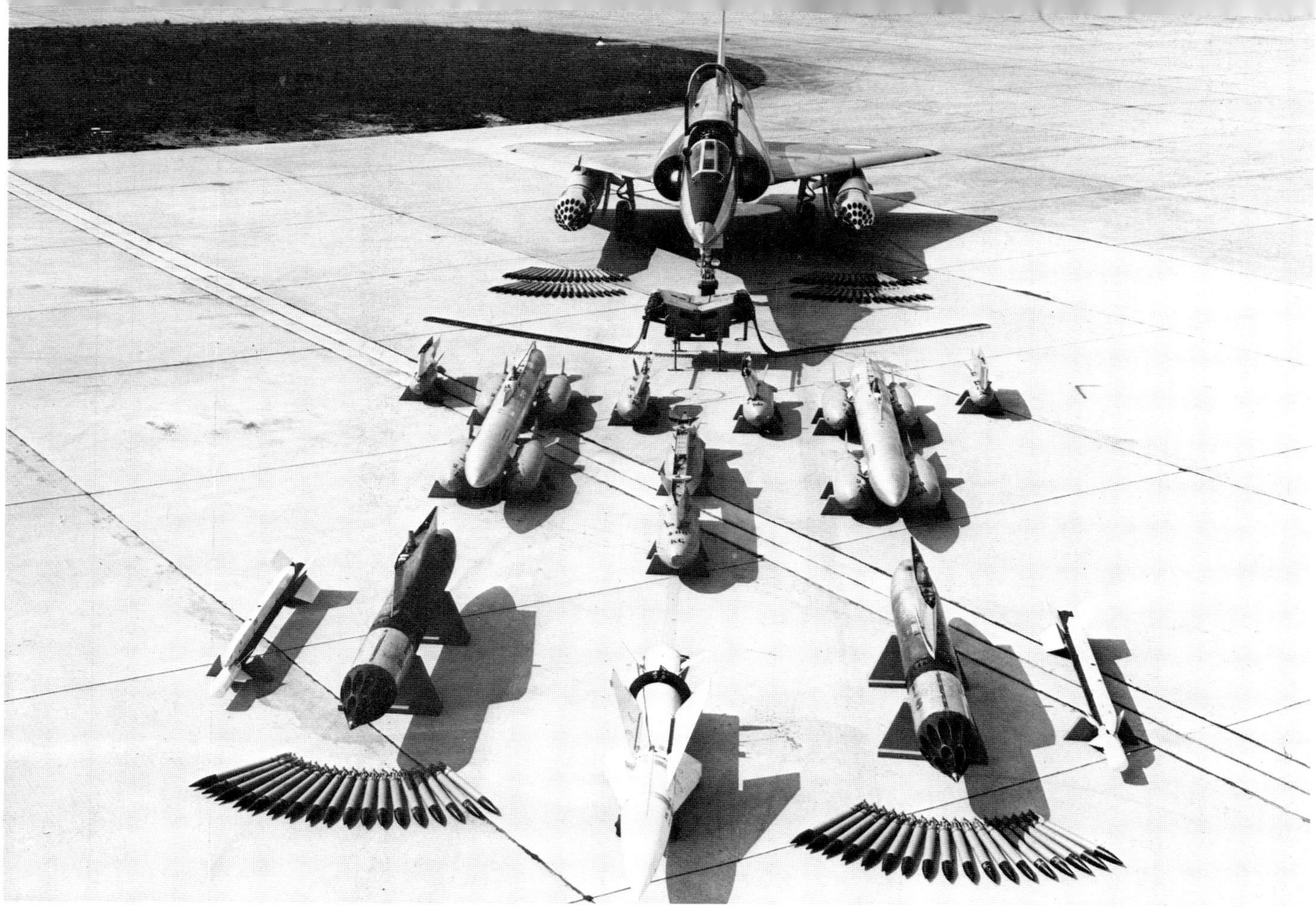

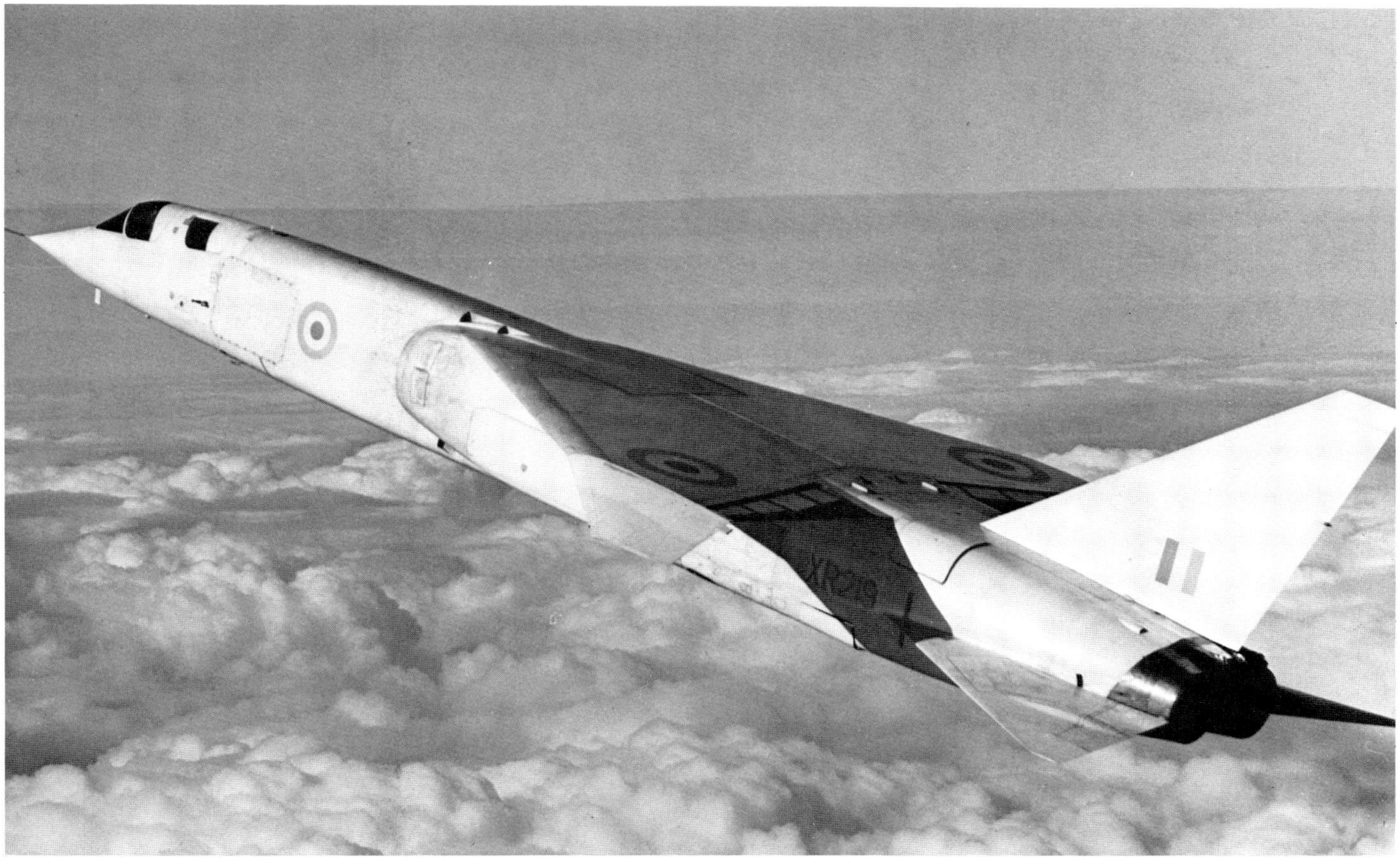

Douglas went on to develop a whole series of big piston-engined transports, the DC-6 of 1947 and the DC-7 of 1953. The final version of this plane, the DC-7C "Seven Seas", had a range of nearly 5,000 miles and it made possible a non-stop transatlantic service for the first time.

Tricycle undercarriages – two main legs in the wings and a small one in the nose – had been adopted, which meant that passengers no longer boarded an aircraft and walked up a slope to their seats.

The DC-4 generation brought about the eclipse of the flying boat as an important long-haul passenger transport. The larger landplanes and the wartime building of great air bases in previously inaccessible places finally dethroned the former "queens" of the skies.

In 1948 the lead that the Americans had established in civil airliners was challenged by a British-made plane, the Vickers Viscount.

It was the first successful turbine transport. Its engines were turboprops – part of their jet thrust was used to drive propellers – and it was one step nearer the modern jetliner.

The Viscount was designed for the short-haul type of air traffic of Europe, but the simpler and smoother turboprops, which largely cut out the noise and vibration of propellers driven by piston engines, had great passenger appeal. So much so that the plane became the first European airliner to go into regular service with American airlines.

And it brought civil aviation to the threshold of a new and dramatic phase of development.

The Wicked Lady

Group Captain John "Cat's-Eyes" Cunningham, the wartime RAF night-fighter ace, was in the pilot's seat when the prototype of the world's first jetliner – the De Havilland Comet – made its maiden flight on July 27, 1949.

He took it up to 10,000 ft above Hatfield aerodrome then, in salute to the men who had made it, he zoomed the sleek machine down to within 100 ft of the runway.

When he landed Cunningham said that the Comet had behaved like "a perfect lady". But before long the perfect lady was to lose her reputation and turn into a wicked lady.

It happened at nine minutes to ten on the morning of January 10, 1954, 26,000 ft above the Mediterranean island of Elba.

British Overseas Airways Corporation Comet *Yoke Peter* had triumphantly begun the world's first scheduled jet passenger service on May 2, 1952 – a weekly return flight from London to Johannesburg, South Africa.

On the morning of January 10 two years later the plane made a refuelling stop at Rome on its way from Singapore to London. With 35 people on board, *Yoke Peter* took off again at 9.31 am and began its climb to 36,000 ft over the sea.

Below, a few miles south of Elba off a part of the coast called Calamity Point, fisherman Giovanni di Marco was quietly casting his nets. He heard the whine of the Comet's Jets but the plane was above the clouds and he could not see it.

Above: *International co-operation has produced the Anglo-French Jaguar which is due to enter service in the early 1970s. A single-seat tactical support aircraft with a speed in the Mach 2 range, it will carry missiles, bombs and rockets.*

Above right: *An American design for an Advanced Manned Strategic Aircraft. It will be smaller than the B-52 and have a swinging wing. Speed is likely to be in the Mach 2·5 range.*

At the controls of *Yoke Peter* Captain Alan Gibson was exchanging routine weather information with another BOAC aircraft flying in the same area.

Over the radio he said to the other pilot: "Did you get my . . .?" then abruptly went off the air.

Giovanni di Marco heard three explosions which followed each other in quick succession. Then he saw a "silver thing" flash out of the clouds pouring smoke. It hit the sea and sent up a great cloud of water. Comet *Yoke Peter* had crashed.

After the accident all Comets were grounded and inspected. But no fault could be found with them. Three months later disaster struck again.

On April 8, another of the aircraft also outward bound from Rome, plunged into the sea off Naples. As before there was no warning. No distress call. No survivors.

The accidents not only shattered two magnificent aeroplanes and the lives of the people who had been in them, but the whole world of flying.

Complete mystery surrounded the crashes. But they had to have a cause. And that cause had to be found.

How the Comet mystery was finally solved is recognised as probably the finest piece of aerial detective work ever carried out. And the results of the investigation, at the Royal Aircraft Establishment in England, had far-reaching effects on the safety and development of the world's jet airliners.

The Naples Comet had fallen into 3,500 ft of water. It was impossible to salvage any of the wreckage.

The Elba Comet was 500 ft down. This was still 300 ft deeper than divers could safely operate but, with the aid of underwater television cameras and giant grabs, the bits and pieces of *Yoke Peter* were gradually brought to the surface.

From all over the world letters came from people offering their own ideas on what caused the Comets to crash. Some insisted that the aircraft had been destroyed by visitors from outer space who were worried about man's progress towards mastering the air. Some claimed that the disasters were acts of God, a punishment for the human race's evil ways.

Other solutions came very near to the truth.

The salvaged fragments of the Elba Comet were painstakingly wired back together over a wooden framework at the Royal Aircraft Establishment. A thousand men stood by to take part in the biggest investigation ever made into an air accident.

Three complete Comet aircraft were handed over so that extra checks could be made. Two of them were flight tested in every possible way and the third was sunk into a giant 250,000-gallon water tank.

By raising and lowering the water pressure inside the submerged cabin every few minutes, the engineers were able to reproduce stresses equal to a normal three-hour flight. In this way the effects of 36 days of flying could be packed into a single day.

One by one the probable causes of the crashes were eliminated. And nothing was not considered.

Above: *Commercial airliners changed very little in the 25 years after the DC-3 was introduced. They were simply stretched to carry more passengers and given tricycle landing gear. Typical of them was the DC-4 Skymaster which gave its name to the DC-4 Generation of transports.*

Above right: *A civil airliner based on the B-29 Superfortress bomber, the Boeing Stratocruiser. It was a double decker plane, the lower portion fitted out as a lounge and bar.*

Right: *The plane that challenged America's lead in civil airliner design, the Viscount. It was the first turbine-powered transport to be successful. Its engines were jets, but they drove propellers.*

Atomic scientists devised a way of making jet fuel radioactive so that any spillage which might have started a fire in the aircraft could be traced. The possibility that a crew member had slipped on the flight deck, grabbed the control column to try and save himself, and caused a high-speed stall was also taken into account.

As the wreckage of *Yoke Peter* was reconstructed it began to give up clues about what happened during the final few seconds before the crash. Something had gone wrong in the cabin which had caused the aircraft to break up.

But what?

The answer came in June 24. After "flying" for 9,000 hours in the water tank the cabin of the submerged airliner split open. Had it not been under the water the plane would have blown itself to pieces like a bursting balloon.

Microscopic examination revealed that the cause of the split was metal fatigue. The constant changing of air pressure inside *Yoke Peter*'s passenger cabin – it was "puffed up" in flight and let down again on the ground – had made the metal skin "tired".

And, under the bending and stretching of pressurisation, it had given way, just as a paper-clip will snap if you keep on bending it backwards and forwards.

When *Yoke Peter*'s cabin was recovered from the sea it was found to be split in the same way as the cabin that had been in the test tank.

With the help of a model and dummy passengers, the investigators were able to reconstruct the moment of disaster. This is what happened:

The cabin burst just as though a bomb had gone off inside it. After three-hundredths of a second seats were being dragged forward as the pressurised air rushed out of the torn fuselage.

After one-third of a second everyone had perished.

After six-tenths of a second the cabin was in complete chaos. Seats were flying about wildly, passengers' bodies were striking the roof or hurtling out of the burst aircraft.

While this was going on the plane had begun to break up.

A large piece of the burst cabin blew out and hit a wing. The aircraft swung into a vertical position and, under the terrific stress, the outer sections of the wings snapped off followed by the tail and the nose. Then the

Top: *The "perfect lady" which turned out to be wicked: the prototype De Havilland Comet, the world's first jet-powered airliner. Note how square-cut the fuselage windows are.*

Above: *Comet Yoke Peter, (upper) the plane that began the first jet-passenger service in 1952, which crashed into the Mediterranean and set off the biggest investigation ever conducted into an air accident. Yoke Peter's remains (lower) wired over a wooden framework at the Royal Aircraft Establishment during the search for clues to the crash.*

Facing page: *The distinctive feature of the Lockheed Constellation was its triple fins. Like the DC-4 it began life as a military transport during the Second World War.*

Right: *Where they found the answer to the Comet riddle: the fuselage of the test aircraft submerged in the 250,000 gallon water tank where it split after "flying" for 9,000 hours.*

centre fuselage caught fire and plunged towards the sea.

The mysteries had been solved.

The world's planemakers were warned of the dangers of metal fatigue and now the airliners of the jet age have special design features so that what happened to the Comets cannot happen to them.

The split in *Yoke Peter*'s cabin was thought to have begun near the corner of one of its square-cut windows. Today's jets have much smaller elliptical or round windows so that there are no sharp corners where stress can start a tear.

Another safeguard is the fitting of double windows – an inner and an outer pane – which prevents the cabin wall blowing out if one of them fails. Better, more "bendy" metals are also in use together with a "fail-safe" device known as a crack-stopper.

These are metal straps which reinforce the cabin skin. They prevent any crack that does develop from reaching a point where it could cause complete failure.

The new Boeing 737 twin jet has crack-stopping straps arranged in a waffle or grid pattern. During tests which simulated a flight at 40,000 ft the pressurised cabin was pierced with a sharp probe, but it did not split.

Just how successful this stiffening process has been was demonstrated in the summer of 1969 when an engine cowling blew off a DC-8 as it flew 31,000 ft over the Atlantic with 260 people on board.

The cowling, from No. 3 engine, smashed into the fuselage ripping out a hole six or seven inches long. It caused a pressurisation leak, but the aircraft held together and the pilot shut down the engine, descended to 24,000 ft and finally landed the damaged plane safely at Shannon in Ireland.

The Comet is now a "perfect lady" again, with a restored reputation. After the investigations into the 1954 disasters, strengthened Comets were flying again in time to start a jet service across the North Atlantic on October 4, 1958.

Three weeks later America's first jet airliner, the Boeing 707, was also flying the Atlantic.

In spite of the Comet being jet powered, it was a conventional aeroplane. Its wings had no more sweep-back than the DC-3 and its tailplane had no sweep-back at all.

But the Boeing and the DC-8, which entered service a year later in 1959, were not conventional aeroplanes. Their design took full advantage of all the benefits of the large jet engines that had been developed for the B-52 bombers.

The 707 began life as a dual-purpose aeroplane. It was intended to be either a transport or a fast military tanker for refuelling the B-47 and the B-52 in flight.

It had swept-back wings and four podded engines slung underneath them. The intercontinental version of the plane was eventually able to carry around 200 passengers at speeds near 600 mph, and it cut down the time for a transatlantic flight to about six and a half hours.

The DC-8's design and performance is basically the same as the 707's. Both aircraft are two of the most successful airliners in the history of flying. Today they dominate the world's long-range air routes and are used by most of the leading airlines.

With them, world-wide jet travel arrived.

But jet transports had another step to take. Airlines also operate over short ranges and, for this type of service, they need different sorts of aircraft.

The first short-range jet airliner came from the French. It was called the Caravelle and, when it went into service in 1959, it set a new design fashion – its twin engines were placed at the rear under the tailplane.

Rear-mounted engines have several advantages. One of them is that they give greater stability to an aeroplane. Another is that they leave the wings completely "clean" which improves their efficiency as lifting surfaces.

A third, and very important advantage for passengers, is that rear-mounted engines mean an almost silent cabin.

The French were able to draw on De Havilland's experiences with the Comet when they designed the Caravelle and they fitted the aircraft with extensive fail-safe devices from the start. They also gave it an identical nose section and a similar flight-deck layout to the Comet.

Since the Caravelle nearly all jet airliners have been designed with engines at the rear. Britain's answer to the 707 and the DC-8, the VC-10, has four jets grouped side by side at the back of the fuselage.

The British Trident and the American Boeing 727, which are both short–medium range aircraft, have three engines at the rear – two either side of the fuselage and one in the root of the tail fin. They are a return to the trimotor airliner of the 1920s. Russia, too, has adopted the layout for its Tupolev Tu-154.

The smaller, "bus-stop" jets, like the DC-9 of America and the British BAC One-Eleven, have the twin rear engines of the Caravelle. And all these aircraft, from the VC-10 to the One-Eleven, have "T"-tails – tailplanes perched on top of their fins.

But there are also disadvantages in having the engines mounted in the rear. Some of the difficulties the new fashion brought cost only money. But some of them were to cost lives as well.

Test pilot Mike Lithgow took up the prototype One-Eleven on October 22, 1963, to make some stall tests. He climbed to 17,000 ft after making four stalls quite safely. During the fifth the aircraft plunged into the ground and all seven members of the crew died.

Lithgow's plane was fitted with two flight recorders. Most airliners today carry at least one. This is the famous "Black Box", though it is usually painted a bright orange so that it can be easily spotted among wreckage. It records on wire or tape everything that happens to an aircraft during a flight.

The recorders in the crashed One-Eleven showed that it had come down rapidly but its forward speed had been very low. During the last, fatal stall test the wings' angle of attack to the air had increased far above what had been expected. The plane had plunged down in a horizontal atti-

Above: *After the discovery of metal fatigue in the Comets airliners were fitted with crack stopping devices. The new Boeing 737, a short-medium range jet, had its pressurised cabin pierced with a sharp probe to test it for safety. The cabin skin did not split.*

Right: *America's first jet airliner, the Boeing 707, began life as a dual-purpose aeroplane. Here a tanker version, the KC-135, refuels an F-4C Phantom fighter-bomber as others wait their turn during a mission over Vietnam.*

tude and all Lithgow's efforts to bring it under control had failed.

He had been caught in a "super-stall".

Three years later a Trident test flight ended with a similar disaster. This time four men died. But before the crash the pilot, Peter Barlow, had been able to radio: "We seem to be in a super-stall." And a man who saw the stricken aircraft come down reported that it had been in a "flat spin", the same attitude that Lithgow's One-Eleven had been in.

The super-stall is now recognised as an ever-present danger in rear-engined aircraft with T-tails.

Engines mounted at the rear make an aeroplane tail heavy. To help restore the balance the wings have to be moved further back along the fuselage and this creates more problems.

The airflow over the wings is likely to cause a reduction in engine power at high angles of attack and it also tends to "blanket" tailplane control surfaces.

So these have been moved out of the way, to the top of the fin, to give us the T-tail. All these things combine to produce a dangerous stall condition.

As a result of the investigations into Mike Lithgow's accident, T-tails were made bigger and alterations made to wings. This type of aircraft is also fitted with a "stick-pusher", or "stick-shaker", a device which moves the pilot's control column to warn him that a super-stall is approaching.

A bigger tail, of course, adds weight to an aeroplane. And with the larger T-tail, rear-engined aircraft there is an extra weight penalty.

The wings have to be made thick and rigid enough to prevent flutter because of the absence of engines to act as balances. It is possible that this is one reason why the VC-10 is heavier and costs more to operate than the DC-8 and the 707, both of which have wing-mounted engines.

These, then, are the aircraft we see in our skies now. And they mark the end of another chapter in the story of the aeroplane.

Development appears to have settled into cycles lasting 20 years: the first, from the beginning of the century until the 1920s, was the pioneer period which saw the appearance of the really practical aeroplane.

The second cycle, between the 1920s and the 1940s, brought larger aircraft and the perfection of the piston-engined transport. The period between the 1940s and the 1960s was the age of the jet.

Now we are about to enter the age of the "superjet".

Above: *A new fashion – rear-engined airliners. This is a line-up of French Caravelles, the first jetliners designed for short-range routes. The rear engines meant much quieter cabins for passengers.*

Right: *The British answer to the big American jets was the VC-10 with its four engines grouped at the rear and a T-tail. But the completely "clean" wings had to be made thick enough to stop flutter and this makes an airliner heavier.*

Above: *Today's three-engined airliners group all the power in the tail.*

Right: *One of the first aircraft to have a three-engined lay-out, the Martin XB-51. Unlike the modern trijet airliners, which use a rear engine mounted in the tail root, its fuselage-mounted engines followed the German pattern and were situated at the front.*

Below: *Passengers board a short-range BAC 1–11 jet. After a prototype crash revealed the dangers of the "super-stall" T-tails were made bigger, wings were altered and a warning device fitted to the pilot's control column.*

Ghastly or sublime?

The aeroplane of the future . . . the supersonic transport . . . will it help the advancement of the world, or turn out to be the most ghastly machine ever created by man?

"In fifty years' time I prophecy that the machines [aeroplanes] will contain all the comforts and distractions of a big ocean liner. Palm courts and orchestras, dance-floors and dining-rooms, lounges together with really comfortable sleeping accommodation, all will be there.

"The journey [across the Atlantic] will take 24 hours. . . . The aeroplane of the future will indeed be at once the most ghastly and sublime machine ever created by the hand of man."

Anthony Fokker talking – in 1922.

He also said that the "utter noiselessness of engines" was only a matter of months away.

Well, it hasn't quite turned out as he prophesied, though some people who live near big airports where jet airliners land and take off day and night, would certainly agree that he wasn't far out about aeroplanes being man's most ghastly creation.

Fokker's views of the future were too ambitious and not ambitious enough, both at the same time. It is a common trap for people who predict trends in aviation, as Louis Paulhan knew only too well.

In 1911, a year after beating Grahame-White in the historic London to Manchester race, Paulhan was asked to forecast the future of flying.

Before putting forward any opinions he said: "To set up as a prophet is one of the most dangerous things to do in flying matters. Men who have done so have lived to regret it. . . ."

And a friend warned him: "Whatever you say you will be accused either of exaggeration, or of not saying enough."

But to Paulhan it was a case of "doing my duty towards the flying movement". Among his predictions: the use of planes for military purposes, the aircraft carrier and enclosed cabins. But he did not think "the aeroplane is likely to be used as a general carrier of goods".

Like Fokker and Paulhan we are also going to look to the future, whatever the dangers of setting up as prophets.

It is easy for us now to laugh at Fokker's palm courts in the sky when we have in-flight cinema shows, his 24-hour Atlantic trips when, for some time now, pilots have been "flying" to New York from London in little more than *three* hours.

And what about Paulhan's conviction that aeroplanes would not be carriers of goods? Freight traffic today is growing faster than passenger traffic.

Fokker's "silent" engines are also sure to raise a smile. The noise of jets is one of modern society's biggest problems – along with other forms of noise of course.

One of them is the sonic boom. The bang caused by modern planes flying above the speed of sound.

The question is: are we, living 50 years after Fokker and Paulhan, able to do a better job of forecasting than they did? Can we say with greater accuracy what aeroplanes will be like 50 years from NOW?

The answer is that we probably can.

Above: *All the comforts and distractions of an ocean liner: The living-room of a "Jumbo" jet on the transatlantic run in the near future. The cabin divider depicting historic aircraft converts into a cinema screen.*

Left: *The Jumbo jet comes into the world: The "star" of the air-buses, the Boeing 747, is rolled out of the company's manufacturing building at Everett, Washington, for its first public showing. An idea of its size can be gauged from the cluster of people standing under and behind the nose and the lone man in white overalls walking near the engine on the right.*

Below: *An in-flight cinema show in progress with one passenger coming down the stairs from the top deck lounge.*

But first, let's see what Fokker would have found if he had lived until the time limit on his prophecies ran out.

He would be about to witness a threefold revolution in air travel. In the immediate future – the mid 1970s – three forms of development will bring dramatic changes to flying.

First, the Jumbo Jets – giant airbuses flying just below the speed of sound with about 500 passengers – will bring mass travel.

Next, the SSTs – the SuperSonic Transports, flying at between twice and three times the speed of sound with up to 300 passengers – will bring faster travel.

Then, V/STOLiners – vertical/short take-off and landing airliners – will bring easier travel.

Commercial V/STOL aircraft are being developed for short-range "feeder" routes – city-to-city and city-to-airport ferrying services which will cut down the time now spent on the ground getting to and from main departure terminals.

Anthony Fokker and Louis Paulhan would indeed have been amazed. Neither of them would have dared prophesy such things.

The Jumbos

Some airlines and manufacturers like to call their airbuses "superjets".

They think that if the gigantic planes become known as Jumbo Jets, people will think of them as slow and lumbering, like an elephant, when really they won't be like that at all.

They will be just as sleek, as fast, and in some cases faster, than the big jetliners flying today.

The "star" of the airbuses is the Boeing 747 because it is the first true airbus. Its development has been very rapid. In the summer of 1965 a party of airline executives visited Boeings to talk about the sort of aeroplanes they would want in their future fleets.

Nobody mentioned the 747. It was an idea that had just not been thought of at the time.

But only two and a half years later, work began on a £13,000,000 extension and addition to the long-haul Oceanic Terminal at London's Heathrow Airport to handle the gigantic flood of passengers the 747s bring in. The first plane touched down at the airport early in 1970, one year later.

Whatever the airliners and the manufacturers think, the Jumbos are aptly named. Everything about them is jumbo-sized.

The 747 is over 231 ft long with a wing-span of 195 ft. The tail rises to 65 ft 6 in – almost the length of a cricket pitch. Other vital statistics, compared with the 707 jetliner the 747 planes:

Weigh twice as much – 300 tons
Carry two and a half times more passengers – 490
Cruise faster – 625 mph
Fly higher – 45,000 ft
Have twice as many wheels in the landing gear – 16

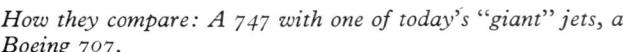

How they compare: A 747 with one of today's "giant" jets, a Boeing 707.

Left: *An artist's impression of how the new DC-10 trijets will look when they go into service. The small-looking aircraft between them is a BAC 1–11 which carries about 90 passengers. The Lockheed airbus is a near-identical aircraft to the DC-10.*

Below: *The rather "plump" looking original design for a European airbus, the A-300, and how it will look on the airport apron next to a Caravelle.*

Have a cabin twice as wide – 21 ft, with two decks instead of one

Are twice as powerful – the four turbofans produce 41,000 lb of thrust at take-off.

The 747 will not be the only airbus. Other Jumbos being planned are the DC-10, a 252-seater trijet, Lockheed's "Ten-Eleven" trijet which will be fitted with the new Rolls-Royce RB-211 "quiet" engines, and the A-300B, a twin jet designed by Britain, France and Germany.

The Jumbos will be able to operate on short- and long-range routes. Their enormous power will allow them to use almost any existing airport suitable for bigger jetliners.

And they will be only "baby" Jumbos.

They will all probably grow later by having their fuselages "stretched" so that they can carry even more passengers.

Present conventional airliners that have already been stretched are the Trident, the Boeing 727 and the DC-8 Sixty Series. Designed for service over intercontinental routes, the DC-8 Super 63 can now carry up to 251 passengers and their baggage 4,600 miles.

The Jumbos will bring a new era of elegance and luxury to air travel. There will be room in their multi-deck fuselages for cinema lounges, cocktail bars, children's nurseries, offices, staterooms . . . even night clubs have been mentioned to provide live entertainment.

But these sort of "frills" will only keep the cost of seats up by cutting down on space for them. The great possibility of the Jumbos is that of cheap fares because of the enormous number of people they can carry.

Though luxury versions will no doubt be built, with all the gimmicks imaginable, the demand is likely to be for what is called "high-density" seating, which means they will be fitted out to carry as many passengers as possible. Airlines are, at the moment, sending out questionnaires to people to find out what sort of aeroplane they want to fly in. The answers they get will determine what kind of services will be provided on the new giants of the air.

The Jumbos will not be the biggest aeroplanes to fly. The Lockheed C-5A Galaxy, the world's biggest aeroplane, beats them for sheer size. Its three-decker fuselage has room to seat 900 passengers – enough people to fill $12\frac{1}{2}$ of London Transport's big Routemaster buses.

The Galaxy is slightly larger than the Russians' Antonov AN-22 turboprop which has been flying since 1965. This is capable of carrying over 700 passengers.

Both aircraft are designed as military cargo planes, and they are slower than the Jumbos, but commercial versions could yet appear at the world's passenger airports.

It may be that the Jumbo will be the beginning of the last phase of development of the aeroplanes we are used to seeing in the skies . . . with their clearly recognisable body, wings, tail and engines.

Less than 20 years ago there was just one type of aircraft, the sort scientists call the "classical" type. It had straight wings and was driven by propellers from piston engines.

Above left: *The DC-8 Super 63: This airliner has been stretched to airbus proportions. It is able to carry up to 250 people. It is 187 ft long, has a wing-span of 148 ft, an overall height of 42 ft 5 ins, four turbofan engines, a speed of Mach 0·84 and a range of nearly 5,000 miles.*

Left: *A mock-up of the European airbus painted on the ground and the number of seats it would have.*

The airbus is a swept-wing aircraft, the second type of shape that came about because aeroplanes began to fly close to, and above, the speed of sound.

Sweeping back the wings delays the build-up of air pressure at high speed, which holds the aeroplane back and causes control problems.

The study of the air flowing over an aircraft's wings, which gives it "lift" to hold it up in the air, has made it possible to think of more new shapes, resulting in aeroplanes which don't look at all like the ones that have become so familiar to us.

The Jumbos may be just a stop-gap, produced because manufacturers know about the problems of swept-wing planes. And the cost of a completely new type of aeroplane is truly astronomic.

The European airbus will probably cost about £200 million to put into production. Each aircraft will be sold to airlines at something like £4,500,000 – just 150 times as much as the DC-3 cost to buy 30 years ago.

Not only is the expense of a new design high, but it also takes time to solve all the problems involved – even with the help of computers to do the designers' sums for them in a fraction of the time it would take a human brain.

Even as plans go ahead to introduce the Jumbos, it is certain that design teams are working on a much more startling project . . . the all-wing airbus.

The all-wing airbus would merge wings, body and power units into a single flight "envelope" – a development brought about by the greater knowledge we have of aerodynamics.

Aerodynamicists – the scientists who study how air moves – are testing ideas for new shapes all the time, to find ways of flying better and faster.

They have discovered that the airflow over an aircraft's wings can be made to behave in a way that cuts down drag dramatically. A plane built to achieve this could:

Fly the same amount of people or cargo faster
Fly at the same speed, but go further

Or:

Fly as fast and as far, but with *less* powerful engines.

It is easy to see how these sort of improvements would cut the cost of flying.

This cheaper, better aeroplane would be an all-wing shape – a "flying wing" in fact – because the aerodynamicists have also discovered that the flow round a fuselage is not as easy to manage as that round a wing. So they would simply get rid of the fuselage and carry passengers or freight in the wing.

Flying wings have been made before, like the American Northrop YB-35 and YB-49 bombers just after the end of the Second World War. But the idea has not yet been perfected.

If the all-wing airbus does come it may be cheap enough to seriously challenge passenger rail travel on short-range commuter routes.

Above: *The world's largest aeroplane, the Lockheed Galaxy, leaves the ground for the first time at Dobbins Air Force Base near Atlanta, Georgia. Note the number of wheels in the landing gear, and the way they stick out from the underside of the fuselage. The plane has to have a large number of wheels because its great weight must be spread over as wide an area as possible when landing. The shock of half a million pounds of metal hitting a runway at up to 200 mph could damage both concrete and aeroplane. The arrangement brings the problem of where to put the wheels when they are retracted for flight. They cannot go into the high speed Galaxy's thin wings, so they have to be given special pods in its belly.*

Below: *Russia's Antonov-22, a turboprop aircraft able to carry 700 passengers. It is 56 ft shorter than the Galaxy.*

Facing page: *Stretching an aircraft: The difference in the size of these two Boeing 727s shows up quite clearly. The plane in the bottom picture has a fuselage that is 20 ft longer than the plane in the top picture. The increase in space means it can carry 49 more passengers.*

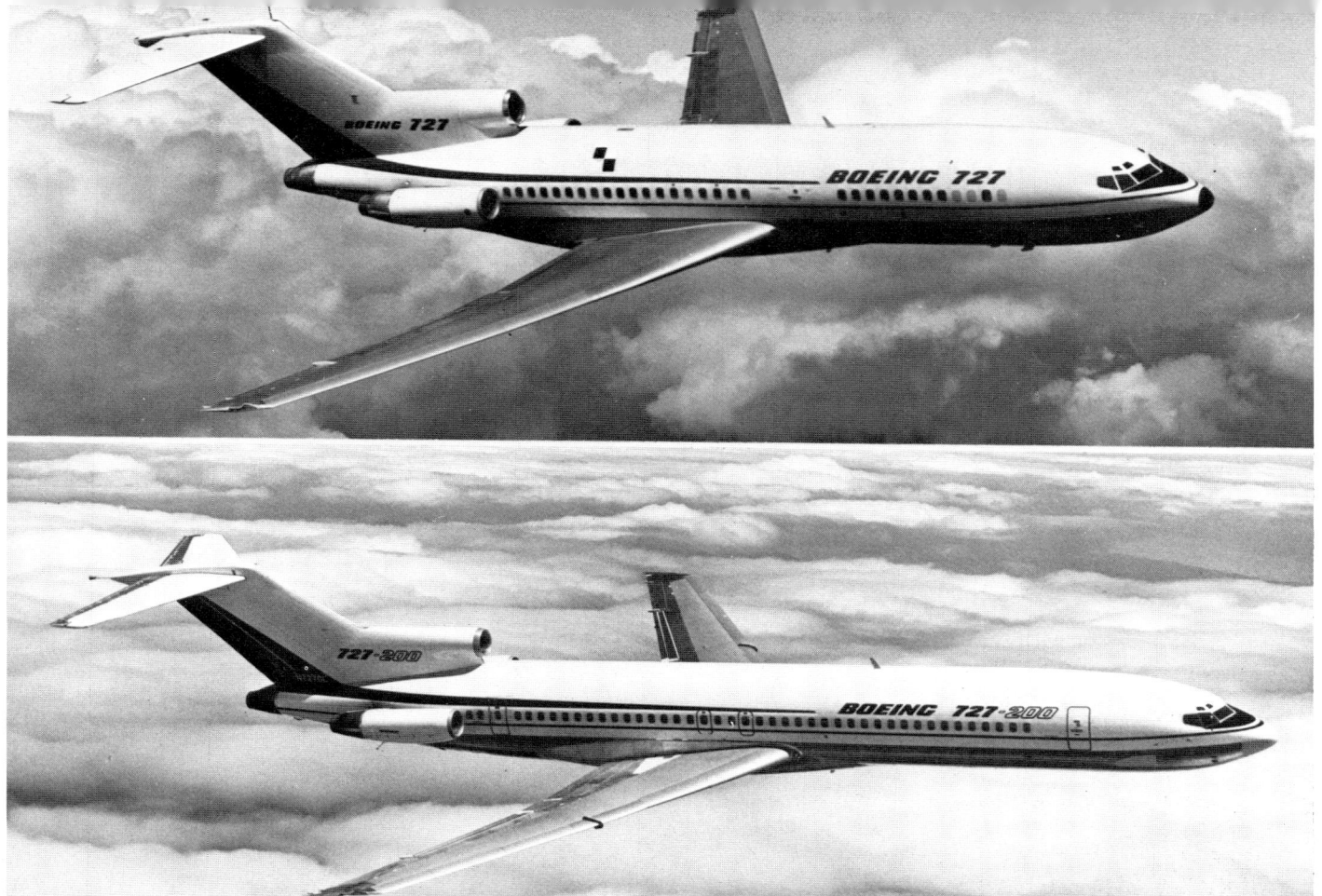

Midway between the swept-wing aeroplanes and the coming all-wing shape is the "slender" shape. This has been developed into the supersonic transports.

The SSTs

The pilots who have been "flying" London–New York distances in three hours – half the time it takes a 707 – have been doing the trip without leaving the ground.

They are the men who are training, in specially built imitation flight decks, to be captains of the SSTs, the airliners that will be flying at up to three times the speed of sound.

In America that means the Boeing 2707-300. In Russia the Tu-144. And in Britain and France, the Concorde.

These are the real superjets.

They are the planes that will make day-return trips possible between Europe and America – an idea that the first European to travel to America, Christopher Columbus, would have found unbelievable. It took him two and a half months . . . one way!

That of course, was in 1492, around the time that Leonardo da Vinci was thinking about helicopters and parachutes.

The look of the supersonic transports is long and pencil-slim. Concorde has delta-shaped wings that sweep back sharply, almost to the end of the fuselage, producing the "slender" outline. And those thin, slender, wings – apart from providing between three and four times the lifting area that other jetliners have – are gigantic fuel tanks inside. They help the SSTs to fly equally well at low speeds during landing and take-off.

As with other delta-winged aircraft, Concorde has a fin but no tailplane. Its four engines are placed in pairs under each wing.

The Russian SST beat its Western rivals into the air, making its first flight on the last day of 1968 over Moscow. The Tu-144 is so like Concorde that it has been called "Concordski", the only outward difference being its four engines grouped all together under the rear fuselage.

Concorde 001, the French prototype, made its first flight on March 2, 1969, at Toulouse, and Concorde 002, the British prototype, took off from Filton, Bristol, a month later. The Americans' SST has yet to fly.

The Boeing was to have been a swing-wing design, which would have made it two aeroplanes in one.

To get the most lift at take-off its wings would have been set at an angle of 42 degrees. Once airborne it would have climbed to between 30,000 ft and 40,000 ft to pass through the sound barrier with its wings swept further back to an angle of 72 degrees.

At this point they would have joined up and locked with the broad tailplane section to form the supersonic delta shape.

On landing the wings would have been brought right forward to an angle of 20 degrees so that it would have been

SUD AVIATION FRANCE – BRITISH AIRCRAFT CORPORATION
Concorde
Concorde

able to retain the right amount of lift to touch down at the slowest possible speed.

But the designers ran into the same trouble that had hit the F-111. Weight.

The swing-wing design has now been abandoned in favour of a fixed wing, Concorde-type, shape. But the wings will not reach so far down the fuselage as Concorde's, and a conventional, horizontal tailplane will be used.

On the ground the SST looks like a pelican at feeding time because of its drooping nose. This gives the pilot, sitting some 36 ft up on the flight deck, the maximum view forward. In flight the nose hinges up to fit flush with the rest of the fuselage to achieve the dart-like streamlining necessary for supersonic flying.

The once menacing sound barrier will hold no terrors for the passengers in an SST. Unless their captain tells them they will not know they are travelling faster than sound.

But the people down on the ground will know. They will be able to hear the boom that the aircraft makes when it goes supersonic. The sonic boom can vary from a noise like a thunderclap to a sound like a car door slamming, depending on how far you are away from the flight path of the plane and how heavy the aircraft is.

But as sonic booms trail along the ground like a carpet many miles wide, the noise could be a nuisance to many people. And the bang has even been known to damage property.

This is one reason why the SSTs are highly controversial aeroplanes.

When they go into regular service flight plans will probably have to be arranged so that they do not make sonic booms until they are clear of populated areas.

A recent survey has shown that nearly three-quarters of the world's international air routes pass over water. Small adjustments to them could raise this figure to four-fifths. So it may not be all that difficult to have SSTs without causing people on the ground too much trouble.

But this is not enough for some. There are societies in Britain and America whose members want the SSTs banned because, they claim, the sonic booms will make life unbearable.

They hope that the cost of developing SSTs – the Concorde bill is expected by some experts to top £800,000,000 – will strangle them at birth.

But though the mountains of money needed to put them into the air seem to go on growing, there is no sign of them being cancelled.

What can people expect when they fly in supersonic airliners?

They can expect to pay a high fare, to begin with anyway. People have been putting their names down to be on Concorde's first flight in much the same way as they have put their names down to be on the first flight to the Moon in a passenger-carrying spaceship.

Facing page, top: *Like a pelican at feeding time: The Tu-144 with its nose in the droop position to give the pilot a clear view forward. Its outward difference to Concorde is the position of its engines – grouped together under the fuselage.*

Facing page, centre: *Revolution: The age of the supersonic transport opens as "Concordski" – Russia's Tu-144 – takes to the air over Moscow on the last day of 1968.*

Facing page, foot: *Concorde 002, the British prototype: This picture was taken after the aircraft had left its assembly hangar at Filton, Bristol, for the first time to be towed to the engine test base. It shows the smooth, pencil slim shape of the SST with its nose hinged up as it would be in supersonic flight. It also demonstrates the sharp sweep of the delta wings and the absence of a tailplane on the rear fin.*

Concorde 001, the French prototype: *With test pilot André Turcat at the controls Concorde makes its first slow taxiing run at about 60 mph on Toulouse airfield. The angle shows how the engine positions differ from the Russian SST's – further out on the wings.*

But the ordinary, everyday passenger lists on SSTs are almost sure to be made up of businessmen. To them time is money, or export orders. They will be able to leave London at breakfast time, put in a full day's work in New York, and be back home in time for dinner.

For both passengers and crew the trip will be luxurious.

They will fly in air-conditioned comfort 12 miles above the earth. There will be little to see from the tiny windows of the passenger cabin, and few will find themselves next to one as seats will be seven abreast.

But they will be able to occupy their time by switching on their individual, retractable, full-colour television sets to watch programmes beamed by satellites.

Outside the aircraft the air temperature at cruising height drops to about 70 degrees below zero Centigrade. But it will be possible to boil a kettle or grill a steak on the metal skin of the SST.

This is the heat barrier.

On a cold day you can warm up your hands by rubbing them together. The heat comes from friction caused by the rubbing action.

The same sort of thing will happen as an SST blasts across the sky at nearly three times the speed of sound. But instead of hands rubbing together it will be an aeroplane and air.

And the faster the plane goes the hotter it will get. There is no way to break through the heat barrier as there is with sound.

The bitter cold at a height of 12 miles will help to cool the aircraft's skin, but it must have other protection. At temperatures of about 150 degrees Centigrade the metals normally used to build aeroplanes start to go soft and lose their strength. New metals have now been found that withstand the heat and hold their strength. One metal that does this well is called titanium.

Concorde is designed to fly at 1,450 mph, or Mach 2·2, a speed carefully chosen to fall short of the need to build the whole plane of heat-resisting metal, which is expensive.

Only certain parts of Concorde's skin will get hot enough to need protecting with titanium – sections round the engines, flying control surfaces and landing gear.

The American SST, which aims at a speed of 1,800 mph – Mach 2·7 – will be built almost entirely of titanium.

Apart from being used to drive the engines, fuel will also be used to absorb surplus heat, and help balance the aircraft.

At low speeds an aircraft flies in a "tail-down" attitude, with the wings "attacking" the air at a steep angle to get the right amount of lift.

The lifting force increases with speed, so the wings do not need to be at such a steep angle. The tail comes up and the nose is forced down.

In the very high speed range of the SST the wings' angle of attack could be negative – leading edge down – which would mean, in an extreme case, that the aircraft might be in danger of flipping over forwards.

To balance any forward tilt the SST's fuel will be transferred to tanks in the rear during high-speed flight. As it slows for landing, and the tail-down attitude is needed again, back will come the fuel to the forward tanks.

At SST altitudes – 60,000 ft and above – any failure in the system that keeps the inside of the aircraft at a comfortable pressure would be very serious indeed. Exposure to the outside air at 40,000 ft would cause passengers and crew to quickly lose consciousness, and body fluids would boil at 63,000 ft.

Because of the time it would take to carry out an emergency dive to a safe height there will be oxygen masks for everyone on board.

Another hazard is cosmic radiation. Earth's atmosphere acts as a giant protecting blanket against the bombardment of high-energy particles from the Sun which are capable of causing serious damage to the body cells of human beings.

In the thinner air at high altitudes the blanket's protection is not so good. And gigantic flares – or storms – on the Sun increase the danger.

SSTs will fly twice as high as today's jetliners. In theory this means their passengers will be taking twice the radiation risk. But this will be more than offset because they will also be flying more than twice as fast, cutting down the time of exposure.

And the Sunstorms happen regularly every 11 years. Pilots will know when they are due and not go above 50,000 ft which will allow flights to be made under the worst of these conditions.

As an added safeguard the SSTs will be fitted with warning systems to alert captains to a dangerous rise in radiation. The equipment will also measure the dosage during each flight so that a check can be kept on the yearly total received by individual crew members.

One Atlantic trip, it has been calculated, will mean being exposed to only one-thirtieth of the amount of radiation you get from a chest X-ray.

The people who build the SSTs might consider including an alarm clock in the pilot's cabin, for if his seat is *too* comfortable he is quite likely to fall asleep!

It will be motorised for one thing . . . he won't have to move it himself unless he chooses to. That is just one of the automatic aids that modern science has devised to help him.

And he will need them because he will be flying faster than he will need to think in some cases. Therefore a lot of his routine thinking must be done for him.

While actually on the ground closed-circuit television will give a pilot views all round his aircraft. In the air as much use as possible will be made of automation.

The navigational system, with a direct link to the automatic pilot, will provide a constant flow of information about the aircraft's position on its route and its estimated time of arrival at its destination.

A moving map display will show the plane's position in relation to the earth below it. Computers will record height, speed, balance, track and weight.

Top: *America's new SST which has a fixed, Concorde type delta wing and a conventional horizontal tailplane.*

Above: *The swing-wing design as it would have appeared in supersonic flight, the pivoting part of the wings have locked with the tailplane and taken on the delta shape.*

Right: *America's design for a swing-wing SST with the pivoting part of the wings set forward for low-speed flight.*

The SSTs will be the most complex airliners ever to take the air. And when Concorde makes its first trip with fare-paying passengers aboard, it will not only be the world's most advanced airliner, but the most tested in history.

The prototype – the original model which will set the pattern for every Concorde that goes into airline service – will have a flight test programme of 4,500 hours, equivalent to spending more than six months in the air.

In spite of the critics, the SSTs are coming.

Man must progress. But the "superjets" are not merely a symbol of that progress. They are also monuments to man's mastery of the world he lives in.

And if the Jumbos promise to mark the beginning of one of the last chapters in the evolution of the classical-shaped aircraft, the SSTs – the slender shapes – promise to mark the beginning of an entirely new chapter in the story of the aeroplane.

Vertoliners

Helicopters have been called the "will-o'-the-wisps" of the air.

The idea of vertical take-off and landing techniques can be traced as far back as the ancient Chinese.

They made a toy by inserting feathers into a spindle which, when rapidly revolved, was able to fly straight up.

But even now, at the dawn of the space age, vertical flight is still something of a will-o'-the-wisp.

There are penalties for being able to fly straight up . . . or down . . . and hover. Those penalties are paid in speed, payload and range, all of which are much lower than those of aeroplanes with wings. A helicopter's lack of wings and a tail also cause control problems.

The first helicopter design in Western history was Leonardo da Vinci's – a small, spring-driven machine with a helical screw rotor.

While his sketches lay hidden many experiments were made throughout Europe. Cayley tried out a device on the lines of the Chinese toy, rotors stuck into corks at each end of a spindle. They were rotated in opposite directions by a whalebone bow, its string wrapped round the spindle. The idea, using propellers made of silk-covered frames, was one

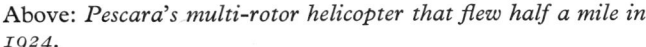

Above: *Pescara's multi-rotor helicopter that flew half a mile in 1924.*

Above right: *Flying bedsteads: Nearly a quarter of a century separate these two machines. D'Ascanio's flew in 1930 . . .*

Right: *. . . and Rolls-Royce made this experimental jet-lift craft in 1953.*

Below: *The next step was the autogiro pioneered by the Spaniard Juan de la Cierva. This model had a standard Avro 504 fuselage and rotating wings.*

Foot of page, left: *The first practical helicopter, the 1936 Focke-Achgelis FW-61, which could reach a speed of 76 mph and stay up for an hour and a half.*

Foot of page, right: *The helicopter appears as a separate aircraft: Igor Sikorsky at the controls of his VS-300. It was, he said, "like a dream" to fly.*

All sorts of shapes and sizes: A hovering man using a small, strap-on power unit. . . .

which two Frenchmen – Launoy and Bienvenu – had successfully demonstrated in 1784.

One of the earliest efforts to solve the problem of vertical flight in a full-sized machine was made by another Frenchman, Etienne Oehmichen. His helicopter had two crossed arms which had four horizontal revolving wings on the ends. Seven other airscrews were added to provide control.

His landing gear was six footballs mounted on shock-absorbers to reduce the bump when he landed.

In 1923 Oehmichen hovered for five minutes with this strange-looking contraption, and a year later made the first circular helicopter flight.

Yes, the vertical flight pioneers created the weird and the wonderful, too.

Like the Marquis de Pescara's multi-rotor machine that flew half a mile in 1924. It was a chassis mounted on wheels with a massive shaft sticking straight up in the middle. Around this revolved four double-bladed horizontal airscrews driven by a 180 hp engine.

The whole thing weighed nearly a ton, but it flew. It managed a flight of 2,550 ft in just over four minutes at a height of six feet.

Then an Italian called D'Ascanio made some flights in 1930. He built a machine that looked remarkably like the Rolls-Royce "flying bedstead" jet-lift experimental rig that was not to be tested until nearly a quarter of a century later.

D'Ascanio's "bedstead" had rotors, of course. He made a vertical ascent of over 20 ft, hovered in the air for one and a half minutes, flew in a closed circuit of one kilometre, and stayed up for a total of eight and three-quarter minutes. The 39 ft diameter twin contra-rotating airscrews were driven by a 95 hp engine.

The next step was the autogiro, which was neither an aeroplane nor a helicopter. Juan de la Cierva of Spain built the first and flew it in Madrid in 1923.

The autogiro looked like a normal aeroplane – a fuselage, with a rudder at the back and an engine in front with a tractor propeller.

But it had no wings.

Instead it had rotor blades mounted above the fuselage

Top: *Russia's giant Mi-10, the world's largest helicopter, in use as a flying crane.*

Above: *One of the first vertical take-off aircraft, the Ryan X-13, sitting on its tail ready for take-off. It was launched from the ramp standing next to it and then curved over into a normal flying position.*

Facing page: *Jump-jet: Hawker Siddeley's Harrier which bends thrust downwards through the rotating nozzle just under the wing root for vertical take-off. For normal flight the nozzle is swivelled to the rear. The Harrier can also fly backwards.*

which turned freely in the slipstream from the propeller – or they could be described as "rotating wings".

After a brief run along the ground the rotor blades would turn fast enough to provide lift for take-off. And therefore the autogiro can claim to be the first modern form of short take-off and landing aeroplane. It could land almost vertically.

At one demonstration, at Farnborough in 1925, the rotors of an autogiro were given a little help to start spinning. A rope was wound round their shaft. On the other end were several men who ran away from the machine as fast as they could while holding on to the rope and pulling as hard as they could.

As the rope unwound, so the rotors began to turn – just as some lawn mowers are started by pulling on a rope.

Later, deflector plates were fitted to the tails of autogiros to force the slipstream up into the rotors to start them turning.

The first practical helicopter – a VTOL machine – was built in Germany in 1936. It was the Focke-Achgelis FW-61 which, like the autogiro, resembled an ordinary aeroplane without wings.

Where the FW-61's wings would have been were two lots of "scaffolding" either side of the fuselage tilted outwards and upwards. At the end of each one was a small rotor. It was capable of flying for one and a half hours, reaching a speed of 76 mph and a height of 11,234 ft.

The helicopter, as a separate type of aircraft, emerged three years later.

Igor Sikorsky, the Russian now living in America, had abandoned his interest in large, multi-engined planes to concentrate on the helicopter – the craft with the now familiar large overhead rotor and the tiny tail propeller which gives stability.

Sikorsky's work resulted in the VS-300 in September 1939, the month the Second World War was declared. He continued to improve his designs until, eventually, the "classic" Sikorsky helicopter, the S-51, went into service in 1946.

It was a four-seater – pilot and three passengers – with a 450 hp engine and a cruising speed of 85 mph.

Helicopters now appear in all sorts of shapes and sizes, from small portable arrangements that can be strapped to a man's back, like the one James Bond used in the film *Thunderball*, to giants like Russia's Mi-10, the world's largest, which can lift a prefabricated building weighing 15 tons.

The "whirlybirds" have proved their value in war . . . in Korea and Vietnam. . . . operating over rough jungle and hilly country, where there are few proper airstrips, to fly wounded to safety and to deliver supplies.

In peace the use of helicopters is almost limitless. They can rescue people from the sea, floods and other disasters, help out as cranes with construction work. VIPs use them – like the British royal family (Prince Philip is a helicopter pilot) and the American President – to take them on official

engagements, they do police and road traffic patrol duties, and are employed in crop dusting work, forestry patrols, fire fighting and in many other ways.

Now there are VTOL aircraft that are both helicopters and conventional aeroplanes at the same time.

This line of development combines the best of both worlds – the vertical take-off and landing abilities of the helicopter and the high-speed forward flight of aeroplanes with wings. It means that the time is not far off when there can be fast city-centre-to-city-centre air travel in sizeable airliners.

Two things have made this possible. Vectored thrust and the convertiplane.

The first VTOL planes, like the Convair XFY-1 turbo-prop of 1954 and the Ryan X-13 Vertijet of 1957, "sat" on their tails for lift-off and then simply curved over into a normal forward flying position when they had enough speed and height.

Vectored thrust allows an aircraft to lift off and land in a normal flying attitude. The thrust from its jet engines is "bent" downwards to push it into the air, then transferred to the rear for forward flight.

Hawker Siddeley have used this method in their Harrier fighter. The exhaust from the single jet engine is funnelled through rotating nozzles on either side of the fuselage beneath the wings. The Harrier can not only hover and fly at transonic speeds, it can also fly backwards.

Another way of using jet-lift is to have separate, smaller engines of fold-out fans for take-off, and a larger engine for cruising.

Ideas like these are being employed in a Hawker Siddeley design study for a future VTOLiner and the Ryan Company's vertifan. They also have the advantage of reducing the noise nuisance of big jet engines.

The convertiplane does exactly what its name suggests . . . it converts itself, taking off like a helicopter, flying level like a normal aeroplane.

It is able to do this by tilting either its engines or its wings into a vertical position to get off the ground, then tilting them back to a horizontal position for cruising.

America's experimental LTV XC-142A (the Downtowner) is probably the most spectacular tilt-winger, and the world's largest non-helicopter.

A four-engined turboprop, it can carry 40 to 50 people and pivot in a circle in either direction within a diameter no larger than its 67 ft wing-span.

The German VFW firm is working on a larger 90-passenger vertoliner. This is an even more spectacular tilt-wing design . . . a tandem. Called the VC-500 it has two sets of wings, one behind the other, with a pair of engines in each set.

An example of the tilted engine technique is the new Westland WE 02, a short-range, 80-passenger transport in the 400 mph range. Because of the extra work the tilted

Above: *Fan-lift: This airliner is landing on a city centre roof with the aid of the fold-out fans at each end of the fuselage. Its two larger cruising engines are at the rear. It is a method that helps to reduce jet noise.*

Left: *The German tandem-wing principle for a vertoliner. Like the XC-142A, the wings tilt vertically for take-off and landing.*

Right: *Convertiplane: A spectacular take-off by the XC-142A showing how the wing is tilted from the vertical position to a normal flying position.*

engines' propellers have to do when raising the whole aircraft from the ground, they are larger in diameter than propellers on conventional aeroplanes.

Coming up in the not-too-distant future are other forms of VTOL and STOL aircraft.

These include the Lockheed idea for a compound transport – a fixed-wing aeroplane with an overhead rotor that folds away in flight.

Then there is the propulsive wing project being tested by LTV. It is called ADAM, the initials standing for "air deflection and modulation". The plane has vertically mounted turbofans within the wings.

Two advances which could provide major breakthroughs in VTOL air travel are the Hughes hot-cycle jet helibus being developed in America, and the British rigid rotor system undergoing experiments at the British Gas Turbine Establishment.

The helibus uses its wings as rotors. High-energy gases from a turbine are pumped through the wings to exhaust ducts at the tips, driving them round to allow vertical take-off and landing. In flight the rotor wings are stopped, locked, and become fixed wings for cruising at 500 mph.

The system is lightweight and does away with complex shafts, gear-boxes and transmission arrangements.

The British rigid rotor scheme is a revolutionary idea that could transform existing airliners into planes capable of rising and descending vertically.

By attaching hollow tubes above the wings and forcing high-pressure air through lengthwise slots in them from the plane's jet engines, much greater lift is produced than from an ordinary helicopter rotor blade.

The tubes could be stowed away in flight and the main jets used to power the aircraft forward.

The 21st Century

Speeds of up to 25 or 30 times the speed of sound are being talked about for the 21st century, only just 30 years away.

The aircraft that will be flying at such phenomenal speeds – up to 20,000 mph – will be the "sons" of the SSTs, the hypersonic transports.

Scientists are already studying designs for an airliner that will be able to fly hypersonically, the speed range that begins at five times the speed of sound . . . about 4,000 mph. They are also considering an aerospace plane that will be able to fly into Earth orbit and return under its own power and control.

One American design suggests an orbital "mother plane". This would be a very large aircraft like a spaceship that would stay permanently in a circular orbit round the earth.

Smaller planes, loaded with passengers, would take off from the ground and dock with the mother plane.

Passengers would then transfer to the main ship, travel in it along its orbit until they were above their destination and board one of the small planes again for the trip back down to the Earth's surface.

The idea is reported to have produced a design for the

mother plane that looks rather like Tower Bridge in London, and weighs about as much – over 12,000 tons.

British scientists are backing a new type of aeroplane called the Waverider.

The Waverider is the fourth shape in aircraft design after the classical, swept-wing and slender shapes. It is called a Waverider because it will produce a powerful shock wave in flight, mainly underneath, which will help to provide lift. Therefore the Waverider will "ride" on its own shock wave.

Looked at from the rear the plane is "caret" shaped – a shallow inverted "V", with wings drooping down on either side of a central ridge.

From above it is triangular, the ridge, formed by the mere suggestion of a fin emerging gradually from the sharp end of the triangle, rising to the squared-off base.

The shock wave will be trapped in the inverted "V". The principle, called the compression lift rule, has already been applied to the giant XB-70A, America's Mach 3 bomber and experimental plane which is being used for research into high-speed flight problems.

Work at America's National Aeronautics and Space Administration (NASA) has produced a similar shape to the Waverider.

Many accepted ideas have had to be thrown away in planning the hypersonic transport.

One of NASA's researchers says: "The fuselage and control surfaces will have to blend into a wing to a degree we have not yet seen."

The Waverider will be gigantic, even by SST standards. It will be a jumbo-jumbo-jet, weigh as much as 400 tons and stand as high as 80 ft.

The reason for this is that it will need vast thrust to reach hypersonic speeds, and great strength to withstand those speeds. It will also be fuelled by hydrogen because today's kerosene jet fuels do not generate enough power for hypersonic flight. Hydrogen has a very low density, about a tenth of kerosene, and needs ten times the space for the same weight of fuel.

Not only has there had to be new thinking in design and fuels, but in engines and metals as well.

The hydrogen will be burnt in a new type of engine called a "scramjet" – a supersonic combustion ram-jet – which uses the high-speed air entering the engine to help ignite the fuel.

The problem of fantastic heat at hypersonic speed – 1,400 degrees Centigrade above Mach 5 – may be overcome by using metals like columbian and molybdenum, which retain their strength at very high temperatures. Here the hydrogen will help, too, because it is also a refrigerant.

The heat problem may make hypersonic airliners "disposable" planes. Parts of them, such as wing leading edges, may only be able to stand up to a few flights at these extreme temperatures, and work is going on into the possibility of replacing entire sections as they show signs of wear.

Hypersonics could change our whole way of life in the 21st century. The prospect of ultra-high-speed forms of

Top right: *Tilting the engines: The Westland solution to VTOL, a method that uses big propellers.*

Right: *The propulsive wing, ADAM: Vertically mounted jets in the wings – note the large air intakes – can use downward thrust for landing and take-off and forward thrust for level flight.*

Below: *Rigid rotor: Existing airliners could be converted into VTOL aircraft by being fitted with tubes like these over their wings. High-pressure air is forced through slots in the tubes for vertical lift and the underwing jets take over for level flight.*

Foot of page: *Hot cycle: The Hughes idea for a helibus which has dual-purpose wings. They rotate to give low speed and hovering flight and are stopped when the aircraft is cruising.*

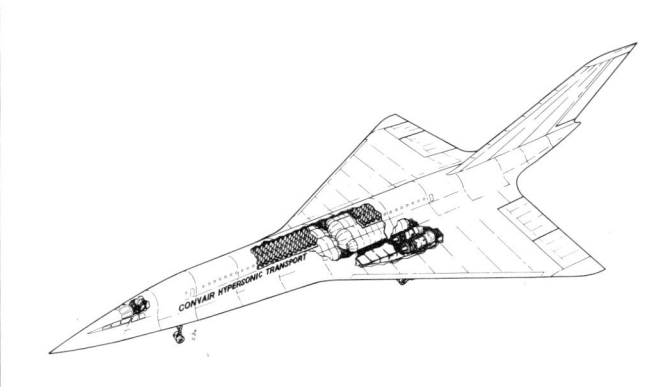

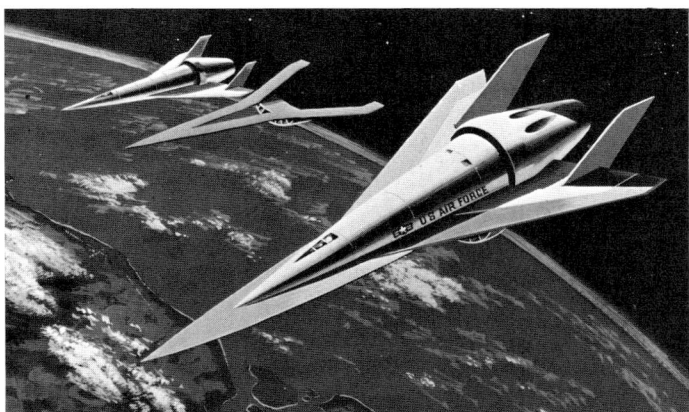

Top: *The flying wing: A Northrop YB-49, the jet version of the propeller driven YB-35. The design has no fuselage which reduces drag. Aircraft like this could challenge rail travel in the future.*

Above left: *Or, it could be like this: General Dynamics' suggestion for a hypersonic transport using hydrogen fuel.*

Left: *Scramjets: These engines – which use high-speed air to help ignite fuel – could produce aerospace planes that could "park" themselves in earth orbit. They would be a combination of spaceship and aeroplane and be used over and over again for space travel.*

Below left: *Atomic power: This is a design for an aircraft with nuclear engines mounted in the tail and two ordinary jets under the wings. It is just one example of the "new" thinking that is going into the sort of aircraft the world will need in the coming century.*

Below: *Surface burning: a revolutionary way of powering an aircraft at speeds up to Mach 15 is the EXTERNAL combustion engine. This form of propulsion ejects fuel into the hypersonic airflow near the thick end of a wedge-shaped aeroplane where it ignites, building up pressure that forces the craft forward. The flying wedge would operate at heights of 200,000 ft.*

transport means that no two places on the Earth's surface will be more than two hours' flying time apart.

This will give town planners the opportunity to design new ways for people to live in communities without having to cram them into the comparatively small areas of our present-day cities, a system that we know causes many human problems.

Within our existing knowledge, the final barrier to how fast we can fly is within our own bodies.

When a spaceship takes off, the Earth's gravitational pull – or "G" force – tries to hold it back. It has to accelerate to 25,000 mph to escape from the pull of Earth.

As America's Saturn V rocket punches its Apollo space-craft into orbit on the first stage of flight to the Moon, the astronauts inside are pushed back into their couches by the tremendous acceleration. The G forces acting on them rise to about four and a half times what they feel when they are standing on earth.

Without special seats and protective clothing to counter-act the G forces, this kind of acceleration puts the human body under severe strain.

Blood is drawn from the brain, causing black-outs. The heart has to pump harder because the blood becomes as dense as molten iron. Vision becomes blurred, there is mental confusion, pains in the chest and it is hard to con-trol the muscles. Hands and feet just won't do as they are told.

Astronauts spend years training in space-medicine centres. In apparatus designed to reproduce the strains of space flight, their bodies get used to the forces they will experience during an actual mission.

When they are blasted away from the Earth's surface they have the added protection of their G-suits, their ship is automatically controlled from the ground, and the period of $4\frac{1}{2}$ G lasts only for a few minutes.

Passengers in hypersonic airliners will not be able to go into training. Even if they could, forces of $4\frac{1}{2}$ G would be more than grandma or the children could stand.

But compared with a spaceship, acceleration in a hyper-sonic airliner will be minute . . . about 0·2 G.

On a two-hour journey from London to Sydney, though a plane would have to reach a maximum speed of about 15,000 mph, it would do it by gradual acceleration over an hour.

At 15,000 mph, one hour out from London, it would then be gradually decelerated again for the second hour. The G force would then never be more than 0·2, which would be quite tolerable for passengers in average health.

Faster flight means higher G. This would cause new problems, for a passenger might find it a struggle to get out of his seat and he would feel much heavier.

So this is where we might have to stop. . . .

Unless scientists have discovered the secret of gravity by then and built an anti-gravity motor!

The idea of finding some form of power unit that will "neutralise" the force of gravity has been dreamed about for years, but existed only between the pages of science-fiction books.

The search to harness gravity has attracted the world's most brilliant mathematicians. Many of the best brains in America and Europe are patiently attempting what, so far, has seemed the impossible.

If they do solve the mystery of gravity they will bring about a greater revolution in power and transport than the discovery of atomic power. The possibilities are fantastic.

Aircraft and spaceships would be able to take off and travel at high speed without strain. They would not have to wrench themselves away from the Earth by the brute force of powerful engines burning expensive chemical fuels.

Astronauts and airline passengers would be free of G forces. Planes would not have to depend on the air for lift.

In theory each anti-gravity vehicle would carry its own field of gravity with it in flight. Then, no matter how fast the acceleration, or how abrupt the change of course, people would feel no more strain than they do now, travelling through space on Earth which is itself a giant spaceship, spinning at more than 1,000 mph, orbiting the Sun at 66,600 mph.

With all these astonishing possibilities opening up before us in the future, are aeroplanes doomed? Will the aircraft we see in our skies today disappear, like the horse and cart has with the advancement of the motor-car?

This is very unlikely according to supersonics expert, Dr. Dietrich Küchemann, the head of the aerodynamics depart-

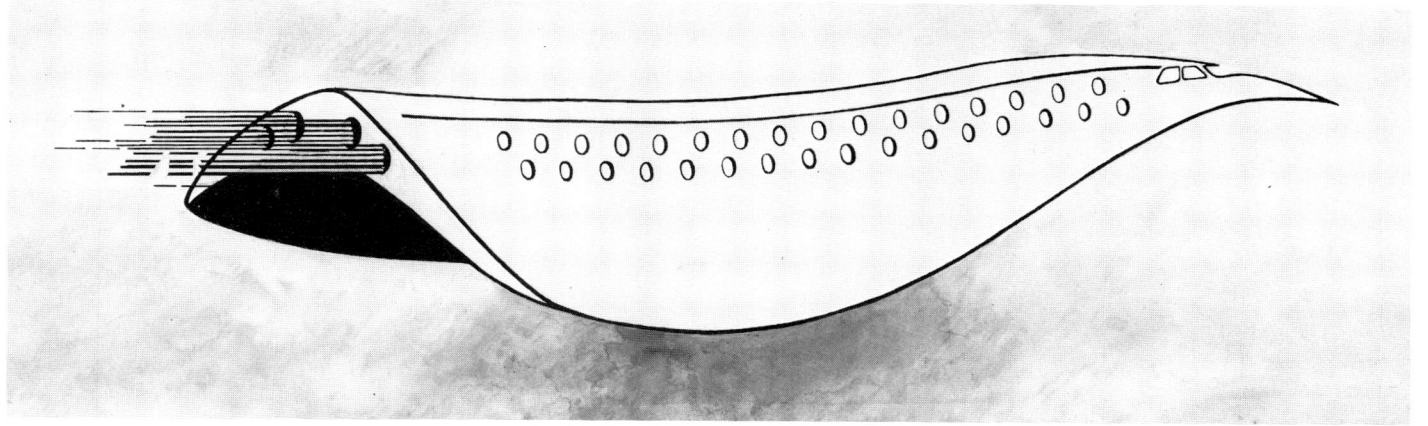

The shape of things to come: The Waverider, a blending of fuselage, wings and control surfaces which will trap hypersonic shock waves in the "V" shape underneath the aircraft. This is the type of plane that could mean a London to Sydney flight of only two hours.

ment at Farnborough. He believes that aviation "is still in its infancy, or at best, just growing up".

The study of fuels, aerodynamics, metals, flows, construction, and the perfection of automatic landing techniques to keep planes flying in any weather, will keep us busy improving the aeroplanes we have until well into the next century.

There is one particular dragon that still has to be slain – Hi-CAT – high-altitude, clear-air turbulence, powerful forces in the upper air that can shake an aircraft to destruction without warning.

Hi-CAT is caused by abrupt changes in wind speed creating pockets of extremely rough air which seize high-flying aircraft, literally in a clear blue sky, with such force that they can be shredded to pieces.

Research flights are going on from which it is hoped to develop a reliable warning system against these invisible storms.

Meanwhile, says Dr. Küchemann: "We can be reasonably confident that classical and swept-wing aircraft are here to stay for flights over short and medium ranges, and that they will continue to develop into a whole family of aircraft of the same kind, from small private aircraft to large airbuses."

He sees no reason why VTOL and swing-wing principles should not be applied to all the major types of aeroplanes. So we could end up with a plane that has everything – a hypersonic, vertical-take-off and landing, swing-wing airliner.

But, because of the spiralling cost of developing new types of aircraft, much more thought is likely to be given to what kinds we shall need in the future.

If our needs are to prove as warlike as they have during the aeroplane's first 60-odd years of life, then Anthony Fokker's prophecy may yet be fulfilled.

The flying machine of the future will indeed be the most ghastly thing ever created by man.

But if it can be used to make man a genuine "superman", to make life better for human beings instead of the instrument of their destruction . . . ?

Louis Blériot, the man who first woke up the world to the promise – and the threat – of the aeroplane, asked a similar question.

"Why," he said, "has this amazing new power been suddenly placed in the hands of man?"

And he had the answer. To Blériot it was this: "Surely it is for the advancement of the world."

Sources of reference

A History of Flying, by Charles H. Gibbs-Smith. B. T. Batsford Ltd., London, 1953.

Adventure of Man's Flight, The. American Heritage Publishing Co., Putnam, London.

Aeroplane, an Historical Survey, The, by Charles H. Gibbs-Smith. HMSO, London 1960.

Aeroplane Magazine, Temple Press, London.

Aeroplane Past, Present and Future, The, by Claude Grahame-White and Harry Harper. T. Werner Laurie, London, 1911.

Aircraft, Aircraft, by J. W. R. Taylor. Paul Hamlyn, London, 1967.

Aircraft Profiles (various), Profile Publications, Leatherhead, Surrey.

Air Dates, by Air Commodore L. G. S. Payne, William Heinemann Ltd., London, 1957.

Air Force and Space Digest – USAF's First Twenty Years. Air Force Association, Washington DC.

An Aerodynamicist's Prospect of the Second Century, by Dr. Dietrich Küchemann. Technical Memo, Royal Aircraft Establishment, Farnborough, 1967.

American Combat Planes, by Ray Wagner. MacDonald, London, 1960.

Aviation: Its Technical Development, by J. L. Nayler and E. Owen. Peter Owen/Vision Press, London, 1965.

Aviation Week and Space Technology. McGraw-Hill Inc., New York.

Battle of Britain, The, by Edward Bishop. Allen and Unwin, London, 1960.

Battle of Britain, The, by Basil Collier. B. T. Batsford Ltd., London, 1962.

Broken Wing, The – A Study in the British Exercise of Air Power, by David Divine. Hutchinson, London, 1966.

"Birth of the Aeroplane, The", by Charles H. Gibbs-Smith. *Journal of the Royal Society of Arts*, January 1959, No. 5030, vol. CVII.

Destination the Moon, by William E. Howard. United States Information Service.

Dumpy Pocket Book of Aircraft and Flight, edited by Henry Sampson. Sampson Low, London, 1960.

"Development of the Aeroplane", by Peter W. Brooks. *Journal of the Royal Society of Arts*, January 1959, No. 5030, vol. CVII.

Encyclopaedia of World Aircraft, by J. W. R. Taylor. Odhams Books, London, 1966.

Evolution of the Flying Machine, The, by Harry Harper. Hutchinson & Co., London, 1930.

Flight into History, by Elsbeth E. Freudenthal. University of Oklahoma Press, 1949.

Flight International. Iliffe Transport Publications, London.

Flight. Life Science Library series. Time-Life International. Life Inc., 1966.

Flight Plan for Tomorrow – The Douglas Story. Douglas Aircraft Co. Inc., Santa Monica, California, 1966.

Flying. Principles of Flight and the Development of Aircraft, by Martin Caidin. Holt, Rinehart and Winston Inc., New York.

Flying Review International (various). Haymarket Publishing Group, London.

Four Miles South of Kitty Hawk. Warren McArthur Corporation, New York.

Friendless Sky, The, by Alexander McKee. Souvenir Press, London, 1962.

Highways in the Air – The Development of British Civil Aviation. British Overseas Airways Corporation, London.

"How We Invented the Aeroplane", by Orville Wright. *Harper's Magazine*.

Hydrogen Bomb, The – The Men, The Menace, The Mechanism, by James

Shepley and Clay Blair Jnr. Jarrolds, London, 1955.

Jane's All The World's Aircraft (various), edited by J. W. R. Taylor. Sampson Low, London.

Jet. The Story of a Pioneer, by Sir Frank Whittle. Frederick Muller, London.

Leader of The Few, by Basil Collier. Jarrolds, London, 1957.

Life and Death of Nazi Germany, The, by Robert Goldston. A Phoenix House Publication, 1967

Man and His Symbols, by Carl G. Jung. Aldis Books, London, 1964.

Military Aircraft Recognition, by John W. R. Taylor. Ian Allan, London, 1969.

Modern Airliner, The, by Peter W. Brooks. Putnam, London, 1961.

Moonslaught – The Full Story of Man's Race to the Moon, by Reginald Turnhill. Purnell, London, 1969.

No High Ground, by Fletcher Knebel and Charles Bailey. Weidenfeld and Nicolson, London, 1960.

Papers of Wilbur and Orville Wright, The. McGraw-Hill Book Co. Inc., New York.

Possible Types of Flying Vehicle in the Future, by Dr. Dietrich Küchemann. Technical Memo, Royal Aircraft Establishment, Farnborough, 1966.

Royal Air Force 1939–45, vols. I, II, III, by Denis Richards and Hilary St. George Saunders. HM Stationery Office, London, 1953.

Royal Air Force Golden Jubilee Souvenir Book. Edited and published by Dr.-Ing. John P. Milford Reid for the Royal Air Force Benevolent Fund, London, 1968.

Safety in the Air, by Maurice Allward. Abelard-Schuman, London, 1967.

Spirit of St. Louis, The, by Charles A. Lindbergh. John Murray, London, 1953.

Their Finest Hour – The Story of the Battle of Britain 1940, by Edward Bishop. MacDonald & Co., London, 1968.

Technical Development of Modern Aviation, The, by Ronald Miller and David Sawers. Routledge and Kegan Paul, London, 1968.

Twenty Years Progress in Aerodynamics and the Changing Shape of Aeroplanes, by Dr. Dietrich Küchemann and John Bagley. Technical Memo, Royal Aircraft Establishment, Farnborough, 1966.

War In The Air – Aerial Wonders of Our Time. The Amalgamated Press, London, c. 1936.

Wright Brothers, The, by Charles H. Gibbs-Smith. Science Museum, HMSO, London, 1963.

"Wright Brothers, The, and the Royal Aeronautical Society, A Survey and a Tribute", by J. Laurence Pritchard. *Journal of the Royal Aeronautical Society*, vol. 57, December 1953.

Acknowledgements

Aerospace International, The United States Air Force Association, Washington, DC.

Air Canada.

Air Registration Board, Redhill, Surrey.

Aviaexport, Moscow.

John Bagley, Royal Aircraft Establishment, Farnborough.

Bell Aerosystems, New York.

Boeing Company, Seattle.

Hilda, Lady Brabazon.

British Air Line Pilots Association.

British Aircraft Corporation.

British Airports Authority.

British European Airways.

British Overseas Airways Corporation.

British Petroleum Company Ltd.

British Hovercraft Corporation Ltd.

Dassault, Avions Marcal.

Dornier, Munich.

Fairey Company Ltd.

Fokker, Amsterdam.

General Dynamics, New York.

Charles H. Gibbs-Smith.

Hawker Siddeley Aviation Ltd.

Hughes Tool Company, Aircraft Division, California.

Imperial War Museum.

International Air Transport Association, Geneva.

KLM Royal Dutch Airlines.

Dr. Dietrich Küchemann, Head of Aerodynamics, RAE, Farnborough.

Ling-Temco-Vought, Texas.

Lockheed Aircraft Corporation, California.

Lufthansa German Airlines.

Martin Marietta Corporation, New York.

McDonnell Douglas Corporation, California.

Messerschmitt-Bolkon GmbH, Munich.

Ministry of Defence, Air Historical Branch.

Ministry of Technology, Royal Aircraft Establishment, Farnborough.

National Aeronautics and Space Administration, Texas.

National Gas Turbine Establishment.

National Periodical Publications Inc., New York.

North American Rockwell Corporation, California.

Northrop Corporation, California.

Pan American World Airways.

Rolls-Royce Ltd.

Royal Aeronautical Society.

Royal Air Force, Inspectorate of Recruiting.

Ryan Aeronautical Company, California.

Science Museum.

Sikorsky Aircraft, Connecticut.

Smithsonian Institution, Washington DC.

Society of British Aerospace Companies Ltd.

Sud-Aviation, Paris.

Tass News Agency.

Trans World Airlines.

John W. R. Taylor.

United Artists.

United States Air Force.

United States Information Service.

United States Navy.

USSR Office of the Air Attache, Great Britain.

VFW, Bremen.

Andy Vincent, IPC Magazines.

Walt Disney Productions, California.

Westland Helicopters.

The reference libraries of: *Daily Mail*, London; *Daily Mirror*, London; *Daily Telegraph*, London.

Illustrations: **Tom Bjarnasson**
Carin Simon
Lee Ives